Engle looked at me. "I thought you was dead, Mister Goldsmith. We took a rocket in the starboard engine. The port engine is overheating. We can barely maneuver. . . ."

Seawolf gunships were rocketing and machine-gunning the south bank at unbelievably low altitudes—as low as twenty feet. I put an M-79 round between the windscreen and tail rotor of one of them. I had fired the round before the chopper came into view. . . .

This was one hell of a firefight: life or death for every sailor on four plastic boats, everyone trying to stay alive by suppressing the fire of the enemy at close quarters but ever mindful of their depleting ammunition, doing their best to save a mortally wounded PBR and shipmates who no longer had a boat to call their own. . . .

PAPA BRAVO ROMEO

*U.S. Navy Patrol
Boats at War
in Vietnam*

Wynn Goldsmith

BALLANTINE BOOKS • NEW YORK

A Ballantine Book
Published by The Ballantine Publishing Group
Copyright © 2001 by Wynn Goldsmith

All rights reserved under International and Pan-American Copyright Conventions. Published in the United States by The Ballantine Publishing Group, a division of Random House, Inc., New York, and simultaneously in Canada by Random House of Canada Limited, Toronto.

Ballantine and colophon are registered trademarks of Random House, Inc.

www.randomhouse.com/BB/

Library of Congress Catalog Card Number: 00-108162

ISBN 0-8041-1921-X

Manufactured in the United States of America

First Edition: January 2001

10 9 8 7 6 5 4 3 2 1

Republic of Vietnam

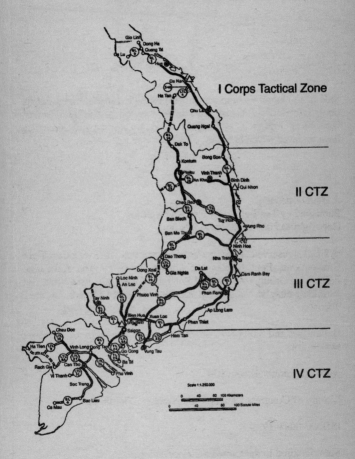

I Corps Tactical Zone

II CTZ

III CTZ

IV CTZ

Gio Linh
Dong Ha
Quang Tri
Ca Lu
Hue
Da Nang
Ha Tan
Chu Lai
Quang Ngai
Dak To
Bong Son
Kontum
Pleiku
Vinh Thanh
An Khe
Binh Dinh
Qui Nhon
Cheo Reo
Ban Blech
Tuy Hoa
Ban Me Thuot
Vung Rho
Ninh Hoa
Dao Thong
Nha Trang
Dong Xoai
Gia Nghia
Da Lat
Loc Ninh
An Loc
Cam Ranh Bay
Tay Ninh
Phuoc Vinh
Phan Rang
Bien Hoa
Xuan Loc
Ap Long Lanh
Chau Doc
Cu Chi
Saigon
Phan Thiet
Ha Tien
Vinh Long
Dong Tam
Hien Tan
Rach Gia
Can Tho
Go Cong
Vung Tau
Ba Tri
Vi Thanh
Phu Vinh
Soc Trang
Bac Lieu
Ca Mau

Scale 1:1,250,000

0   40   60   100 Kilometers

0   40   60   100 Statute Miles

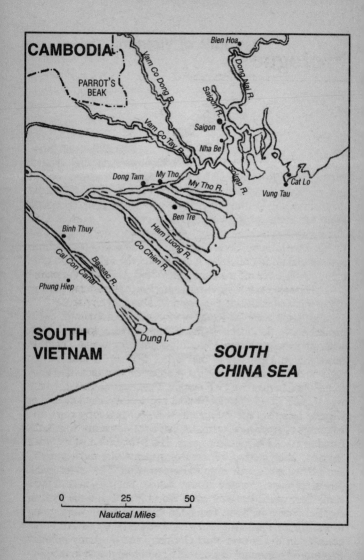

CAMBODIA

PARROT'S
BEAK

Bien Hoa

Vam Co Dong R.

Dong Nai R.

Vam Co Tay R.

Saigon R.

Saigon

Nha Be

Dong Tam

My Tho

My Tho R.

Soirap R.

Cat Lo

Vung Tau

Ben Tre

Binh Thuy

Ham Luong R.

Co Chien R.

Cai Con Canal

Bassac R.

Phung Hiep

Dung I.

SOUTH
VIETNAM

SOUTH
CHINA SEA

0   25   50

Nautical Miles

Prologue

This book is not intended to be a history of the U.S. Navy's PBR (patrol boat, river) river rats during the Vietnam War. It is a personal account of my experiences in an unusual combat environment over thirty years ago with those little fiberglass boats. It is an incomplete first-year record of a great U.S. Navy unit that existed for only twenty-two months. One unit of two dozen or so, formed in the cauldron of war, with no history and no future. A force assembled for a short-term mission to help stave off a communist victory in South Vietnam.

The mission was a short-term success, but ultimate failure. The boats and their sailors were not failures in any sense.

The boats were basically off-the-shelf commercial cabin cruiser/sport fishermen hulls, painted green, loaded down with machine guns and ammunition, and sent to war. The little boats got into combat in the spring of 1966, within ninety days of the signing of the first production contract. The Uniflite Boat Company of Bellingham, Washington, delivered the first vessels of an initial 120-boat run within schedule and at slightly less than the estimated $100,000-per-copy cost. The whole production line of that small-boat company was dedicated to the Navy for three years. The $100,000 cost included engines, water pumps, all control systems, the radar system, acceptance trials, and even the green paint. The government furnished guns, ceramic armor, radios. The .50-caliber guns came from stock left over from World War II and the Korean conflict. Some of those venerable guns probably were going to war for the third time. They had been fired by 8th Air Force gunners on B-17s over Nazi Germany and by Army infantry or armored personnel in Korea. The additional cost to the government to fully equip a PBR for combat was probably less than $5,000 total per boat. Altogether, the cost of each of those boats delivered into combat was a slight fraction of the cost of a patrol plane or fighter bomber, which, even in 1966, cost the taxpayers a couple of million dollars each.

The little fiberglass boats were first intended to replace Navy land-and-sea-based patrol craft monitoring enemy movement on the waterways of the Mekong Delta. The Navy was using both Lockheed P-2 (land-based) and Martin PM-5 (seaplane) aircraft to patrol the waterways of Vietnam at low altitude, but the aircraft were expensive and ineffective on that mission; they had been designed to seek and destroy submarines.

Second, the boats were to identify and engage enemy watercraft using the waterways, something that fast-moving aircraft, even at low altitude, could not accomplish.

The PBRs did that and more. They saved friendly outposts by the hundreds, medevacked wounded friendlies by the thousands, saved a couple of provincial cities during Tet 1968, and were the main tools for sealing off the Cambodian border as the United States exited the war. Those boats got American sailor warriors face-to-face with the enemy on the water and in a platform suited for the mission. The PBR was a great example of how the United States government and industry can work together on an emergency basis to deliver an effective, cost-efficient weapons system.

The first combat patrols in 1966 showed that the little boats were vulnerable to concentrated enemy fire from fortified positions on the riverbanks. They needed reliable air cover, and reliable intelligence. The Seawolves (helicopter gunships) came first. The Navy gratefully accepted old UH-1B Army gunships, and combat-experienced Army gunship pilots provided training to Navy helicopter aviators trained to battle submarines. They provided reliable air cover.

The SEALs (sea, air, land), the U.S. Navy commandos, came second. They were to provide reliable intel.

It was the sailors on our boats who made them such an effective implement of war. Most of them were captained by first class petty officers or CPOs (chief petty officers), sometimes by second class petty officers, occasionally by a guy with only one vee stripe under his crow (a third class petty officer). When they engaged the enemy it was usually with a small tactical unit of two boats commanded by a first class, a CPO, or a junior officer (usually a lieutenant, j.g.). The little boats went to a war where there was no top-heavy command controlling their actions. Patrol, seek, engage—that loose doctrine was interpreted differently by each PBR commander.

A typical PBR unit performed a tough job exceptionally well. A first class or second class (E-6 or E-5) was the boat captain. Every river rat at the time probably knew that he was not in the real Navy and that the Vietnam War was not a real war. But it *was* combat. A lot of the guys really wanted that experience. They were, for the most part, young guys— middle-class Americans who wanted to support their country. Guys who proudly enlisted in the Navy and volunteered for PBR duty because they knew that they would be tested under fire. They were tested. About 50 percent of the nearly 6,000 PBR sailors who served in Vietnam got Purple Hearts. Three hundred or so gave their lives.

My story is typical of the stories hundreds of PBR junior officers who served in Vietnam could have written.

I was a son of the generation that had grown up and suffered during the Great Depression, had desperately fought in World War II, and had prospered ever since. I was like most of my generation.

In the spring of 1967, when I received my orders to PBRs, I was not a volunteer for the boats or, even, Vietnam. I had a regular Navy commision. I wanted a West Coast destroyer. I wanted a blue-water challenge. I wanted to be part of the ever-increasing high-tech Navy during a period in which the ships were at a high degree of readiness and often in danger zones off the Vietnamese coast. I wanted to be a part of a surface Navy that was not shortchanged because of the Vietnam War. The minesweep force on which I served out of Charleston was being stripped of men and materiel to wage the war in Vietnam. I wanted to go to sea with a full complement of trained sailors going in harm's way. I was tired of cumshawing men and spare parts—a cook here, an electrician here, a piston head there—just so my ship could get under way for local operations.

In Navy lingo, cumshawing basically means "borrowing

and bartering." Stealing, or "midnight requisitioning," was often used under the cover of cumshawing. The COs and XOs winked at such stuff, part of a long Navy tradition to get the job done, and to hell with procedures. The brown-water river rats I knew could out-cumshaw anybody.

I also wanted to visit exotic ports of call in the Pacific, and a home port different from Charleston. I had heard a lot of good things about "Dago," as San Diego was known in the fleet. A town where you never had to wear foul-weather gear, a town where you never felt as if you were being treated as second class by the locals because you wore a military uniform. In Charleston polite society, only the Citadel-gray and Confederate-gray uniforms got respect. "Yankee" sailors and dogs had to keep to the sidewalks. The rough-and-tumble North Charlestown municipality, with its plethora of bars, pawn shops, strip clubs, and gambling· dens respected and loved the Navy. The Navy was a cash cow to those folks. The tourist-oriented, historic downtown Charleston community south of Broad Street (the SOBs) with all the fine dining places, fine homes, and fine young girls of the community, was virtually off limits to sailors in uniform. I dated a couple of those fine young SOB women, and I was warned never to show up in uniform. Even though I was a son of the South and descended from a long line of Confederate warriors on my father's side, my mother's grandfather (just off the boat from Germany) had fought for the Yankees. I never got comfortable with those ladies or their families.

I just wanted to be close to the action on a blue-water destroyer out of San Diego. A job as DCA (damage control assistant) and assistant engineering officer on a destroyer doing Yankee Station (South China Sea operations area for U.S. Navy carrier attacks) would have been fine with me.

Eventually I got to spend a lot of time in San Diego.

The Vietnam War SEALs have received a lot of attention over the past decades. Many books about tough, brave, in-your-face, gritty, bloody SEALs have been published. PBRs are mentioned often in the personal accounts. Not often enough and not correctly though, so readers might think that PBRs were just transportation for SEALs.

Five PBR sailors were killed in action for every SEAL

killed in action. Five Navy ships were named for PBR river rats killed in action, only one for a SEAL.

The Navy had an easy job of filling the billets of the enlisted PBR units. The boat captains were, for the most part, young petty officers in nontechnical ratings who had already determined to make the Navy a career, and who had a couple of years to go on their current (usually four-year) enlistments. They were proud of their chosen profession and wanted to make rank as fast as the technical ratings in the dawning of the age of computers were making their additional stripes. They were professionals, trained for war, and they wanted that combat experience. They also knew that a tour in Vietnam would accelerate their advancement. It was typical that Vietnam E-5 (petty officer second class) or E-6 (petty officer first class) PBR boat captains went on to retire as CPOs (chief petty officers) or as commissioned officers. The fleet appreciated their dedication and leadership. The sailors appreciated the respect they received once back on blue-water ships.

The young gunners (E-3s when they arrived in Vietnam) had a different collective experience. Some of the PBR sailors who served as gunners had almost their entire Navy experience on the little boats. A lot of them were eighteen-year-olds right out of boot camp or gunner's mates G-school ("G" for guns as opposed to missiles). A minority of gunners who survived one tour extended for another, then another, until they were rotated back to the fleet for their final year to make the Navy a career. A few of them stayed on in Special Warfare, the SEAL-dominated combat boat community. Many of them were surveyed from the Navy with disabling wounds even before they completed a year's service. Most simply left the service to resume their education, marry, and start successful civilian careers after their first experience with the realities of blue-water shipboard life. True to their often-heard declarations, they were not "lifers."

The commissioned PBR officers filling the two top spots of a river section (later designated "division") for the most part were regular Navy junior officers. Lieutenants with a couple of two-year sea tours and five or more years' experience were designated OinCs (officers in charge). Lieutenants completing four years' experience were given the operations-officer billet.

Most of the other PBR officers were lieutenants (j.g.) with a two-year sea tour under their belts. Less than half were regular Navy. Most were college guys fulfilling a three-year obligation. When they left Vietnam, they separated from the Navy. Some, like me, were Naval Academy or regular NROTC guys with a four-year obligation. Whatever their source of commission, CPOs (experienced chief petty officers) usually were in charge of a typical two-boat 12- to 14-hour combat patrol.

The enemy was different. They were usually not professional warriors. Most of the ones we faced were conscripted locals under the tight rein of a minority of zealots operating on home territory. The dedicated enemy soldiers did have the advantage of fighting on home turf. They fought until they died or until the Americans and the Saigon forces were defeated. Mostly they just existed as ordinary folk until they were called to battle. They farmed, fished. They worked in secrecy. A quarter of them were full-time soldiers living in secret base camps. They had only a couple of combat assignments a month. For the most part we were just passing through on one-year tours; the Viet Cong were led by guys with twenty years' fighting experience. They were supported by powerful forces off limits to us. We had the firepower, communications, and maneuverability. They had the staying power.

As soon as the PBRs were introduced in early 1966, they denied the Viet Cong use of the waterways during the day. The boats became targets from the riverbanks. In the beginning, the enemy fire was usually ineffective sniper fire, but the enemy learned to deal with PBRs. They created diversions like sniper attacks on one stretch of water to direct attention from crossing points. They used English-language propaganda and fake messages on our radio frequencies. They mounted elaborate ambushes with evading sampans the bait. For the most part, the PBR sailors were too smart to take the bait. Even when the little boats ran down some small canal to catch a skunk, only to be met with rockets and machine guns, the boats usually came out whole with no major casualties unless a rocket hit the fuel tanks. PBRs were agile and packed a lot of punch.

Most of our duty was spent as foreign policemen in a civil war. We were not trained or inclined to be diplomats. We had to adapt. We did. But sometimes we were "ugly Americans." Usually we were the only reliable American forces in the Mekong Delta that could and would safely medevac wounded civilians regardless of their political persuasion. PBR sailors often saw the same people twice a day, every day. In the morning, peasants went to market towns in motorized sampans, and in the evening the same peasants went home, many of them to enemy-controlled villages. PBR sailors got more familiar with the Vietnamese peasants than most Vietnam GIs so the PBR sailors had a much different experience than most of the other American combat troops during the Vietnam War.

We just hoped that we could wear down the enemy. We did our best. We learned from mistakes. We outwitted our enemies more often than they outwitted us.

We did know that the Navy appreciated what we did, and that kept us motivated.

This book describes a typical tour of a junior officer on PBRs during 1967–1968 in the Mekong Delta. I have attempted to make it as truthful as possible by using real names, dates, and places taken from old monthly combat-action summaries, oral interviews with old shipmates, and even photocopies of their war-time diaries. Mostly it comes from my own memories. I have a lot of memories, but my story could be written by most of the PBR sailors who served in the Vietnam War. Each has a story to tell. Some of their stories would definitely be more exciting than mine.

PBR enlisted sailors in Vietnam were for the most part typical sailors of the time in their ratings. Those ratings were primarily the ones on the low side of the technical scale—the boatswain's mates, the gunner's mates, the signalmen, the quartermasters. But at the E-4 or higher level, their ratings required both seamanship and leadership in an age where naval warfare was becoming increasingly electronic. Those ratings were becoming obsolete in the mid-1960s. World War II cruisers—with teak decks, a full array of 8-inch, 5-inch, and 40mm guns, and all their manpower requirements—were being superceded by smaller ships armed with missiles. The same goes for a lot of destroyers with batteries of 5" guns being replaced by helicopters and ASROC antisubmarine weapons.

The new ships operated as units of small task groups rather than as part of massive armadas of surface vessels as in World War II. Those were relegated to screening aircraft carriers, the Navy's "big stick." The Navy was adjusting to the nuclear age. A massive global communications and radar network of both fixed bases and patrol aircraft kept the ships in close contact with the Pentagon. Communications with reliable and encrypted modern FM systems replaced the old flag hoist. The sextant was being replaced by sophisticated radar charts, radio beacons, and even satellite signals. The days of surface-ship captains setting sail independently to seek and destroy the enemy were long gone. That mission was even being taken away from the submarine force attack submarines. The silent service had by then been mission-oriented toward other kinds of submarines.

I saw a lot of those regular Navy guys coming to the boats. Every one was first a volunteer in time of war. The Navy always made its manpower quotas with volunteers during that time. Most, but not all, of the seasoned petty officers on the boats had volunteered for small-boat combat duty. The E-4 through E-6 enlisted sent to the boats had requested small-boat combat duty to further their advancement in the ranks. They wanted to prove to themselves and the Navy that they were still relevant.

My combat experiences were far less than those of some enlisted sailors I knew. Some of my old shipmates' stories, related to me, are included. I hope the book is read by a lot of people because our story needs to be remembered. I hope other long-in-the-tooth river rats write their stories. The SEALs have gotten a lot of black ink from their Vietnam experiences. Those Vietnam SEALs stayed together. A lot of them stayed on in Special Warfare and spent enough time in the service to retire with their SEAL designators. Most of the young SEALs during the Vietnam War are probably like me and the PBR river rats: they got out of Vietnam and got out of the Navy. Unlike the river rats, they stayed in touch. The SEALs are bonded better than the PBR river rats and it is only natural—the SEALs operated in small teams and went out on specific missions. PBR sailors never knew from day to day what lay ahead or who was going to be their leader for the day.

This book's beginning was in Maui during the summer of 1995. My family was on a once-in-a-lifetime Hawaiian vacation. While my wife and daughter stayed at the condo, I went fishing out of Lahina on a sport-fishing boat. As I walked down the pier and approached the boat, I recognized its lines. It was a Uniflite 31-foot cabin cruiser/sport fisherman. It had been over twenty-eight years since I had been on one of the fiberglass boats. The fishing boat had a head, a flying bridge, a spacious cabin, and plenty of afterdeck space for a half dozen anglers. No machine guns, splinter shields, gun tubs, rifles, grenade launchers, boxes of ammunition, or cases of C rations that were on the PBRs back then. Even with screws and not water pumps, painted a bright white, not dull jungle green, it was the same platform that I had been on for nearly 3,000 hours on the waterways of Vietnam in hot sun, cold rain squalls, night and day, experiencing combat, boredom, excitement, fear, pathos, and victory. Every PBR sailor who served on one of the little fiberglass boats must have had similar experiences. Some of them probably spent thousands of hours more on those boats than I did; some guys kept extending their tours. Life on the boats was usually more interesting and enjoyable than in the rack or being pressed to clean up some mess. Sailors definitely preferred time on the boats to time at base.

As the boat sped out of the harbor I reflected on the action thriller I had read on the long flight from Atlanta. Another one by Jack Higgins. It had been enjoyable but predictable. I thought I could write something better. But what was I going to write? The humming diesel engines and the spray from the chop gave me an inspiration. I would write an adventure story about the Vietnam river rats. I knew the violence, heard about all the spying/double-agent intrigue, and could well imagine the sex scenes. I sure could describe some unforgettable characters.

As soon as I got back to Roswell, Georgia, I began to write. I wrote 120,000 words in four months, but had written only a small part of what I wanted, and decided to make what I had written the first of a trilogy. I spent months trying to interest a publisher. I had some interest but got nowhere. The reading public was not interested in Vietnam War fiction. A couple of literary agents suggested that I write a personal account of my experiences with the brown-water navy. There was still a market for such accounts, according to Ethan Ellenberg, the literary agent who agreed to pitch this work.

Thank you, Ethan.

Chapter 1

June 26, 1968. Another day at war, but it was different to me. I believed that it would be my last "special" patrol. I was afraid that it could be my last patrol. I still thought that I would get out of Vietnam alive. I just did not want to be shipped home early with tubes stuck in my mangled body to spend the rest of my life as a crippled veteran. I knew that I had been lucky. I also knew that I had to make that luck hold. I was in charge on this operation. There would be no one to blame except bad luck or me if it turned sour and I got myself killed or totally disabled. That thought was a comfort to me. I still felt lucky that day. Get through the day and I would soon be off to Australia for almost a week of debauchery, followed by a month-long wind down of routine patrols before I left for the World—back home, the good old USA.

My year of being a brown-water sailor in a strange war with strange happenings would soon be a memory. I wanted the experience to be over. I had seen enough. This war was not like the wars I had read and heard about from my high school teachers. My shipmates and I had been fighting on the same water, the same riverbanks, the same canals on which the French had fought twenty years earlier. During that time scant progress toward victory had been made. I was a little depressed that day, but somehow I pumped myself up for what was to come.

Most of all, I was prepared. I told myself over and over that I was no longer a dumb-ass. Not like my wardroom buddy, Bill Dennis, killed the week before. Bill had made a stupid mistake. A dumb-ass mistake. He had given a little old mamma-san in a sampan the benefit of the doubt and taken a couple of boats up a narrow channel to chase her down. The same fucking channel where a buddy of mine and five other sailors had been seriously wounded four weeks ago. The boats were led into a deadly ambush. Bill and two other sailors were killed. A PBR had been destroyed. The Viet Cong had patiently waited days for their little ambush.

Bill had been a full lieutenant (O-3, equivalent to an Army captain), USN, an XO (operations officer/executive officer). A man who did not have to go out on regular combat patrols, Bill still pulled more than his share. He was a full man. A regular Navy man with a wife and kids, he did his job extremely well. He made sure the sailors were prepared and ready. The 535th's sailors were some of the best. Some riverboat section's XOs went out just one or two times a month; they did not have to go out at all. Four weeks of inactivity around that canal had probably just made Bill a little complacent.

Bill Dennis had also been a compassionate man. He had spent hours tending to two wounded Viet Cong in our custody a week before he was killed. Just the day before, those two young men had been turned over to the South Vietnamese, who tied them to fish stakes at low tide. Then the tide did its thing. Those two patched-up tenderly cared-for Viet Cong teenagers endured hours of anguish before they died. Some sailors just laughed about their fate. I did not. I knew that the locals would exact their revenge; the execution had been seen by hundreds of villagers.

Bill was probably still pissed at the behavior of Dai Qui Thom—the South Vietnamese district chief in Cho Lach who had staged the slow execution—when he went after that lady and her evading sampan. Bill wanted to bring in a live suspect to show the locals that American sailors were not butchers or torturers. Instead, he and two other sailors got eternity in a few seconds.

Perhaps it was just fate that got Bill killed. Bill was really no dumb-ass. He was a thoughtful man. He believed that he and his sailors could capture that sampan with no sweat. Going in and out of a narrow tributary off the My Tho River in a few seconds would have been an easy job for a PBR. Bill had probably weighed all the possibilities. The Cong in the area were on the run. No activity around for days. Bill took his chance. Bill lost. Bad luck happened that day.

I had been a dumb-ass more times than Bill. The difference was that I had been lucky.

I could have been killed several times if a round had been closer, a boat had been slower, my head had been turned another way, and so forth. Bill took his chance. He and two other sailors lost. I had to steel myself into thinking that Bill had been unlucky. Shit could happen to even the best and brightest. Just to be sure of having good luck, I did all the right things before my boats went up that enemy-controlled canal.

I was a seasoned river rat and knew what to expect. Small arms and machine guns were bad, but rockets and command-detonated mines were the worst. I was mentally prepared for everything. I was confident in the men, our boats, and the Navy helicopter gunships. We were prepared. I just hoped that my luck would hold.

It was 1400 local time. The hot tropical sun was still very high in the sky, with only scattered puffs of cumulus clouds. It was the hottest, most miserable time of the day. That was good; it was siesta time in the Mekong Delta. Perhaps the Viet Cong defenders of the barrier had left their bunkers and spider holes for the shade of the tall palms in the hamlet two hundred meters southwest of the objective. Even better, the water was high and slack. The SEALs could jump off the boats to the top of the canal bank without wading through sucking mud. Maybe this SEAL platoon would not fuck up.

Our radio transmissions were minimal. A minute earlier I had made a radio check with the two-ship Seawolf Huey helicopter (UH-1B) fire team orbiting the Ham Luong two miles to the north. Next came a three-word cryptic transmission from the SSB (SEAL support boat) indicating that it was within thirty seconds of entering the canal. I had been following this boat's movement with my glasses in the shimmering reflections from the river. As the little, green, shallow-water boat made its turn, I touched the shoulder of the first class gunner's mate beside me and looked into his eyes.

"Hit it, Pappy. Let's see if this boat can get on step with an extra load."

Boat commander GM1 "Pappy" Sheppard smiled at me and rammed the throttles home. As the boat leaped up to speed I could see through my binoculars that Chief Stevens's two PBRs were kicking up rooster tails one thousand meters south and ahead of us. I looked behind to see another PBR keeping the fifty-meter interval. The six SEALs on my boat stood up to enjoy the breeze. Two of them worked their way forward on the narrow aluminum gunwales to the bow of the boat. Once they were forward of the cowling that shielded the coxswain's flat, others passed them their weapons: a Stoner 5.56mm automatic weapon with its 150-round box of belted ammunition, a CAR-15 carbine with a 40mm grenade launcher under its barrel, and haversacks that I assumed carried explosive charges and extra ammunition. The other four SEALs then sat down on the engine covers and checked their equipment.

I stuffed my soft, floppy hat into the right pocket of my jungle fatigue blouse and grabbed my helmet and flak jacket from their place on the deck behind the coxswain's flat. The other gunners and the boat commander also put on their battle gear. The four SEALs behind me slapped each other on the shoulders and began making the animal grunts SEALs use to psych themselves for combat. They were not wearing any protection except for some camo greasepaint on the face of the one without a beard or handlebar mustache. Two of them were wearing cutoff camouflaged jungle fatigues and bright red bandannas carefully tied over their heads. Today it would be called the Deion Sanders do. With long facial hair and long locks spilling over the back of the neck and protruding from a bandanna, each resembled a scurvy pirate from the seventeenth century. Two carried standard M-16 rifles with three thirty-round banana magazines taped together. The magazine in the middle was in the well. Another had an M-79 grenade launcher. The fourth cradled a duck-billed, 12-gauge Ithaca pump shotgun. The shower shoes on the feet of two of them completed the picture of third-world, scruffy, ill-disciplined commandos. They were the antithesis of what I expected from such highly trained and superbly conditioned U.S. Navy frogmen warriors—and they were about to storm a fortified bunker complex in broad daylight. At least these guys had operated as a team for a month or so. None wore the uncomfortable black beret that SEALs and river rats were officially sanctioned to wear as a badge of distinction. A U.S. Navy propaganda photo once showed a SEAL storming ashore wearing his black beret and cradling a submachine gun. The photo caption said the operation was along the Mo Cay Canal, where we were now headed. The photo must have been staged. Even the most dumb-ass SEAL would never go into combat in the Delta midday heat wearing a hot, uncomfortable wool felt cover, especially not up that Mo Cay Canal. Or would he? SEALs were famous for their courage and combat effectiveness. In my experience, they often lacked common-sense smarts.

I knew that if I were going ashore at that bunker complex, I would be wearing a helmet, flak jacket, and jungle boots with double nylon or aluminum inserts. I had seen what could happen in that canal. I knew about the toe-popping booby traps widely laid out around enemy fortifications. The guy with the shotgun, who was wearing a complete fatigue uniform with jungle boots and a floppy hat, had the right idea. His grease-paint was mostly under his eyes. That was practical: it could help him spot a fast-moving target under high sunlight.

If I had questioned him, the lieutenant junior grade SEAL OinC of the platoon on the SSB would probably have said that his SEALs felt more comfortable in the cutoffs and that the shower shoes were well adapted for the Mekong's mud. The shower shoes did not leave distinctly American foot tracks. The greasepaint and flashy red bandannas would put the fear of God into the enemy. His SEALs were elite warriors, the men with green faces who terrorized the enemy in their own backyard by night.

But it was broad daylight.

Far be it from me—the river rat full lieutenant (just promoted from j.g. three weeks earlier) and tactical commander for the little operation—to question the attire of the guys who had to do the heavy lifting once the boats reached their objective. I mused that maybe the bright red bandannas would at least keep the SEALs from shooting at each other once ashore. I knew from experience that the SEALs could get separated and fire on each other.

The SEAL SSB (a thirty-foot, armored-steel, shallow-draft craft designed to carry eight SEALs into combat) was thirty meters into the Mo Cay Canal as my lead PBR entered. We closed up to ten meters before we slowed down to the twelve-knot max speed of the steel craft ahead of us. The other three PBRs were at ten-meter intervals astern.

I had been down this canal before. A hundred meters down, it had a bend to the south (port side). Past that bend the landscape changed. The tall grass on the bank gave way to raised mounds, earth-covered palm logs covered by palm leaves—Viet Cong bunkers. Some of them might be reinforced with concrete. They could withstand direct hits from gunship 2.75-inch rockets. The west end of the canal was blocked by steel cables and tons of logs so the PBRs and the SEAL boat would have little room to maneuver. If trapped in a firefight, the river rats would need to silence the gun ports of those bunkers with machine gun fire, 76mm rocket fire from our LAWs (lightweight antitank rockets), or demolition charges from the SEALs. This was not a pretty prospect. We hoped that the bunker complex would not be manned.

I had seen what a fully manned bunker complex could do to the Mobile Riverine Force despite the heavy firepower of its cannons and its flame-throwing armored assault craft. Four months earlier I had a two-boat PBR patrol on station on the Ham Luong just south of the Mo Cay when a mobile riverine assault group had conducted an operation down the Mo Cay. Seventeen brown-water sailors and U.S. Army 9th Division soldiers had been killed. Most of the dead were Army draftees on the armored assault boats. It had taken the firepower of fixed-wing aircraft and five-hundred-pound bombs to silence the bunkers. I doubt if the number of enemy killed was anywhere near the friendly casualties caused by booby traps and RPG warheads (B-40 shoulder-fired rockets) bouncing around inside the armored Tango boats (LCM-8s configured as riverine troop carriers).

A month later, while the bunker complex was being rebuilt, I had led four PBRs carrying a company of South Vietnamese troops down the canal to assault the complex. Upon seeing the magnitude of the rebuilt fortifications the South Vietnamese commander and his U.S. Army major adviser decided not to disembark the troops, so sixty little soldiers on the four overloaded U.S. Navy fiberglass PBR gunboats hosed down the bunkers with bullets and 40mm grenades. The PBR sailors also did some firing. It had been a waste of ammunition but a good tension reliever.

Before we began the barrage that day I had to restrain the adviser, who was almost beside himself in demanding that five sampans in the canal a hundred and fifty meters west of us be taken under fire. The sampans were being beached on the north side of the canal and the Vietnamese were attempting to disembark into the nipa palms. Through binoculars I saw thirty or so old men and women frightened out of their wits. Of course these old people were Viet Cong. The only way the VC would let them go on sampans out to the main river was for them to be absolutely "politically correct." Their sons and daughters probably built bunkers, made booby traps, and manned the lookout posts for the main forces that could be trusted with automatic and heavy weapons. Some of their offspring were probably full-time Viet Cong fighters. But to me the old folk were civilians, noncombatants. And some of them probably did provide valuable intelligence to friendly forces back in Ben Tre once they had reached the market town. I had probably touched or at least talked to most of those people when PBRs had body-searched anybody coming or going to the Mo Cay from the main river over the last few months.

Reluctantly, I gave in to the demands of the adviser and the Vietnamese infantry commander. I told the forward gunner to fire some bursts from his twin .50-caliber machine guns over the sampans. GM3 Wayne Murray's gunner's aim was true. Fifty or so rounds passed cleanly at least a foot over the heads of those old people before the last of them disappeared into the nipa palm. The honor of the South Vietnamese soldiers was regained. The adviser seemed pleased.

A few weeks later a SEAL platoon wanted another crack at the Mo Cay. I guess they figured that they were much better at daylight assaults than the local friendlies. Some of their teammates from earlier adventures had had good luck in the area in clandestine nighttime forays.

I had been on the Ham Luong near the Mo Cay when the SEALs brought out a bunch of enemy weapons in the early morning light. The SEALs had been led by a *hoi chan,* a Viet Cong who had turned against his comrades, who knew where the weapons were buried. That was the first time I saw a B-40 rocket launcher and its rocket round close up. Before that I had seen only what those rocket rounds could do to boats and sailors.

The first SEAL off the first 534th PBR on our daylight operation got gut-shot. Then it was a race back to the main river to save the guy's life. And command-detonated mines almost destroyed a 534th PBR when the four boats tried to exit the canal with the wounded SEAL.

The boat commander of the first PBR down the canal that day, GM1 Ned Caldwell, later described that incident to me in one word—"dumb." When Caldwell had asked the SEAL officer in charge how far down the canal the boats were to go, the SEAL told Caldwell, "Just to where we get the first rounds of gook fire." That first round told the tale.

Today the troops would go ashore regardless of the number of reconstructed bunkers—as long as the bunkers were not spitting rockets and machine gun bullets in sufficient volume to render the mission impossible. No Vietnamese watercraft were on the canal. I remembered days when the canal had been full of sampans and junks coming out just as the 0600 morning curfew lifted. The salad days before Tet. Now that canal was like the front lines on the western front during the fall of 1918. The Cong were basically beaten but still had their pride. They would not give up sacred, hard-won territory in the district that had first given birth to the National Liberation Front many years earlier. (If I had read Bernard Fall's *Street Without Joy,* 1964 edition, before going to Vietnam, I would have been really uptight about those Vietnamese coming out of the Mo Cay on sampans. Many were probably the hardest of the hard core. They had lived for years under communist control, under the guns of NVA cadre disguised as "liberation fighters" for reform and democracy. Any dissident got eliminated. Those folks went along to go along. Those who were bold enough to give intel to the friendlies in Ben Tre were often quickly and painfully eliminated because the South Vietnamese police were infiltrated by Viet Cong agents.)

The barricade appeared in front of the SEAL boat. It

looked like a green ribbon of flotsam with all the palm leaves lashed to the logs by steel cables. I knew that it was strong enough to stop LCM-8s (landing craft medium, eight-ton carrying capacity—heavy landing craft that could transport M-60 tanks), much less thirty-one-foot, fiberglass PBRs. The SEAL support boat edged into the south bank ten feet from the barricade. I told Pappy to beach the PBR behind the SEAL boat. Pappy landed the boat against a relatively straight length of canal bank approximately thirty feet behind the SEAL support boat. He positioned the midsection of the boat against a small, clear patch.

The seven SEALs from the first boat were already on the bank and securing the area where the steel cables were anchored. The SEAL support boat backed off and made slow, lazy turns in the water with two guns aimed at the west bank. Four SEALs from my PBR leaped to the bank from behind the coxswain's flat and started moving inland. They were to scout beyond the bank with the intention of covering the others from any enemy who attempted to enter the area from the tree line two hundred meters away. The two guys on the bow of the boat had to lower themselves from the elevated bow into some vegetation. The first one gingerly eased himself off the boat, found a path, and moved quickly into the underbrush. As the last SEAL was about to go over, there was an eruption of automatic weapons fire and explosions ahead of the PBR. It was the distinctive staccato roar of a Stoner (the belt-fed, 150-round, 5.56mm machine gun used by SEALs), and the *whoomph* of grenade blasts inside bunkers. The SEALs on the first boat were clearing the bunkers and the fighting holes around the barrier. The last SEAL on my boat jumped from the bow into the green bushes to join his buddies. He leaped right onto a pungi stake.

I heard his scream above the sound of the weapons. I rushed forward on the port gunwale with an M-16 in my left hand. The boy (probably around twenty years old) was on his back in the mud. Ten inches of barbed bamboo stake protruded from the top of his right foot, just behind the rubber thong of his shower shoe. Another dumb-ass SEAL! I momentarily had a vision of the mission turning into another

SEAL team disaster. This time I would be in the middle of it and not, as before, safely in the middle of a river. This time the body parts picked up by the survivors could be my own.

I yelled to Pappy that a casualty had to be lifted back onto the boat. The plan had been for our PBR to join the other three PBRs performing lazy-eight patterns in the canal until the SEALs were ready for extraction. So much for the plan. I ordered the forward fifty gunner to get out of his mount. I gave him my rifle as soon as he pulled himself up from the gun tub, then I eased over the bow and onto the bank, carefully looking at each square foot of ground. I looked at the face of the young, blond, baby-faced SEAL. He was sweating, crying, and in a lot of pain. His brief military career was probably over. He would be lucky to use that right foot for walking again, much less running. The fire-hardened bamboo had probably been smeared with human feces. Unless treated quickly and properly, the wound would fester and amputation might be required.

Following my hand movements, Pappy positioned the bow of the boat close enough to the injured SEAL for me to ease over the bow. I knelt down beside the boy's chest, took my canteen from my pistol belt, and gave it to him. I spoke some words of encouragement so the kid would know that he was not alone. He would be all right. But first I had to cut off the pungi stake buried in the mud. The gunfire had stopped. I could concentrate. The man had been lucky in that he fell forward after the stake had penetrated his foot. There were dozens of other stakes between his feet and the water's edge. I used my ten-inch Buck knife to probe the area. I saw that I could scoop out enough mud around the offending stake to bring the knife-edge to the stake. The knife handle was slippery. I wished that the blade had saw teeth, or that I had a Marine Corps K-bar knife with its handgrip of leather rings. As I cut a notch in the stake, I was surprised at how easily the knife cut through the half-inch bamboo. Maybe the Cong fire-hardened only the first foot or so of the stakes. I put the knife back in its sheath, then, still kneeling, I tossed the SEAL weapons up to the forward gunner. I stood up and looked for solid ground behind the man. I would need all the leverage I could get to lift him.

As I moved forward I saw a small object half buried in the ground—an old American MK-2 pineapple grenade. It had probably been rigged as a booby trap and if I disturbed it enough, the lever would spring, strike a percussion cap, and ignite a black-powder charge instantaneously. Viet Cong boys would have pulled out the inch-long fuse and replaced it with powder. Two young American sergeant advisers, who had turned over to me two prisoners their troops had captured, had been killed by an instantaneous grenade booby trap within minutes of my meeting them. The VC flag at a crude tax collection stand had been their undoing.

I told the young SEAL to lean forward. He did, and the ground this movement uncovered appeared solid. I bent down and put my arms around his waist and lifted him in a fireman's carry position. Pappy saw us and pulled the boat forward to a place that I indicated with my right hand. Somehow I managed to carry the sailor to the waiting arms of the after gunners, who lifted him aboard. When I'd climbed in after them, the injured SEAL was already on the deck behind the coxswain's flat. The young M-60 gunner, whose name I did not know because he was so new, had broken out the medical kit and was bending over the SEAL. The gunner was shaking in fear. Evidently Pappy had ordered him to look after the wounded man but there was little anyone could do there; we did not have morphine syringes. I sat down on the engine cover to get my breath.

An explosion violently rocked the boat and rained mud and debris all over. A chunk of dirt hit my cheek. The gunner jumped back to his gun. Pappy put the boat in full reverse perpendicular to the bank. It took a few seconds for us to realize that we had not been hit by a rocket but by the fallout of C-4 charges the SEALs had set off to destroy the barricade. By that time the PBR was in the middle of the canal. After another thirty seconds the friendly firing of small arms started again.

After another minute of high anxiety I could see that the SEAL support boat was taking on troops for the extraction. The SEALs were firing their weapons as they backed up to the support boat. I told Pappy to close the SEAL boat. The SEAL platoon leader was the last one on the bank. He counted noses

including the wounded man on my boat. He shouted to me
that they were receiving fire from the tree line to the southwest and that the gunships should cover our exit. Viet Cong
were running to the canal through the tall grass behind us.

"Have your boats hose down that bank when we start firing
on the way out. We got beaucoup VC coming this way!"

I grabbed the radio mike just as our PBR went alongside
the SEAL boat, and three SEALs jumped aboard. One SEAL
knelt beside his wounded comrade. The other two inserted
fresh magazines in their weapons and looked toward the south
bank of the canal. I requested the Seawolf Huey fire team to
make a firing run on the tree line and then clear the area. We
would be coming out hot after their pass. All five boats were
ready to exit the canal in planned order. The gunships commenced their run within ten seconds. They flew over us at max
throttle at about three hundred feet with their flex guns roaring and rockets lighting off in pairs. By the time their run was
over, our little armada was under way back to the Ham Luong.
Chief Stevens's two boats led the way. They maintained ten
yards ahead of the slow SEAL boat, which was in the middle
of the formation. I radioed Chief Stevens to have the after
gunners on his boat, the second boat in line, aim in the same
direction as the SEAL boat's guns once they started firing.
The shooting commenced as soon as the SEAL boat rounded
the turn to the right. The target area was inches above the bank
and into the four-foot-high grass. Soon at least ten machine
guns and a dozen or so small arms from our boats were firing
into the grass for a hundred-yard stretch. Any Viet Cong near
that bank dare not raise his head. After about fifteen seconds
the SEAL boat ceased firing. The other PBRs' guns went
silent. The lead PBR was almost out of the canal.

I then realized that the M-60 machine gun on my boat continued to fire as fast as it could—over ten rounds per second. I
looked behind me, then ran back between the engine covers
and grabbed the arm of the young gunner. His eyes were completely closed and the terrified boy's finger remained clenched
on the trigger of the M-60. He had fired almost all of the four
hundred rounds in his ammo box. The gun's barrel was white-
hot and had gone plastic and rounds were corkscrewing all
over the place. I took my helmet off and banged his helmet

with it. That did the trick. The young gunner opened his eyes and finally relaxed his finger on the gun's trigger. He was crying. I cleared the breech of his weapon before more rounds could cook off. The hot gun barrel drooped at a thirty-degree angle. I told the gunner to sit down. Pappy would deal with him later. I wondered if the young gunner had what it would take to survive a year on the boats. After all, he had another three hundred and fifty-something days to go. I had less than two weeks before my oft-postponed out-of-country R & R. Then it was only forty days and a wakeup before I flew back to the World, as many in Vietnam had taken to referring to the United States. My last "special" was over.

As our boat exited the canal, I turned my attention to the wounded SEAL. Evidently his buddy had administered some painkiller. The man's head was elevated and he seemed comfortable. I decided against calling in a dustoff; we called in medical evacuation helicopters only in life-threatening emergencies. I remembered seeing a lot of wounded with more serious injuries transported by boat. Besides, a PBR could have him delivered to the Dong Tam Field Hospital within a half hour. A medical chopper would have saved only a few minutes. I radioed the Seawolf fire team leader and thanked him. If the SEAL had been in shock or had a sucking chest wound, I would not have hesitated requesting one of the gunships to land on any one of the uninhabited islands nearby to evacuate him. The aircrew would have put their lives at risk in a heartbeat. I shouted for Chief Stevens to have the 7-14 boat come alongside; GM1 Ned Caldwell's PBR was a fast boat. The SEAL was lifted over to the 7-14 boat as the SEAL boat closed us. The "jay gee" (lieutenant junior grade, i.e., paygrade 0–2, the equivalent of a first lieutenant in the Army) SEAL platoon leader checked out his wounded man and agreed that a dustoff was not necessary. The 7-14 boat sped off to Dong Tam.

For the next few minutes the boat crews policed up all the spent brass and reloaded the ready trays as we cruised up the Ham Luong. The postcombat exuberance of the river rats almost matched that of the SEALs, who were headed back to the YRBM-18 (yard, repair, berthing, messing), our floating PBR support base, for some early rounds of cold beers. I decided that my river rats deserved some early cold beers also. We sped ahead of the SEAL boat. Returning from a patrol early was not usual for PBR crews. Today was an exception. I was pleased with the way the operation had gone considering what could have happened.

I made a couple of cryptic radio transmissions using the daily shackle code to the op center of the YRBM-18 and to the Kien Hoa Tactical Operations Center at Ben Tre to indicate that the mission was a success. I figured that the operation did not merit a combat action report. A verbal report to my boss, Lt. Ron Wolin, OinC of River Section 534, would be sufficient. Let the SEAL platoon leader telegraph the world that one of his men took a pungi stake through a shower shoe and was the only casualty, friendly or hostile, in the action.

Shortly after the Kien Hoa Tactical Operations Center operator acknowledged my encrypted transmission, I heard my voice callsign on the Kien Hoa MACV net channel.

"Pineapple Bowl Charlie, this is Howling Pistol Bravo, over."

I smiled as I picked up the mike to respond to the familiar drawl of Lt. Jack Harrell, USNR, a fellow Georgian, who was the U.S. Naval Intelligence officer in that part of the eastern Mekong Delta.

"Pistol Bravo, this is Pineapple Bowl Charlie. Roger. Over."

"Pineapple Bowl Charlie, this is Pistol Bravo. What's a smart Jawja boy like you doing down the Mo Cay Canal? Don't you know that you can get your ass killed down that canal?"

"Pistol Bravo, this is Pineapple Bowl Charlie. That canal was not half as dangerous as your dinner party."

Jack laughed as he acknowledged and signed off. Even a CIA-funded swashbuckler like Jack knew when to stop chatter on the airwaves in a war zone.

Jack and I were far away from the pine trees of Georgia.

Chapter 2

I arrived in Vietnam like tens of thousands before me and more tens of thousands after me. A canary-yellow Braniff Airways 707 landed at Saigon's Tan Son Nhut Airport around noon in the September tropical heat of 1967. About one hundred and fifty passengers got off the chartered flight from Clark Field in the Philippines. Most were American servicemen like me. I suspect that, like me, most were new hands to the war. A few of the Army men had ribbons on their Class A uniforms indicating that they were returning to the war zone. Many of the young soldiers still had the short haircuts from Advanced Infantry Training and were wearing new, bright-green jungle fatigues. I guess they had changed uniforms somewhere before this final stop on their trip.

When the World Airways charter carrying me had left California a week earlier, all the troops had on Class A uniforms. Most of those passengers had spent the night in transit barracks in Guam before flying to Vietnam. Several other Navy men and I had orders to the Philippines to attend jungle survival school. We caught a flight to Clark from Guam without spending the night there. The most interesting thing to me about the stopover in Guam was seeing the scores of big B-52 bombers parked across the runway. It was an impressive display of military might. I realized that those mighty dark-green monsters were punishing the enemy in South Vietnam and that they could turn on a moment's notice to level Hanoi and bring the war to a quick conclusion—my feelings at the time.

I was nursing a hangover from having too many cheap (half-dollar) beers at the officers club the night before. As I walked down the aisle to the plane's exit, I managed to return the smile of the blond flight attendant with whom I had danced and played slot machines the evening before. She was about thirty, at least five years older than me. I should have known that she would be leaving the club with a male crew member, probably the pilot. I should have hit the rack as soon as she left the club. At least I did not lose any money on the slots after she left.

The attractive flight attendant grabbed my hand and wished me luck as I exited the plane. I believed that she was sincere.

The heat hit me as soon as I left the plane for the tarmac and the waiting buses. My tropical khaki uniform became soaked with perspiration. A lot of the young soldiers were probably too young to drink so they did not share my pain. But even those young guys started to sweat. The buses took us to the terminal area, which was crowded with waiting servicemen. Cliff Willis and I got together and made for a young Vietnamese boy selling Coca-Colas from a cart. The boy seemed a little upset that we paid him in quarters instead of dollars; I still had a pocketful of quarters from playing the slot machines. The Cokes were cold and tasted just the way they did back in Atlanta. I wished that I had a couple of aspirins to wash down with the Coke.

Cliff and I were both regular U.S. Navy lieutenants (j.g.). We had trained together in California for a couple of months and were finally getting to our new assignments—river patrol duty on thirty-one-foot fiberglass gunboats, PBRs (patrol boat, river).

When Cliff and I had been commissioned out of college NROTC two years before, we had not heard of PBRs. Over the last year and a half we had become aware of the little boats. All the sea-service magazines had articles about the expanding brown-water navy and its exploits. Blue-water sailors like Cliff and me had seen men on our ships who had a couple of years to go on their enlistments being sent to Vietnam. A lot of them went to the brown-water navy. Many had requested small-boat Vietnam duty for patriotic reasons. Some probably figured the adventure, combat pay, and chances for spot promotions far outweighed the danger, and sure beat the shit out of chipping paint and preparing for yet another inspection or deployment. In late 1967 the squared-away (or not so squared-away) sailor volunteers from the fleet were assigned to coastal patrol boats (PCFs), river patrol boats (PBRs), or the hundreds of Mobile Riverine Force boats that carried a brigade of the Army's 9th Division into combat in the Mekong Delta. There were still plenty of Navy jobs in Vietnam even for sailors not squared away because the support ships and bases of Vietnam required more men for duty than the combat boats. I'm sure that a lot of those guys were even more squared away than some of the river rats I knew. The U.S. Navy, like any large organization, chooses assignments based simply on manpower availability.

Cliff and I were not volunteers; five months earlier some computer in the Pentagon had spat out our names. We had become pigs in a pipeline, and the pigs had reached the terminus.

The day after I had received my orders was the day the Charleston-area junior officers expecting new duty assignments could meet their NAVPERS detailers, the Navy "human resources" people who were supposed to be looking out for the careers of young officers. I had received good fitness reports from my commanding officers. I was a fleet-qualified OOD (officer of the deck), even if I had earned my qualification on a slow MSO (ocean minesweeper) and not on a fast destroyer. I figured that my choice of a San Diego–based tin can (destroyer) for a duty assignment had a good chance of coming true. But when I received my orders to PBRs, I was only a little disappointed. In 1967 that could still be a good billet for a naval officer. I was told, and believed, that a year of combat duty could not hurt my career path. What the hell. I was free, white, and three years older than twenty-one. I would come through a year on riverboats unscathed. As my buddy, Lt. (j.g.) Ed Stokunis, USNR, the new first lieutenant aboard my ship, the USS *Fidelity* (MSO-443), had said to me after I told him of my orders, "Goldie, you have a whole year of boredom interspersed with moments of sheer terror in front of you." Easy Ed, a flight school washout with little interest in the surface Navy, spent most of his free time with stock market reports. He is now probably a Wall Street big shot, and he was mostly right about my year in Vietnam. But Easy Ed never mentioned how long those moments of sheer terror could last in someone's mind.

I went to the briefing the next day with my new orders in hand. The junior-officer detailer addressing us in the Charleston Naval Base theater responded to the first question. A young jay gee wanted to know the chances of getting his choice, PCFs (patrol craft fast—basically a sixty-five-foot civilian offshore support boat of the kind used to service Gulf oil rigs, but loaded down with guns), for his next duty assignment. The detailer replied with a straight face that the number of volunteers for PCF and PBR duty far outweighed the number of billets available. Evidently the questioner had missed the big draft by a month or so. My MinDiv 52 minesweeping buddy Ron McAlphren, married and with a new baby, who had received orders to PCFs the day before I received mine to PBRs, swore under his breath. Ron had requested sea or shore duty in Charleston, where his wife taught school.

I resolved to never again believe a NAVPERS detailer as long as I lived.

Cliff and I had been in the military long enough to expect confusion and delay in getting out of the airport so we were both surprised at how quickly we located our seabags and B-4 soft suitcases that had been loaded on trucks following our buses. We soon found a Navy enlisted man to check our orders and direct us to a bus stop. A pale-gray school bus with stenciled black lettering, steel mesh over its lowered windows, and a middle-aged Vietnamese driver took us about a mile and a half and deposited us at our home for the day, the Annapolis BOQ/BEQ, a squat, two-story concrete structure with heavy wire mesh covering the open windows. The petty officer at the desk looked at our orders and told us to make ourselves comfortable. A bus would take us to the Navy's Saigon Support Center at 0800 the next morning for further processing.

Even by September 1967 most BOQs (bachelor officers' quarters) and BEQs (bachelor enlisted-men's quarters) for transient naval personnel in Vietnam had been named after some sailor or officer killed in action. Not this dump. Maybe nobody wanted to dishonor the dead with a rat hole like the

Annapolis BOQ/BEQ. Perhaps some supply corps commander with a wry sense of humor and a hard-on for U.S. Naval Academy graduates had named the former Vietnamese flophouse. Perhaps the Saigon warriors wanted to show the guys being sent to combat assignments that Saigon was not really the soft life. Whatever. The Annapolis was several steps down from a Mexican whorehouse. The communal bunk rooms were not separated from the toilet area, which had no individual stalls and only holes in the floor for human waste to be deposited. The septic odors, the flies, the mosquitoes, and the lack of air movement all compounded my hangover. I felt I was going to be bowl-hugging sick, a condition I frequently had after University of Virginia fraternity parties in my past life, before I had become an officer and a gentleman.

I decided right away to go for the hair of the dog. Cliff, who was tired but not sick, decided he was tired enough to rest on his bunk. The petty officer in the lobby gave me directions to the nearest safe watering hole, just two blocks away. The strange street smells of Saigon were a welcome relief after those of the BOQ. I watched the locals on the crowded street and was amazed by the number of little Vietnamese men, in and out of uniform, driving Honda motorbikes with lovely girls whose *ao dai* costumes fluttered behind them as they hugged the driver's waist. War was not always hell.

I found the place, a standard three-story Vietnamese hotel that had been requisitioned for use by U.S. military officers. The place reminded me of an old Humphrey Bogart movie set: a large lobby, ceiling fans, comfortable chairs, and a cafe on the top-floor terrace. I went up to the cafe and ordered a San Miguel from the young Vietnamese barmaid. I had acquired a taste for the Filipino beer while at Subic Bay to attend jungle survival school.

A USAF first lieutenant joined me at the table. We introduced ourselves. He said the war was going well judging by his two months' in-country experience. There was never any enemy activity in Saigon except for probes of the air base perimeter at night. He said that I should come back to the rooftop cafe at sunset and watch the movie or the gunship action that took place a mile and a half away because the tracer rounds around the air base were sometimes a better show than the movie. Tonight there would be two-dollar steak dinners. Happy hour would last until 2000. It sounded like a good deal.

After a couple of San Miguels and snacking on beer nuts and pretzels, I finally felt more fatigue than nausea so I went back to the Annapolis. Before I took off my uniform and crashed I spoke to the young man on the bunk beside mine. He was reading a paperback and seemed a little on edge. He was a jay gee who had been in Saigon over a week. It seemed that nobody in the Navy knew where he was to meet his ship. He had been flown from the States to Japan, where he expected to find his ship, only to be told he was to meet it at some to-be-determined port in South Vietnam. But nobody in Saigon had ever heard of his ship, the *Pueblo*. It did not sound right to me that the Navy could not get an officer to his duty assignment. I knew that beginning the next morning at 0800 I would be fully assigned and dispatched to wherever the Riv-Sect 535 boats awaited me so I would not have to wait around for an undertermined time in the Annapolis flophouse. I could be in combat within days, if not hours. Somehow I felt good about that. The man with orders to the *Pueblo* would probably have a really dull time aboard a survey ship that the Navy seemed to have forgotten.

The steak dinner was well worth the two dollars. The movie was something else. It was a cowboy movie starring, of all people, Roy Orbison. Orbison was a popular country and western/pop singer of the time. He had emerged from the South during the same period that Johnny Cash, Elvis, Jerry Lee Lewis, and Carl Perkins had brought forth the rockabilly sound to teenagers of the mid-fifties. I was of that generation. I liked Orbison's singing. I did not like his acting in this (I suspect) his one and only film. The best part of the movie, which was probably part of a trend of spaghetti westerns filmed in Spain by some Italian director with B-grade American stars like Clint Eastwood, was Roy Orbison's singing. I still enjoy Orbison's songs whenever the local oldie station plays them. His *In Dreams* recording still stirs my emotions.

The Air Force officer was right. The streams of red tracers from the helicopter gunships around the Tan Son Nhut perimeter were of more interest to me than the movie.

The next morning I was feeling almost as full of piss and vinegar as I hoped I would appear when reporting to my combat command. I was wearing new tropical jungle fatigues with shiny silver bars on the collar tips of the blouse. On my head was my new Marine Corps–style utility cap that I had purchased back in Subic. The cap had the black crossed-anchors-and-shield insignia of a U.S. Naval officer stitched in front. I still have the cap on the back shelf of a closet. It is covered with paint stains from many housepainting jobs over the last thirty years.

Processing at the Saigon Naval Support Center was fast and professional. I was told that I was going to the Nha Be river base only twelve miles away to report to River Section 534, which had just been commissioned, rather than 535. There was no explanation of my assignment to a different boat section. A corpsman took a quick look at my medical record, which had a lot of gun-decked signatures of Medical Corps officers on it attesting to my having had a complete medical examination back in California. Of course, no U.S. Navy Medical Corps doctor had examined me since I was enrolled in the NROTC program back in 1961. The E-3 corpsman striker who had done my "complete physical exam" in San Diego back in June was a fantastic speed man with a pencil; he completed a four-page form that had hundreds of little boxes in under a minute and a half. At least he asked me if I had any medical complaints or was taking any kind of maintenance medication. My "Nope" bought me a hint of eye contact from the overwhelmed young sailor. Even the weight on the completed exam was my weight years earlier.

The last stop was the armory, where I got an opportunity to check out my choices of personal weapon for my tour. My options were limited to a .30-caliber M-1 (semiautomatic) or M-2 (fully automatic) carbine, with or without a folding stock, or the standard .45-caliber 1911A1-model semiautomatic pistol, a sidearm that had seen action in all the American wars of this century. The first class gunner's mate showed me a beauty of an M-2 (automatic, single-fire, selective) .30-caliber carbine he had just received. It looked brand-new and came complete with three banana-shaped thirty-round magazines. There was not a scratch on its highly polished walnut stock. The GM1 said it had belonged to a Navy chief gunner's mate who had just completed his tour in Saigon. It was very clean and probably had never been fired over the last year. I hefted the little rifle of the type used by infantry officers in Korea and World War II. It was immaculate, but not what I required. If I had invested in a 9mm Browning or .380 Beretta automatic as a lot of my PBR officer classmates had done while back in California, I would have snatched up the little carbine. But unlike a lot of budding river rats, I had entered Vietnam unarmed. A pistol was certainly more convenient than some old but pretty carbine whose ammunition might not be readily available on the boats.

I settled for a .45 that appeared to be in good condition. There were millions of bullets in stock for that old weapon. I hoped it did not have a defective sear like the one I used in Vallejo the month before. I had been squeezing off the first round of a five-shot magazine when suddenly the pistol went full automatic. The last round had gone off just above my right ear.

As I was signing the custody cards for the pistol, the GM1 asked where I was going. I told him PBR duty in the Delta. He told me that I had made a good choice.

"You river rats can always get your hands on shotguns or automatic rifles. Pistols are in short supply." I think that was the first time I ever heard the term "river rat."

The trip to Nha Be in the back of a Navy Ford pickup truck soon got under way. Before we left the support center compound, the second class yeoman driver asked if one of us wanted to ride in the cab beside him. Cliff and I both decided we preferred the open air of the truck's bed. Cliff took the 12-gauge Remington shotgun offered by the driver and a sackful of rounds. Cliff said he had a similar gun back home. We sat down on our seabags as we went off to do our part in the war.

The road leaving Saigon ran parallel to the Saigon River. A lot of vital war materiel was shipped up that river. We saw a couple of merchant ships moving upriver. Perhaps my cousin Don Cross, who had narrowly avoided the draft by getting his merchant marine ticket as a radio operator, was on one of those ships. My mother had recently written to me that he served aboard a ship that was ferrying stuff to Vietnam from

California. If Don was aboard a freighter going up the Saigon River, he would be earning the equivalent of an extra month's wages for the short trip. If the unloading at the docks took the ship into the next month, the crew got two months' extra pay. Ships had been sunk and civilian sailors had been killed on the Saigon River. I did not begrudge the merchant sailors their extra pay. With combat pay, tax breaks, free housing, and cheap food bills (the standard $47.50-per-month allowance) the eight thousand dollars I was to earn this next year could mostly be banked. I could buy that new Corvette with cash and still have a sizable down payment for a home in Charleston, Norfolk, or San Diego, whichever was the port of my post-Vietnam assignment. That was every unmarried sailor's dream if the sailor still had time to serve after Vietnam.

The river resembled Charleston's Cooper River in some ways. It was only a couple of hundred yards wide, and the far bank, with its scrub brush and marshes, could have been South Carolina low country. But the road we traveled was no Meeting Street. It was a narrow track of broken pavement. Shacks and little military guardposts were on the right side of the road. Sometimes there would be a half mile of rice paddies before the next populated area. We saw little sign of war.

As the truck passed through a built-up area of Vietnamese wooden and tin structures with signs in English advertising laundry services and beer, I knew that the naval base was near. They were typical of business enterprises outside naval bases all over the world. Soon I noticed servicemen along the muddy street. I stood up in the truck bed and saw the entrance to the base.

The Nha Be Naval Base was a work in progress. On the waterfront a couple of dredges were pumping out river bottom. Pile drivers were setting up pilings for new piers. There were a couple of weathered Quonset huts. Most of the buildings appeared brand-new. They were white clapboard, one- or two-story structures, just like the standard "temporary" U.S. military barracks or mess halls hastily constructed in the 1940s that still served as base housing for thousands of recruits on their way to Vietnam. Even the shiny, dark-green plastic sandbags stacked to the first-story windowsills of the buildings looked new. Other buildings were in various stages of construction. There were even some large, open-air tents set up in the brown mud. Gravel paths and wooden walkways connected the buildings.

I reviewed the waterfront as I dismounted the back of the truck. The piers were crowded with familiar Navy boats. Most were the thirty-one-foot MK I PBRs that I had trained on back in California. There were some LCM-6s (landing craft, medium, six-ton) and a couple of LCM-8s (eight-ton landing craft). There were also four wooden fifty-seven-foot MSBs (minesweeping boats) that I had seen for two years at the Charleston Naval Base. The MSBs had been priority sea-lifted to Vietnam eighteen months previously from Charleston to counter the mine threat to the Saigon shipping channel after old Russian-moored contact mines had seriously damaged a couple of merchant ships in the river approaches to Saigon. It had been big news back in Charleston when those boats had been rushed to war. The boats now looked different. Never pretty, they now appeared ugly, marred by the boxlike, armored, steel machine gun platforms that had been erected on the deck behind the pilothouse. War is a matter of expediency. The mine threat was from moored mines, not magnetic bottom mines, so the nonmagnetic signature of the wooden boats was sacrificed to provide the seven-man crews with protection against bullets coming from the riverbank.

Within a few minutes I found myself in long single-story building that housed the offices of the various riverboat commands at Nha Be. I walked down the center aisle until I stopped at the stenciled sign of River Section 534. There were two desks. A chubby, pink-faced young man in a dark-green T-shirt was standing and conferring with a lieutenant seated at one desk. The lieutenant paused to look up me. I had dropped my bags and was holding only my personnel file in my left hand.

The lieutenant gave me a wide smile that did not seem possible on such a long and narrow face. "You must be Goldsmith. First name is Wynn, isn't it? We have been expecting you." He left his chair, walked over, and shook my hand. "I'm Bill Earner, the XO of the 534th. Welcome aboard."

Lt. William A. Earner Jr., USN, Annapolis class of 1963,

demonstrated that day the charm that would serve him well throughout his career. Bill retired in 1996 as a vice admiral. I'm sure that even today, as executive head of the Navy Federal Credit Union, he is still the quick-witted, easygoing, hardworking man I knew thirty years ago.

Bill explained the 534 situation to me. The new MK II PBRs had not yet arrived in country because of shipping delays. Many of the officers and men assigned to the new unit (it had been commissioned just five days before) were being assigned temporary duty to other river sections. Some of the fifty-five enlisted coming from existing sections scattered throughout the Delta would remain with their old units until the boats arrived. Only a small cadre of officers and enlisted would remain there at Nha Be. I was to be farmed out to the 522 River Section down on the Ham Luong River as soon as transportation could be arranged. Bill had emphasized the word "transportation" while raising an eyebrow. After the new boats arrived and were outfitted, the rest of the section would join me on the Ham Luong. The CO (at that time the official designation was officer in charge, OinC), Lt. Ron Wolin, would further explain my assignment when I met him.

Bill and I chatted for perhaps five minutes. I asked about the two other junior officers in my PBR class who had orders to either the 534th or the 535th, Rich Sloane and Jerry Letcher. They could not wait to complete the rain-delayed jungle survival school I had attended the previous week at Subic Bay. Bill told me that they had been farmed out within the last few days.

Bill asked where I had gone to school. I replied, "Mr. Jefferson's University."

Bill smiled and said, "UVA had a pretty good lacrosse team this last year." I interpreted the comment to mean that the Cavaliers had beaten the Navy in that sport, which was popular in colleges around the Washington, D.C., area. I had noticed Bill's big Naval Academy ring on his hand as soon as I met him.

The young man in the green T-shirt, YNSN (yeoman, seaman, E-3) Bruce Burns, took me to see my guide for my short stay in Nha Be. The yeoman even helped me with my bags. We entered the cubicle of the sleeping Lt. (j.g.) Burkie

(Frank) Walker, USNR, in a nearby junior officer barracks. I deposited my gear on an unoccupied bunk in the cubicle and left the room to meet my new commanding officer.

When I first met Ron Wolin, he was putting the finishing pencil touches on his sketch for a River Section 534 emblem, a red dragon spitting fire against the background of the yellow-with-red-pinstripe South Vietnamese flag. The shield-shaped border was green with a stripe of yellow. Ron was copying the Air Cathay dragon artwork from an ad in a magazine. He explained to me that he had first seen the dragon ad in an airline magazine while flying to Saigon several weeks earlier.

Ron was tall, dark, and narrow-waisted but with a muscular upper body. His arms and chest were covered with thick black hair. The hair on his head was also jet black, but fine and thin. Ron said he was from some Massachusetts town whose name I soon forgot. To me Ron was always from "Baasston." I figured his ethnic extraction was a mixed bag. Perhaps German or Dutch with some Portuguese. He was from the Boston area, but definitely not Irish or Italian. His name suggested Dutch or German ancestry. Over the next year we would share some interesting experiences. Ron was a real hero to the young 534 river rats. To me he was a great commanding officer and a friend. I have long forgiven him for his stubborn streak that almost got me killed.

Ron showed me a chart of the area where I was being sent. It was in the eastern Mekong Delta about fifty miles to the southwest. The Navy had recently moored the YRBM-16 on the Ham Luong River at the mouth of the Ben Tre River to accommodate River Section 522. The YRBM-16 was where River Sections 534 and 535 were to be based once the new boats arrived in country. I was to be sent to River Section 522 to learn the operations area and to keep an eye on the 534 sailors who would be TAD (temporary attached duty) to the 522 before the new boats and the rest of the section arrived. River Section 522 was to be sent north to I Corps to guard the river approaches to Hue. I had never heard of Hue but I was familiar with the Ham Luong River and Ben Tre from training classes and instructor sea stories back in California. It was a bad area. Meaning that I could expect a lot of combat. I had been chosen for the assignment because I was the senior jay gee assigned to the 534th. I was even to have the title of senior patrol officer. It was a job similar to that of operations officer on a Navy ship. I was to be third in command of the ten-boat section, just behind the OinC and the XO.

As Ron finished describing my assignment, a bulky young sailor wearing a black beret and carrying some sort of automatic weapon entered the office and interrupted us. The sailor was bursting in pride.

"Mister Wolin, the operation was a success! We got the jeep now in the automotive shed ready for painting."

Ron Wolin smiled that sly, thin smile of his to the young sailor.

"Good work, Tatum. What have you got in your hand? It looks like a French MAP-47."

"Sir, I don't know what it is. I won it in a craps game last night from a SEAL. Figured you might be interested in it."

Ron took the weapon in his hand. It was clean but shiny where the bluing had worn off. The sheet-metal receiver and long straight magazine were ripped by bullet holes. Even I could tell that the weapon was useless.

"Tatum, this would be valuable if it had not been shot up. I don't know any gunsmith here that can make it serviceable. Thanks for showing it to me. You can probably get somebody to pay you twenty bucks for it."

Ron turned to me and said, "Wynn, let's go see your transportation down to the YRBM-16."

The automotive shed was crowded with shirtless sailors huddled around a gray jeep that had USAF-stenciled lettering on its hood. Two sailors were removing the license plate and registration plates under the hood and on the dash with screwdrivers. Others were masking the vehicle with tape. Another sailor was fiddling with a compressed-air-driven paint gun, test-spraying a box cover with dark-green paint. Within ten minutes the U.S. Air Force jeep that had probably carried some officer on a shopping trip to the Saigon Cholon U.S. Military Exchange two hours earlier had been transformed into a U.S. Navy vehicle. This was my introduction to how the river rats of the 534th would operate.

Chapter 3

The next two and a half days at Nha Be went quickly. I went back to my quarters and met an awakened Frank Walker. We were both young southerners surrounded by officers from places such as Boston and Chicago. Frank was a very open and friendly guy from Cajun country, Baton Rouge, with a business degree from LSU. We shared a fondness for things southern. Frank was impressed that I had gone to high school with the recipient of the flea-flicker pass that the University of Georgia had used to defeat Alabama in 1965. I was impressed that Frank had gone to high school with the rock singer who now called himself Johnny Rivers. We became fast friends.

Frank showed me the ropes. Instead of waiting in line in front of a U.S. Navy Supply Corps disbursing officer, I cashed my government check at Ba Nhu's place, a combination beer joint and laundry just outside the base. Ba Nhu reminded me of a portly Bloody Mary from the show *South Pacific*. The pockets of her big dressing gown held thousands of U.S. dollars, Vietnamese piasters, and U.S. military payment certificates (MPC, scrip good only in U.S. exchanges). She probably even had gold coins stashed away in some pocket of her big sarong. Her monetary exchange rates were supposedly the best in the Saigon area. The beer in her joint was cold and cheap. The laundry service was good and fast. I got my name and rank insignia sewed in black thread on two sets of fatigues in the time it took me to suck down a couple of beers. I purchased my first and only black beret, complete with the CTF-116 (coastal patrol force) patch. I suspect the comely Vietnamese girls serving the beer had a lot more to offer the troops during slack business hours but I never got to know for sure.

I went out with Frank on my first patrol that evening. It was on a MK I PBR from 542 Section based at Nha Be. Frank, who had been in country for six whole weeks, was in charge of the two-boat patrol from the Nha Be 542 section, which was glad to get some relief for its own patrol officers. The patrol was twelve hours of tension for me. I was new to the Rung Sat Special Zone. Frank and the other sailors could somehow navigate by landmarks on the twisting channels of the branches of the river—the Soi Rap, the Long Tau, and so forth. To me there were no discernible landmarks, only darkness and desolate riverbank defoliated by chemicals and gunfire. To determine the shape of the river around the boat, I constantly went over to the coxswain's flat to look into the rubber hood covering the Raytheon Pathfinder radar scope. A cigarette smoker like most Navy men of the day, I had to overcome my addiction for the duration of the patrol. That was tough for me. The only interesting thing to happen that night was seeing tracers and hearing gunfire around 0400 when a SEAL team was being extracted from an ambush position under fire about a mile away.

The next afternoon was spent in the little O club that served snacks and beer on a volleyball court in the Nha Be sand. After an hour's play the junior officers defeated an enlisted-men's team (that's my story and I'm sticking to it). On the way back to the barracks I met John Smock, another jay gee and a familiar face from training in California. Like me, John was awaiting the new boats. We laughed over the irony that his original orders were to River Section 534 and mine were to the 535th, to which he was now assigned. He also was TAD (temporary assigned duty) to River Section 542 until the new MK II boats arrived. John said he was going to take a boat downriver for some weapons training. He asked if I wanted to join in. I did.

That day I was introduced to the LAW (lightweight anti-tank weapon), a 66mm shaped-charge rocket fired from a disposable fiberglass tube. Remove the plastic caps at each end of the tube, extend the weapon by a wire bale, line up the target in the sights, uncover the firing button, fire the weapon, and throw the tube away. I had not seen the weapon in training. Clint Eastwood introduced it to movie fans many years ago. In the movies it did wondrous things to bad guys in San Francisco. The day I fired it at a VC bunker months later, the round barely unsettled the dust on the outside of the bunker. The LAW's shaped charge was designed to penetrate armored vehicles, not earthen bunkers. That is, unless the shooter could put the round through a six-by-four-inch firing slit. Then the LAW would do a number on the bunker dwellers. If shrapnel did not get the bad guys, the blast energy surely would. River Section 534 boats would all carry LAWs. Much later in my tour the weapons performed extremely well in a couple of emergencies.

That day in the Rung Sat I fired two LAW rounds. Each was literally a blast. The weapon had no recoil but the back blast sounded like a clap of thunder and was deadly to anyone fewer than twelve feet behind the weapon. My second round chopped down the tallest palm in sight. Already missing its top fronds, I just wanted to put the tree out of its misery. A sailor commented that I had just destroyed a familiar navigation mark. I did not care. I felt comfortable with a new weapon.

On the boat ride back to the base, John Smock gave me some very serious scuttlebutt. He was to be River Section 535's senior patrol officer like I was to be the senior patrol officer of RivSect 534. John told me that we might both get very personally involved in a project recently dreamed up by some glory hound of a river-division commander named Don Sheppard down on the Bassac River, the western branch of the Mekong in the Delta region. Lieutenant Commander Sheppard had proposed that each river section form something called a MACE team. Capt. Paul Gray, commander of CTF-116, the operational commander of the River Patrol Force, had bought Sheppard's concept. MACE was an acronym for mobile assault command element. A MACE team would consist of the senior patrol officer of each section plus six volunteer sailors from each section. Whenever a PBR received low-intensity enemy fire from the bank of a major river, the MACE team would storm ashore armed with flamethrowers and demolition charges and root out the enemy snipers.

I just looked at John and told him that he could not bullshit me. I knew the Navy was not buying into anything like that crap. Still, despite what I said to John, I had my doubts. I had seen a picture of Don Sheppard, the so-called "Bassac Interdictor," in the pages of the recent edition of *Jackstaff*, the Navy's in-country monthly magazine. From the engine covers of a PBR, he was drawing a bow with a flaming arrow. The accompanying article said that Sheppard had destroyed an enemy hootch with his flaming arrow. I said that I thought Sheppard was a showboat. He reminded me of Squirrelly Squires, commander, USN, MinDiv82, back in Charleston. Squires was a man who would do anything to get attention.

John Smock, who had been on a Charleston-based destroyer at the same time I was on the Charleston-based minesweeper, gave me his opinion of Sheppard.

"Don Sheppard is a flaming asshole! Why use flaming arrows when good, old-fashioned Willie Peter (white phosphorous) grenades or Willie Peter mortar rounds will do the trick. Rooting out snipers is not our job. I think Sheppard is a pompous megalomaniac. I will show you the messages that confirm that Captain Gray has bought into this MACE team bullshit."

When later that day John showed me classified messages from CTF-116 directing all river sections to organize MACE teams for imminent training and outfitting, I became depressed. I felt that I would soon die on a muddy, boobytrapped riverbank doing a poor imitation of John Wayne. My dreams of glory had always been to cross the T of a VC armada at night on a river much the way Admiral Oldendorf had done in the Battle of Leyte Gulf. My boats would have detected the VC armada by radar a mile away. I would turn my boats broadside to the enemy at a range of one hundred meters. We would illuminate the enemy with a flare round from our 60mm mortar. Then our eight .50-caliber machine guns would destroy the enemy flotilla.

I never realized my fantasy. But, more important, I never got a chance to play John Wayne. As soon as Admiral Veth, COMUSNFORV (Commander, U.S. Naval Forces, Vietnam), read a report about several PBR sailors' being seriously wounded by booby traps while practicing MACE team concepts in an abandoned enemy bunker complex, he put a stop to that foolishness. God bless the admiral.

That night I enjoyed a poker game with Frank Walker and five others in the junior officer barracks. A couple of the card players were SEALs. This was the first time I had socially met any SEALs. I had seen them training in Coronado when I attended the required counterinsurgency/Vietnamese language classes. While attending classes I had seen and heard the brutality of UDT (underwater demolition team) training during "Hell Week," when would-be frogmen were put through a week of twenty-hour days of rigorous physical and mental activity. They ran, four men to a heavy inflatable rubber raft, which they carried over their heads, everywhere they went for a whole week from exercise to exercise. The "exercises" could be swimming for miles, running for miles in the soft sand of the Silver Strand, endless push-ups, endless squat thrusts, etc. A UDT/SEAL-trained Navy corpsman was always present to see that the trainees did not die. Once a man passed the UDT training, more extraordinarily rigorous training lay ahead if he had been selected for SEALs.

I held my own in the poker game. The five-dollar limit was mild compared to the table-stakes games I had played at the University of Virginia. I remember all-night games back in college in which car keys were traded back and forth even in my first-year dorm recreation room. The secret of my poker skills lay in my instinctive ability to count cards and weigh possibilities. I am a conservative poker player. Unfortunately for my poker playing, I have few of the other attributes of a winning poker player: I cannot mask my expressions, and I do not have a killer instinct. Fortunately the other players, and especially the SEALs, were not serious poker players.

I quickly discovered that SEALs are not supermen. They reminded me of college jocks; they ran their mouths and guzzled beer. I sipped my beer that night. I was more interested in their talk than the cards: the story of one guy's skinning his knee the week before when he jumped into the uncovered engine compartment of a PBR that was being scrambled during a nighttime mortar attack. The "wounded" men thought he deserved a Purple Heart. The SEALs laughed at his case. The story of the crude VC mine, caught in the drag chains of an MSB, that detonated at a pier full of curious spectators, killing some and wounding many more. The story of some unfortunate Vietnamese woodcutters who had been "greased" in a SEAL ambush two nights before. How the dead woodchoppers were added to the SEAL team's tally of enemy killed. How Lyndon Baines Johnson, the only person for whom I had cast a vote in a presidential election, was referred to as "Lying Buying" Johnson. I had been in the Navy for over two years; until that night, I had never heard a derogatory remark about the commander in chief from fellow Navy officers. Within a few months I would join the chorus.

The next morning after breakfast I met the driver who would take me down to the Delta, a young, heavyset quartermaster second class by the name of Robert Hunt. Hunt helped me store my gear in the back of the jeep. On the floorboard on the passenger side were a couple of filled sandbags. As I entered the jeep and put my feet on the sandbags, Hunt handed me a very heavy green haversack. He then handed me an M-14 fully automatic rifle. As Hunt got in the driver's side, I looked into the haversack. There were at least a dozen hand grenades along with two extra twenty-round magazines for the M-14. Most of the grenades were the standard M-26 fragmentation variety but a couple were larger white phosphorous grenades and one was a thermite grenade.

"I think I've thought of everything, Mr. Goldsmith. Hope you don't have to use the rifle or the grenades. If we get ambushed we're on our own. Kill as many gooks as you can. Save a grenade for yourself if we are being overrun. I keep a grenade in my pocket, just in case, everywhere I go over here."

I looked at the sailor. Hunt was perhaps even younger than me. He seemed full of both exuberance and fatalism. I was not that much concerned with the danger of the trip; Ron Wolin had told me the drive down Highway 4 to My Tho was safe. He had done it a couple of times. I was more concerned with being caught in a stolen jeep. I now became concerned about the mental state of my driver.

"Hunt, what if we get stopped by military police looking for stolen jeeps? Don't we have to have some sort of paperwork showing the jeep assigned to our unit?"

"Don't worry about that, sir. The Army's CID (Criminal Investigation Division) pukes came here yesterday looking for the jeep. Why do they always suspect Navy river rats when something gets stolen? Don't the Army have guys with enough balls to liberate stuff from those Saigon warriors? This jeep passed muster. The serial numbers belong to a NAV-SUPT jeep in Saigon. Those dumb-asses only looked at serial numbers on the plates under the hood. We could have saved ourselves some grief by not grinding down the engine's serial number. As far as paperwork is concerned, I even have a motor-pool chit signed by a made-up lieutenant commander, even though Nha Be don't have a motor pool. And besides, MPs never look at GIs leaving Saigon for the Delta. They only question guys driving into town."

During the two hours it took us to drive to My Tho, Hunt filled me in on the details of stealing the jeep. A set of bolt cutters to cut the chain around the steering wheel was all it took. The Navy "liberation" team Hunt had led scouted out several jeeps. Only Air Force jeeps were considered targets because the Army had the responsibility for tracking down thefts of military equipment in Saigon and our team thought that maybe the Criminal Investigation Division would not press too hard in a case of stolen Air Force property. This jeep was practically brand-new and it had been parked close to an easy escape route. In those days military vehicles in a war zone never used keys for the ignition system. The big security device was a padlock on the gas cap to prevent sappers from putting a grenade into the gas tank.

Hunt told me that he had been a seaman assigned to after-steering on a destroyer accompanying the USS *Maddox* when it was engaged in the famous Gulf of Tonkin incident in August 1964, which was used by LBJ to escalate the American buildup against North Vietnam. Hunt said that he wanted only to kill gooks and become a PBR boat captain. He told me some questionable war stories. I was more interested in the passing panorama of rice paddies, water buffalo, military checkpoints, and war scars on an otherwise idyllic country-side. Bomb craters were scattered randomly. Some were close to built-up areas. Some were in the middle of fields. Hunt continued to tell me tales of the war.

Traffic delays at bridges over narrow waterways made the forty-mile trip slow going. Each bridge seemed to have a

South Vietnamese armored personnel carrier (APC) and a couple of sandbagged machine gun positions. There were dozens of bridges. Very young Vietnamese soldiers with M-1 carbines directed traffic at the bridges, which allowed for only one-way flow across the waterways. Most of the traffic was civilian: old buses, aged black French Citroën automobiles straight out of *Casablanca,* some Volkswagens, and a lot of Honda motorbikes and three-wheeled Lambretta cyclos with small cargo beds behind the passenger and driver.

On the outskirts of My Tho we encountered a South Vietnamese armored column turning down a dirt track to our left. Hunt told me that they were from the 7th ARVN (Army of the Republic of Vietnam) Division and were "a bunch of worthless bastards." I thought that at least those nineteen-year-old drivers of the APCs and two-and-a-half-ton trucks could drive their big vehicles. A year before most of them had probably driven only water buffaloes from the rice paddies. A tangible result of billions of dollars already spent.

Highway 4 went right through the center of My Tho, past the Victory Hotel on the left and the Carter Hotel on the right. Hunt explained to me that the hotels had been requisitioned for living quarters and offices by the river rats of the 533 and 532 sections. Commander River Division 53, in charge of the three PBR sections in the eastern Delta, had made the Victory Hotel his headquarters. Our jeep continued past a traffic circle and into the gates of the U.S. Navy Support Center, a sectioned-off portion of a South Vietnamese naval base that had been home for the French brown-water navy during their war years here.

Hunt went off to look up some river-rat buddies. I walked down to the quay wall and piers. On one pier was a nest of a dozen PBRs. A couple of other boats were up on skids, being repaired by shirtless sailors. I was more interested in viewing the My Tho River. This easternmost branch of the Mekong was at least a mile wide. In another thirty miles the mighty river would flow into the South China Sea, completing the water flow that had started over twenty-three hundred miles away in the mountains of Tibet. The dirty, brown river had a small chop of surface waves. A couple of flat, open islands were visible in the expanse between the banks. The river reminded me of the Mississippi from the Vicksburg side. The opposite bank looked like solid vegetation. Dark-green nipa palms and taller coconut palms. Numerous watercraft were visible on the river: colorful water taxis, junks loaded with bundles of who knew what, and hundreds of smaller sampans, each with one or two passengers wearing conical straw hats. Most of the sampans had a little lawn-mower engine in the stern. I had finally reached the waters of the Mekong Delta, where I would either be on boats, on patrol, or on anchored barges for most of the next year.

The officer I talked with at the My Tho operations center told me it was not advisable to continue on to Ben Tre that day because there was only one more ferry crossing the river and no other military traffic was crossing on it. I was advised to wait until the next morning when an armored resupply convoy was scheduled to head to Ben Tre. I wanted to get to Ben Tre posthaste, but I also wanted security. I sought other opinions.

I found Hunt talking with some enlisted SEALs (distinguishable by their long hair, khaki shorts, and the weapons they were cleaning on a table) outside a Quonset hut. I told him that maybe we should probably wait until the next morning before continuing on to Ben Tre. Hunt protested. His arguments that the YRBM-16 had air-conditioning and better chow than the Victory Hotel mess were strong as far as he was concerned, but I just did not want to face another day of Hunt's bullshit. I also rationalized that the Viet Cong probably did not expect us to come down that road that day. If they were smart they would wait for the scheduled convoy the next morning. I figured the enemy was smart.

Our jeep was the only military vehicle on the ferry. There were a lot of cyclos, motorbikes, and a couple of small trucks carrying goods from the My Tho marketplace across the river. A lot of the passengers were old women afoot in conical straw hats. They had betel-nut-stained teeth, and their *chogi* poles had wicker baskets at each end packed with produce. Several small Vietnamese boys, perhaps five to seven years old, approached me in the jeep. They giggled and seemed extremely interested in the hair on my arms. Some of the bolder ones came up and touched the hair. I guess it was a game of who would be the first to touch the strange hair on the arm of the barbarian giant.

The village on the south bank was almost an armed camp. Dozens of armed Vietnamese soldiers could be seen on the street or in the confines of a couple of earthen forts on either side of the ferry landing.

From the landing, the road south was just a dirt track. About two hundred yards down the road we encountered a bamboo-pole barrier and a squad of Vietnamese soldiers. It took some convincing and all my Vietnamese language skills and two years of high school French to get them to lift the barrier. Hunt had not been all that helpful; he wanted to drive right through it.

After about a mile of driving through a dark tunnel of palm trees that only partially masked little villages from our view and crossing a small bridge surrounded by Vietnamese soldiers, we encountered our first mine crater. It was in the center of the road, twelve feet across and four feet deep. Peasants wearing black pajamas were filling the hole with earth and lengths of palm log. Other Vietnamese, in green uniforms and with drawn rifles, watched as Hunt maneuvered the jeep around the mine crater. They shouted what were probably warnings but neither Hunt nor I understood.

After another half mile, the roadside began to change. There were no longer any visible signs of human life, just trees. Then we entered a really dark and desolate two-hundred-yard stretch where all the vegetation seemed black and oily. The tops of the trees had all been blown off and the trunks bore further scars of war. We came to yet another crater in the road and nobody was around to fill it. Again Hunt drove the jeep around the crater. We saw some ashes of what had probably been hootches. We drove past the burnt-out wreck of an armored personnel carrier. The front of the armored vehicle looked like a tin can perforated by .22-rifle fire. When I was thirteen years old I loved to shoot up tin cans with the J. C. Higgins bolt-action .22 that I had received from my parents (via the Sears and Roebuck catalog) on my previous birthday. A .22-caliber rifle definitely did not produce the holes in the APC, which had probably been caused by a 75mm recoilless rifle. Some of the vegetation in the area was still smoldering, a sign that the battle had taken place recently.

Hunt sped up. He told me to take off the safety on the M-14 and to shoot at anybody I saw. I was nervous but my driver was a maniac. The jeep got up to forty miles an hour as we bounced down the track. It was all I could do to stay in the vehicle much less steady the heavy rifle over the dash.

After a few hundred yards the track went into an open area about a quarter of a mile long. Fallow rice paddies. Then, a hundred yards ahead, we met more trees and vegetation. I saw armed men in the middle of the road. They were wearing black pajamas and conical straw hats. Hunt yelled for me to open fire. Fortunately I did not. Hunt drove the jeep so fast, the men had to jump out of its path.

The men in the black pajamas were armed with M-1 rifles and M-1 carbines, the first line of defense for Ben Tre, which was another two miles south. They were Popular Force irregulars, home guard soldiers who had been armed to defend their villages. This particular village happened to be close to the Ben Tre airfield, a source of employment to nearby villagers, who got paid for being human trip wires. Thank God, for them and me, their rifles were never pointed at our jeep. The M-14's safety was off and the selector was switched to full automatic. Two M-26 fragmentation grenades were cradled at my crotch. The first for them. The second for them also. I could still get to the sack for the one for me if it came to that.

After passing through the little village, the dirt track went into another open expanse of dried-up rice paddies. That one extended for almost half a mile. Ahead on the right was the single asphalt runway of the airfield. I saw a couple of huts and a small single-engine plane that resembled a Piper Cub parked near a wind sock pole. But this airfield had no control tower and none of the revetments for parked aircraft that I had seen at Tan Son Nhut. I felt relief. We were close to Ben Tre.

Ben Tre surprised me. With a population of over thirty-five thousand, it was much larger than I had expected, and it had a lot of well-maintained houses and businesses undamaged by the war. Many buildings were stucco or brick and had red-tile roofs. I had expected thatched roofs on mud huts. The road curved around to the left of a small lake complete with a grove of tall palms someone had planted. It must have dated to the French colonial period. The area was some sort of park, and it was being used as a park. Women and children were walking around the lake admiring the hundreds of ducks in the water and along the shore. A very tranquil scene. We then entered a wide and long open-air market surrounded by two- and three-story masonry buildings. It was full of old men and women and children. The only young men were occasional Vietnamese national policemen walking around with old Thompson .45-caliber submachine guns strapped to their shoulders. Some of these guns were without their wooden stocks, making them into just really big machine pistols. But they did appear to be nifty, menacing badges of authority when slung over the shoulder of some young buck of a peasant wearing a splendid white shirt and a peaked police officer's cap.

We found the USMACV compound just where it had been indicated to us on the old French ordnance survey map I had unfolded after we passed the airfield. The compound was on the north bank of the Ben Tre River and just a hundred yards west of the river boundary of the marketplace and the imposing steel bridge that arched at least a hundred yards across the river.

Much later, after I had gone under that bridge many times on PBRs, I learned that the long steel bridge was unique in the Delta. The bridge was on pilings that penetrated over two hundred feet into the Mekong mud before they reached bedrock. That bridge could accommodate trucks up to two and a half tons. In the Delta, other streams as wide as the Ben Tre River required ferry boats. That bridge was something special.

We parked the jeep outside the riverside entrance to the compound. At the entrance, two soldiers—one Vietnamese, the other an American—were manning a sandbagged guard post under a large sign in two languages with the MACV logo handsomely painted on it. I told the American soldier that I needed to contact the U.S. Navy representatives in Ben Tre. The heavy gate swung open and Hunt drove the jeep into the compound as the American soldier asked how we had reached Ben Tre. When I told him we had just driven down the road from the My Tho ferry landing, he saluted and said, "Sir, you are a lucky sonofabitch."

In the next twenty minutes I checked out transport to the YRBM-16, ate at the MACV* mess, and met a couple of characters. Five months later, one would give Peter Arnett one of the most enduring clichés of the Vietnam War. The other would show me what it took for the Navy to fight the enemy in the Delta. We got to know each other in the mess hall.

USAF Maj. Chester Brown was a forward air controller who flew a little L-19 observation plane from the Ben Tre airstrip in support of ARVN ground operations. In 1945, Chet had been a twenty-year-old pilot of a B-17G dropping strings of bombs over Nazi Germany while flying in formation with scores of other bombers. Now he flew his little Piper Cub–like aircraft at treetop level over the waterways of the Delta. The major ordnance on his little spotter plane were the smoke rockets used to mark targets and the Swedish K 9mm submachine gun that he fired with one hand at the VC from treetop level at a hundred knots or slower.

Jack Harold was a USN(IR) lieutenant. He and I shared Georgia accents. I was from Atlanta. Jack was from Quitman, a small south Georgia hamlet. Very different areas of a big state. But in 1967 a lot of people in the other forty-nine United States automatically assumed that white folks from Georgia were backward racists. Jack and I probably had shared a lot of the put-downs from others while in the Navy. Jack welcomed me as another "Jawja boy." He was a naval aviator, a qualified jet pilot on the Navy F-4 Phantom jet. He had been trained to shoot down MiGs with radar-guided rockets but he was in naval intelligence. He said that he and his Kit Carson Scouts worked closely with PBRs, SEALs, and PRUs. I did not ask him what Kit Carsons or PRUs meant as I did not want to appear ignorant to him.

Jack, who at six feet and at least three inches looked much too big for the cockpit of an F-4, told Chet that I could be his

---

*The MACV compound was a full square block of barracks, administrative offices, armories, etc., surrounded by a ten-foot masonry wall. Nearly one hundred U.S. Army advisers operated out of there as well as over two hundred Vietnamese command and support troops for Kien Hoa Province. It was a choice military target for the Viet Cong.

ticket to a meal in the wardroom of the YRBM-16. I told the major I would get him invited to a meal in the wardroom as soon as I could arrange it. I got the impression that Jack Harold was persona non grata at my new base, that he simply did not enjoy the wardroom company on board it, or he did not want to be with regulation naval personnel. Major Brown simply wanted to enjoy some good Navy food.

When I told them about my ride from Nha Be in the stolen jeep, they both laughed. Jack told me that only fools or smart warriors would do that last five miles of the trip in a lone jeep. What was I? I replied that I was a fool, of course. I had just arrived from the States. They told me that the VC in that area were lazy part-timers; as long as the VC in the vicinity did not expect a vehicle to come down the track, the vehicle probably would not be taken under fire. They only carried out operations when ordered by the cadre of full-time VC fighters who stayed in secure areas miles away. Jack and Chet both said that they were looking forward to working with River Section 534. Jack was most appreciative when I told him that Ron Wolin wanted the purloined jeep handed over to the senior Navy officer at Ben Tre. Jack smiled and said that the jeep must belong to him, then.

"Ron knows that's me. I'll put that sucker to good use."

I realized then that the war would be somewhat different from what I had imagined. It was a local war, and I had better get used to the locals.

Chapter 4

A gray LCM-6 came down to the small dock beside the sea-
wall on the north side of the Ben Tre River at the MACV compound. Five or six young sailors wearing green uniforms and
black berets jumped off and headed for the marketplace to
spend their money. Hunt and I carried our gear aboard the
steel landing craft. I stored my stuff beside the pilothouse and
met the coxswain. He and the other crew member were wearing the familiar Navy working uniform of blue denim trousers
and chambray shirts. Only steel helmets distinguished them
from a liberty boat crew from some amphib ship in Naples,
Palma, Hong Kong, or wherever sailors went ashore on
LCM-6s for some fun. Two M-14 rifles were leaning against
the steel plates of the pilothouse and two .50-caliber machine
guns were mounted on stanchions behind the pilothouse. The
petty officer in the pilothouse asked me if we were the only
passengers to be picked up. When I replied in the affirmative,
the boat cast off in a roar of diesel engines. I got the impression he did not want to stay too long at that boat landing.

The thirty-minute boat ride down river was uneventful but
the number of watercraft on the river fascinated me. There
were hundreds of them. The coxswain watched out for sampans in front of the boat while the other crew member
watched the south bank at the port side machine gun position.
I studied that south bank. Scores of little streams almost
covered up by thick vegetation flowed into the river from it.
Through the vegetation I glimpsed bamboo and thatch
hootches. The south bank was home to tens of thousands of
poor Vietnamese farmers and fishermen living in little hamlets that were almost like subdivisions. Instead of roads and
quarter acres, the six-hundred-square-foot dwellings had per-

haps two thousand feet of land for gardens and tiny canals as their roadways. In peacetime the people enjoyed good lives. Fish, fruit, and vegetables were in abundance. As long as there was a good rice crop, the Vietnamese peasants in the Delta lacked for nothing. Except, perhaps, for some political respect.

The YRBM-16 was visible almost a mile away as the LCM-6 made a slow turn to the left. The base looked like a big white ark. It appeared to be anchored almost directly in the mouth of the Ben Tre River where the Ben Tre and Ham Luong rivers joined. As we approached I could tell that the base was in fact anchored to two mooring buoys along an axis parallel to the wide Ham Luong and only two hundred meters from the mouth of the Ben Tre. It looked too close to shore for me.

Once aboard the YRBM-16 I felt comfortable in the familiar surroundings of gray-painted steel bulkheads, air-conditioning, the hum of big diesel engines (for the electrical generators), government-issue furnishings, shiny linoleum decks, even the diesel-fuel fumes. I was most appreciative of the air-conditioning. I even had a made-up lower-rack bunk waiting for me in a stateroom that had steel locker drawers for my gear. I was home! Except for the fact that the junior-officer bunk room was much more spacious, it reminded me of my quarters aboard the *Fidelity*. Probably something like what junior officers on aircraft carriers enjoyed.

After iced tea in the wardroom, I checked in with the executive officer of the 522 River Section, Lt. Bill Larsen, USN.

I remember little about my six-week stay on the YRBM-16 other than what happened on patrol, my dislike of Larsen and my worrying about doing the job right. I feared that I would let others down. I feared that I could not make the right decisions in combat to save the lives of the sailors under me. I knew that I would have to overcome those fears. I knew that I would have to trust people under me. Larsen had not gotten to that point. I bet he never did.

Perhaps Bill Larsen was overcome by his responsibilities. He had a lot of administrative problems. River Section 522, which had recently been sent to Ben Tre, would be ordered to I Corps (the northernmost of South Vietnam's four corps tactical zones) as soon as the 534 and 535 River Sections became operational and relieved them. The 522, which had been in combat over a year, had just become acclimated to the Ham Luong. Now they were to be sent north, near Hue. A move like that required a lot of logistical support, and Larsen was responsible for making sure that everything was done in accordance with Navy regulations. All the admin reports on personnel and equipment status had to be brought up to date. Inventories of classified material, weapons, ammunition, and spare parts had to be made. Shipping containers had to be located and carefully packed. Charts of the new op area would have to be obtained. Boats "down" for various casualties would have to be fixed. All requests for out-of-country R & R by eligible troops would have to be reviewed. All the award citations put forward by men engaged in combat for their buddies, all the nonjudicial punishments (those not involving court martial) against disorderly sailors, all the inspections that even the brown-water navy required, were the bailiwick of a river section XO. Perhaps Bill Larsen was stressed out and overwhelmed.

Nah. I figure that Larsen was just a born asshole. He created his own stressful demons. I've seen a bunch like him over the years.

The morale of the troops was low. The 522 River Section river rats felt they were being jerked around; the luxury accommodations of the YRBM-16 were to be given over to new outfits; they would have to go aboard some rusty old LST (landing ship, tank) and get bounced around until they reached some godforsaken river near the DMZ. They all thought they were being sent on a suicide mission and wanted to know what they had done to earn the new assignment. All these things must have weighed heavily on Bill Larsen. Unfortunately, from what I saw, he was not up to the task. He could not delegate and did not trust junior officers, much less the petty officers.

The first thing Larsen wanted was for me to bring charges against Hunt for being disrespectful to a superior petty officer. No "Good to meet you. Welcome aboard. Good to see you" stuff, like Bill Earner's greeting.

Evidently QM2 Robert Hunt had pissed off the first class

gunner's mate in charge of the YRBM-16 armory when he turned in the M-14 rifle and sack of grenades. Hunt had acted surly: he had demanded a receipt! The first class (paygrade E-6) had assumed that Hunt was a chief petty officer (paygrade E-7). He gave Hunt a receipt. But Hunt had cursed him when the first class had asked where the custody card for the rifle was located. Hunt had no clue where the custody card was and told that to the first class, using profane language.

The first class petty officer soon found out that Hunt was only a recently promoted Ho Chi Minh second class. (Ho Chi Minh promotions basically meant that sailors in Vietnam got promoted as soon as their time in service permitted regardless of examinations or completion of courses.) The first class bitched. His bitch found its way to the RivSect 522 admin office within an hour. Now Larsen wanted me to make amends by disciplining Hunt. I respectfully told Larsen that I had no administrative powers to discipline sailors from the 534th. I would be happy to counsel Hunt and to report the incident to Lt. Ron Wolin, OinC of my unit. Larsen seemed even more pissed off. He warned me that he would remember my lack of cooperation.

I was not intimidated. Stronger officers than Larsen had threatened me. Most of the threats had come from my first CO on the *Fidelity*, Lt. Comdr. Stephen Belechek. That hardnosed, up-from-the-ranks, former EOD (explosive ordnance demolitions) specialist, who had cleared underwater obstacles in Korean waters in a combat environment fifteen years before, would not tolerate best efforts that failed. He demanded perfection, even from junior officers just out of college. Captain Belechek often threatened me when I did not perform my job as engineering officer to his standards. If I failed he would have me transferred to be the "inspection officer on the scuttlebutts of some bird farm." This meant that he could see to it that I was assigned to an aircraft carrier, where junior officers were regarded as lower than whale shit. The engineering department on his ship would pass every INSURV inspection or there would be hell to pay. Once, just before my first INSURV inspection, I told him that some stainless steel ladders between decks had steel (magnetic) bolts attaching the ladder runners to the deck instead of the prescribed stainless steel bolts.

Captain Steve just looked at me and told me to get the non-magnetic bolts within two days even if I had "to shit them."

I did not tell him about the classified publication that was missing. Like several of my predecessors, I had signed for it sight unseen. Only I had subsequently inventoried and page-checked the classified pub safe and found that the publication *Operations in Arctic Waters,* classified as NATO Confidential, was missing. I decided to solve that problem the hard way. I went to the classified publication control library at nearby COMINLANT ready to kneel on my sword and confess to the missing publication. There I found out that the particular publication had never been issued to any Charleston-based MSO! Over the preceding nine years, hundreds of signatures in the ship's records had verified the presence of the publication. I quickly wised up to the real Navy world of letting the chicken stuff slide and concentrating on the important stuff.

I solved the problem of the missing nonmagnetic bolts the easy way, by telling a first class engineman that I would up his semiannual evaluation in the area of resourcefulness if he had some contacts at the shore-based machine shops who could fabricate the bolts on short notice. The petty officer came through. The fact that I had the collateral job of supply officer on the ship, and could write off ten pounds of coffee as barter payment, made the deal easy.

I told Lieutenant Larsen that both Hunt and I would be available for patrol assignments immediately. He was free to put Hunt under the thumb of his toughest boat captain. I would take out any boats assigned to me. My attitude seemed to placate Larsen. He gave me a two-boat patrol for the next morning.

Later that day I met the OinC of River Section 522. Lt. Jim Dykes was the most laid-back officer I met in Vietnam. When I first saw him he was sunbathing up on the helo deck and wearing nothing but a Speedo-type bathing suit. He had a dark tan and his thin body was covered with suntan lotion. He reminded me of the movie actor George Hamilton. He was not the least bit concerned about going up north to the Perfume River. He was more anxious that a recent directive had put an end to waterskiing behind PBRs.

"Can you believe someone would be dumb enough to put out an after-action report indicating a PBR was taken under fire while towing a skier? Now that dumb-ass has spoiled a lot of recreation for sailors. We had four sets of skis, including a great new slalom model. Now they are locked up. I used to love skiing out here in this area of the Ham Luong."

Jim Dykes had a southern accent. I soon found out that he had graduated from the NROTC program at Auburn and that he planned to go back to destroyers when he left Vietnam in a couple of months. I asked about our patrol area on the Ham Luong. He said it could be dangerous if the boats started chasing sampans up the little canals off the main river and advised me to stick to the main river, and to be careful in Ambush Alley, a crossing corridor just a mile and a half south of where the YRBM-16 was anchored. He said that the presence of PBRs on the main rivers was causing the Viet Cong problems in moving men and supplies. We were doing our job just by being there. Going off the main rivers in search of Viet Cong was the job of the Mobile Riverine Force and the ARVNs. Jim had a sensible approach to what he regarded as a "little pissant of a war nobody will remember thirty years from now."

I asked Jim why the base was anchored so close to the mouth of the Ben Tre River. He replied that it was a political decision made against the wishes of both him and the base OinC. The LDO (limited duty officer) lieutenant (O-3) in charge of the base was very concerned about a swimmer/sapper attack at night launched from the south bank of the Ben Tre River, but, to placate the Kien Hoa Province chief, the powers in Saigon wanted a powerful American presence near the Kien Hoa capital, but not actually in the city. The province chief was a Vietnamese Army officer handpicked for the job by President Thieu, so Saigon had overruled the on-scene commanders for political reasons. To placate the YRBM-16 OinC, a SEAL team had recently surveyed the situation and determined that the local Viet Cong lacked the personnel and equipment to mount an attack by swimmers because the current was too strong for the locals to handle. Lookouts and a roving patrol by an LCM-6 boat would be sufficient to thwart any attack by surface craft. That was the

conventional wisdom at the time. In late November it was
demonstrated that conventional wisdom in the Vietnam War
was just blind stupidity.

The next morning at 0600 I had the opportunity to lead my
first patrol in that "little pissant of a war."

Chapter 5

A normal daylight PBR patrol from the YRBM-16 would usually begin for the crews and patrol officers with a red flashlight being shined in their faces around 0500. In the junior-officer bunk rooms, the man with the flashlight would usually be a young Filipino steward's mate. Then it was a matter of visiting the head and returning to the bunk room to dress by red-lensed flashlight. The standard dress was tropical jungle fatigues, combat jungle boots, and some sort of hat. Flak jackets and steel helmets for the crews were left on the boats but patrol officers, who had no assigned boat, had to carry that heavy gear with them from the bunk rooms. The two patrol officers for the two departing boat patrols would then usually go to the communications center to get briefed on what had happened overnight. The radiomen manning the comm center would relay any information that they felt might be of interest: outposts that had been attacked; incidents involving enemy fire against PBRs in our area of responsibility or adjacent patrol areas assigned to other sections; friendly operations under way or expected; and any changes in callsigns for friendly forces. The friendly forces were usually company-size Vietnamese Regional Force infantry and their U.S. Army advisers located in district capitals, or the Vietnamese Popular Forces often clad only in black pajamas and equipped with World War II–era weapons, stationed at villages outside the district towns. The Popular Force troops were part-time soldiers who had to guard their homes at night. District capitals were usually small towns with populations of a few thousand Vietnamese, most of whom lived in the numerous hamlets surrounding the district towns. The "secure" districts, with their hamlets, were in turn mostly surrounded by "contested areas," or places where the Viet Cong ruled the night and, often, the day.

Usually there was nothing of interest in the briefings for PBR patrols. Outposts here and there would have received harassing fire; friendly forces were to make daylight sweeps. The day-in and night-out tempo of small-unit actions throughout the Delta was typical of the way the war was being fought. The patrol officers would note callsign changes on their charts and then go down to the mess deck to have a big Navy breakfast. An officer with a light appetite would breakfast on sweet rolls, juice, and coffee in the wardroom.

By the time the patrol officer arrived on his assigned boat the engines were running, the ice water and cases of C rations were aboard, and the radios had been checked. There was no need to check the fuel or ammunition load. Every boat was refueled, rearmed, and had its guns cleaned before being secured from its previous patrol.

At some predetermined coordinate shortly before daylight, the two departing boats would rendezvous with other boats that had been on patrol. The turnover points were randomly selected, but usually close to known enemy crossing areas. The boats would detect each other by radar and get together. The boat carrying the patrol officer for the new patrol would come alongside the nearest boat from the on-station patrol. This nearest boat would usually have the patrol officer from the retiring patrol aboard. The two boats on patrol would usually be a half mile or so apart. They would be within visual range and close enough to give mutual support, but still provide good coverage of the known crossing sites. The patrol officer from the boat to be relieved would pass on any significant information about the previous night's action: outposts that had been attacked, "contacts" on the water that had evaded fire or had led to being taken. If the boat being relieved carried a 60mm mortar that the new patrol required, the tube and several cases of ammunition would be transferred to the relieving boat. All of this was done with no lights while talking in whispers. Once relieved, careful not to indicate by the noise of their engines that an exchange had just taken place, the incoming patrol boats would gather speed. A half mile from the exchange site the crew would kick up to over twenty-five knots and head as fast as they could for hot chow and sleep in air-conditioned comfort before they would have to be out on the river again.

Shortly before dawn, little blips began to appear on the radar scope. Most of them would be innocent sampans carrying peasants on early trips to the market. Possibly some of them would be Viet Cong decoys. The judgment of the PBR patrol officers and boat captains determined which radar targets were intercepted. A lot of local boating activity took place just before dawn. Most of the Vietnamese peasants just wanted to get moving to market as soon as the 0600 curfew was lifted. Depending on the weather conditions there could still be an hour or so before full daylight had burned off the morning fog that was prevalent especially in the monsoon season, May through November, in the Mekong Delta.

My first patrol was in the area north of the YRBM-16. All the radar blips were hugging the east bank of the Ham Luong, heading south to market. None were going west to the "free-fire zone" on Tan Tan Island.

Tan Tan Island was four miles long. It hugged the west bank of the Ham Luong and was separated from the riverbank by a narrow (thirty-meter-wide) channel, the Cai Cam. The southern tip of the island was on a line between the YRBM-16 anchorage and the Ben Tre ferry landing on the east bank of the Ham Luong. The southern portion of Tan Tan was considered a secure zone, and several Vietnamese outposts guarded the ferry landing on the west bank of the Ham Luong. From the ferryboat landing an unpaved road led to the Mo Cay district capital five miles to the southwest. The road was dotted with outposts all the way to the district town of Mo Cay, which was not really the true district town. The more populous and traditional district town was firmly in the hands of the Viet Cong at night and usually even during the day. It was the scene of never-ending battles. The northern portion of Tan Tan Island was so securely held by the Viet Cong that it was designated a "free-fire zone." (That phrase was abandoned late in the fall of 1967 and replaced by the more politically correct "specified strike zone.") Whatever these areas were called, they were clearly marked on PBR charts by diagonal red stripes, and the meaning was the same: basically, anybody ob-

served in those areas was considered fair game for any gunships spotting them from the air, and PBRs could test-fire their
weapons at will after confirming with the MACV net that no
friendlies were in the area. Anybody evading by sampan into
such areas could be taken under fire without the customary
warning shots dictated by the established rules of engagement.
Sampans leaving such areas would be thoroughly searched.
The slightest bit of contraband or improper identification
cards (*can couics*) would cause the occupants to be regarded
as VC suspects, and they would be hauled off to the Vietnamese national police at Ben Tre for interrogation.

My first patrol on the Ham Luong was like most of the one
hundred sixty or so patrols I did on my tour there. It was
strange but unremarkable. We were not fired upon but did see
evidence of the war that was all around. On day patrols the
river rats would inspect sampans and junks at random. The
sailors would trade cigarettes and C rations for fresh vegetables. The Vietnamese on the sampans would mostly be old
women or men and children under the age of five. Children
from five to thirteen would be in school if possible. Even during a destructive war, the Vietnamese people knew that education for the young was paramount even if the school was in a
thatched hut in a bombed-out village under Viet Cong control.

All the young men would be either in the uniform of the
South Vietnamese Army or in Viet Cong base camps. The
Vietnamese people on the main river never showed antago-
nism about the American sailors' interrupting their trips to
market. PBR sailors were usually the only Americans encountered by Vietnamese in the Mekong Delta. The peasants knew
that we might kill their Viet Cong friends or relatives. They
knew that we would defend and protect their families and
friends who were against the Viet Cong. They also were very
appreciative of the tens of thousands of little 2.5-horsepower
lawn-mower engines that the U.S. government gave them under the USAID program. They all smiled and graciously accepted our gifts of chewing gum, candy, and occasional
propaganda leaflets. If an older kid was aboard a sampan or
junk we inspected, he or she would invariably say in English,
"PBR sailors number one. You give me candy?"

After a few hours the sun and humidity would start to take

their toll. The young sailors would want do something less boring. Any excuse to visit an outpost, go to the marketplace, or run into some canal or Mekong tributary off the main river would be a welcome relief to being a customs cop on a drifting PBR.

The only diversions on my first two patrols were shopping runs into the Ben Tre marketplace and the Army PX at the Dong Tam base five miles west of My Tho on the My Tho River. Since the 522 sailors knew that they were soon to be headed to I Corps, they wanted to stock up on things that might not be available in the ship's store of an LST. The Ben Tre marketplace was a black market cornucopia of uniforms, toiletries, and cheap souvenirs, and was considered a routine patrol area. The Ben Tre cafes also offered excellent bakery items such as French bread and pastries. To take my first patrol into the marketplace, I rationalized that Ben Tre was in my patrol area. I was smart enough to follow the suggestion of the first class commander of my boat to order that at least two sailors were to remain on each craft at all times, one in the coxswain's flat and the other in the forward .50 turret with his guns trained on the south bank.

Dong Tam was out of our patrol area but it was close enough that 522 boats could respond to emergencies in its area. Sometimes referred to as Dog Town, Dong Tam was quite a sight. Its six hundred acres was home to thousands of GIs from the 9th Division and and sailors from the Navy's Mobile Riverine Force (CTF-117). It had its own airfield. It had a hospital. It even had Red Cross girls. When the full Mobile Riverine Force was present at the anchorage on the north bank of the My Tho River, a half dozen large naval craft such as YRBMs and LSTs and hundreds of landing craft were present. Most of the landing craft were tied up to pontoons lashed to the sides of the larger naval craft. A lot of those landing craft had been converted for river warfare. They were painted jungle green and bristled with cannons and machine guns. Some had a small helo pad attached for helicopter medical evacuation. Some were command-and-control boats for infantry company and battalion commanders. They were obvious from the many antennae sticking up from the control center. Most of the boats had steel bar armor surrounding their exposed freeboard. That was to prematurely detonate enemy armor-piercing rockets and minimize the effect of the shaped-charge warheads. The bar armor was effective against 57mm recoilless rounds. Sometimes it would even slow down the destruction of RPG-2s (B-40) and RPG-7s (B-50).

PBRs tied up to Navy piers inside a little harbor carved out of the east bank of a man-made canal that formed the western boundary of the base. It must have comprised hundreds of acres of rice paddies that had recently been filled in with sand and mud dredged from the My Tho River. The western bank of the canal into Dong Tam harbor was lined with little palm-thatched tin huts with signs proclaiming the availability of everything from sex to cold beer. A lot of the signs had full-color paintings of comely nude oriental women and bore legends like "Scientific Bath Massage," "GI Pleasure Palace." Most of the signs were pockmarked with bullet holes. The buildings on that western canal bank consisted mostly of off-limits whorehouses. Somehow they kept in business. At night the Viet Cong would move into the area to fire rockets and mortars into Dong Tam. When that happened, the 9th Division soldiers on perimeter guard duty along the eastern bank of the canal would respond with defensive fire ranging from guard-post machine guns to artillery pieces firing beehive rounds filled with antipersonnel flechettes.

The harbor also had an asphalt ramp for the Navy's PACVs (patrol air cushion vehicles). The strange hybrids—half helicopter, half boat—were sixty feet long, ten-ton, heavily armed, seventy-mile-an-hour hovercraft based at Dong Tam. The PACVs were flashy, noisy, expensive, and ineffective. Later I got a ride on one of them. The OinC was a washed-out airedale jay gee. Even at the time I thought those monsters were a waste of taxpayers' dollars.

On my third day-patrol, my two boats came under sniper fire from the thick nipa palms along the bank of Tan Tan Island. *Pop! Pop! Pop!* Bullets kicked up water in three-round increments just behind the path of the PBRs. I followed the then-standard PBR doctrine: the two boats picked up speed and increased the distance from the sniper to four hundred yards, then made a firing run using the machine guns. Then we turned around and went by the area without firing. Again we

Canal. There was no intel to be passed, and the relieved boats proceeded to gather speed for the ten-minute trip back to the YRBM-16. The crews on my patrol were at general quarters, the men manning their guns and wearing flak jackets and helmets. Cool ground fog blanketed the river. We used our Raytheon radars to maintain our positions, as the two boats did lazy figure eights on the river, and to monitor the east channel of the river. I recognized what had been described to me in training in California as Ambush Alley. On the radar scope I could see the islands, the cuts between the islands, the curvature of the river, the Mo Cay Canal.

I realized that I was less than a mile from where a company Viet Cong had destroyed a PBR and wounded a bunch of ors who had grown complacent. They had responded to a r attack in the same manner they had on numerous other ions. When they slowed down and closed the bank a hundred yards, with their guns blasting at the sniper's hole, they had been clobbered by 57mm recoilless ri- heavy machine guns from camouflaged bunkers along ard-wide stretch of river near the sniper's position. after the one-sided firefight, the Ruff Puffs (Re-rce/Popular Force South Vietnamese troops) had bank from which the fire had come. The Ruff Puffs sualties from booby traps but determined that the d taken weeks to prepare the site. Their holes and ns had been established over many nights. All been done by dozens of laborers and the posi- used by nearly one hundred fighters. Their hard off; the Viet Cong had made the PBR sailors r the trouble they had been causing the Viet ations network.

ed not to let my boats get waxed by a supe- losing in on a decoy sniper. After all, that t of the half-hour training session back in tablish a pattern in an area where the en- rbanks around you.

nspecting sampans leaving the Mo Cay en Tre marketplace, the patrol cruised western channel to the end of the mid- yond. I wanted to make contact with

were fired on. Three-shot bursts that had the angle right but fell short by fifty yards or so. Again the two PBRs went on a firing run. The bullets from our PBRs were in line with the sniper's position, but many of them hit short and skipped off the water.

I decided to use my training and prerogative as patrol officer. After settling the boats slightly to the south and at least three hundred meters from the sniper position, I got on the radio and called for some artillery support from the Dong Tam fire support base. I knew that the Vietnamese artillery batteries within range would not waste their precious rounds against a sniper shooting at American patrol boats. I double-checked the coordinates. The artillery at Dong Tam had 155- and 175mm guns that were well within range. They also had a lot of ammunition.

Just as I was to give the "commence fire" order on the radio for the first spotter round, the boat commander of the PBR I was on, BM1 Tony Summerlin, a slow-talking man from South Carolina, gave me a good piece of advice. Tony was one of a half dozen 534th sailors TAD (temporary attached duty) to the 522d like me. He would later become a great 534th PBR patrol officer and brown-water legend before he retired as a master chief boatswain's mate.

"Mr. Goldsmith, I suggest we get our boats away by another three hundred yards or so. Them Dog Town gunners are not used to firing on coordinates from our charts."

Tony's advice was good. The first round was an airburst almost a hundred and fifty meters from the bank and over the river. It burst nearer to where our boats had been than the sniper's position. The following four rounds were corrected by me to get the last one close enough to the sniper to at least give him an earache if he was still in his spider hole. He had probably run back to a fortified bunker deep within the nipa palms before that last round was fired. I decided that artillery fire was not all that great for snipers but that it beat my leading a MACE team into the jungle.

Off-patrol routine on the YRBM-16 was the easy life. Airconditioned sleeping quarters with a more comfortable rack than I'd had aboard the minesweeper. Good Navy chow served in a wardroom setting, complete with individualized napkin rings for the white linen napkins. Movies in the wardroom after evening chow with plenty of fresh coffee. The movies were generally John Wayne–style western "shitkickers" or war movies. Recent reruns of the *Combat* TV series (starring Vic Morrow, who would be killed years later while filming a movie about combat in Vietnam) that had been transferred to film stock were also popular.

One movie proved to be a major disappointment. The Navy supply corps officer on the YRBM-16 probably thought he would be a hero because he had traded only two recent westerns for *The Playboy of the Western World*. Everyone in the wardroom the night of the show expected to see some soft-core sex and beautiful babes. So much for the cultural IQ of the brown-water navy officers, including me. The movie was, of course, a film rendition of an old Irish play by John Millington Synge that depicted family strife in the Irish Aran Islands at the turn of the century. Even the Irish-American officers from the Boston area were pissed off. Instead of a lot of female skin and action, the movie was all rustic, costumed characters. No action. Plenty of words. All in hard-to-understand accents. Many years later I would take my Irish bride and our two-year-old daughter to the Aran Islands. I finally appreciated Synge and his work.

Cold beer (even if it was only 3.2 percent) was never more than twenty-five cents MPC. MPC (military payment certificates) was the "funny money" issued to the troops in lieu of U.S. currency and coins. Sometimes there would be happy hours when the beer was only ten cents. Beer was served on the "beer barge," a sixty-foot pontoon lashed to the side of the YRBM-16. The beer barge was our way around the U.S. Navy's prohibition against serving alcohol on in-service ships and vessels. The beer barge even had music piped in from the guys up in the comm center. On Sunday afternoons steaks and lobster tails were grilled outside. Beer drinkers like me could then feast while downing suds and listening to good ole rock 'n' roll music in the waning tropical skies. If you could forget about the war all around you, you could really savor the fact that it was a great life in the tropics. All that was missing was round-eyed women. A favorite topic of conversation was how to lure a contingent of female USO entertainers or a group of Red Cross girls from Saigon down to the YRBM-16.

Chapter 6

Over the next few weeks I got sniped at a couple mor[e]
began to enjoy night patrols, and captured my first pr[…]

Two miles south of the YRBM-16 anchorage, th[e …]
ong River divided into two channels separated b[y …]
habited islands. The deepwater channel wa[s …]
alongside the eastern boundary of the Mo Cay[…]
Hoa Province, where once-prosperous vill[…]
had enjoyed fertile rice paddies and farm[…]
trict was a never-ending battlefield. Vie[…]
former district town. South Vietnames[e …]
new district town with its popula[…]
(mostly refugees) by maintaining t[…]
forts all around the town and alon[g …]
landing opposite the Ben Tre fer[…]
The main channel from the [… …]
(VC-controlled) district tow[n …]
Both ends—from the Co [… …]
Luong end in the east—[…]
Cong. The Mo Cay Ca[…]
tions route from wes[t …]
the Mo Cay–Ham [… …]
tween the uninha[…]
path to the Ba [… …]
area fifteen m[…]
the unmole[…]
fortress of [… …]
that group [… …]

My first da[y …]
boats under my c[…]
loitering on station in [… …]

the PBRs patrolling the lower part of the river. The river became wide, but its color indicated that most of it was very shallow. Not too shallow for PBRs, of course, but for any LST or other Navy support ship with a draft over six feet. The channel deep enough for ships was narrow and often shifted. Months later I would see an LST PBR-support ship high and dry at low tide on that stretch of the river. It had made its run upriver during an ebb tide and had run aground. It had taken hours for the next full tide to lift the ship off the mudflats. A normal course of business on the lower Ham Luong for American support ships. In peacetime and in less hostile waters, an LST skipper who allowed his ship to run aground would probably lose his command or, at least, receive a severe reprimand.

After a few miles we saw a couple of PBRs tied up to a small pier in front of a Viet fort on the west bank. Only one sailor manned each boat. The rest of the crews and the patrol officer were up in the little mud fort, fifty meters to the west. I jumped off the bow of the PBR and walked to the mud fort, which was in an open, flat area. Most of the sailors from the boats went with me. A well-defined path led from the landing to the fort, and I was not concerned about mines or booby traps. The river rats from the other boats were still trading stuff with the Ruff Puffs, C rations and pop flares for fresh vegetables, etc. I met the patrol officer, a young but aging chief gunner's mate, who was chewing the fat with an American Army sergeant adviser. The CPO-531 patrol officer was pleasant to me. He said that more and more of their enemy contacts had been closer and closer to the area patrolled by the 522d. He wagered that if my patrol went back into Ambush Alley, we would receive fire close to the mid-channel cut to the Mo Cay Canal. He had taken a prisoner to the Ben Tre police the day before and his boats had been sniped at from the eastern bank of the Ham Luong in Ambush Alley. I told the chief that it was my intention to run Ambush Alley within ten minutes.

"Lieutenant, just make sure you don't do nothing stupid. Don't make a big deal over a sniper. Shoot a belt of grenades around him and go to full speed. Don't ever make a combat action report. Them Saigon warriors will try to do something stupid. Like ordering a SEAL platoon or a RAG [river assault group] to sweep the area if they can't get the Ruff Puffs to make a sweep. Friendlies will be wasted by booby traps. Those Cong have controlled that bank for over twenty years. Let them keep it as long as we can control the water."

My two boats ran down Ambush Alley at near max speed. Just past the mid-island cut near the Mo Cay Canal, sniper fire was received. In three-round bursts. By the third burst, the third shot was getting close to the boat I was on. The gunners on both boats returned fire. Most of their bullets either bounced off the water or were high. We had no room to increase the range parallel to the sniper's position. We had to outrun his shots by going north. After distancing the boats from the sniper by three hundred yards, we turned around. We went back at full speed with both M-79 single-shot grenade launchers and the M-18 Honeywell grenade launchers doing the fire suppression. The sniper opened up again and we responded. The third round from my M-79 appeared close, but the sniper kept on shooting until the Honeywell gunner on my boat found his mark while firing single-round bursts. Then he started cranking the handle to send another twenty rounds into the sniper's location. The Honeywell gunner on the cover boat also concentrated his rounds on the same position. Then we turned around and went back at full speed. There was no more sniper fire. We cleared Ambush Alley. A sailor later discovered that a bullet had penetrated the fiberglass hull and struck a CO_2 cartridge on one of the inflatable vests stored in the forward compartment. The result was a short action report back at the YRBM-16 that probably was not forwarded to Saigon or Binh Thuy but another red pin would be stuck into the chart back at the ops center in an area of the chart covered with red pins.

If the sniper had gotten lucky and wounded a sailor or damaged a boat there would have been a radioed combat action report. Enough reports and the Ruff Puffs would probably sweep the area. Then there would be some serious casualties. The enemy always seemed to be waiting for sweeps over riverbanks they controlled. They would ambush the Ruff Puffs from a tree line with machine guns and automatic rifles or they would put down a few well-placed mortar rounds in their midst. Even without an established ambush party awaiting them the Ruff Puffs would suffer losses from mines and

booby traps. Seeking out and destroying enemy emplacements on the riverbanks was a dangerous business. The ordinary Ruff Puff knew that. The ordinary PBR river rat knew
that. It was only the desk-bound Saigon and Binh Thuy warriors who seemed not to understand that nothing would be
gained from the sweep and much would be lost.

My first night-patrols on the Ham Luong were interesting
if only because night was the time that the Viet Cong really
became active. The Mekong Delta was flat as a table. There
were no mountains or hills to obscure all the nighttime war
action, and during the rainy season the sky was sometimes
partly clear. Firefights could be seen from miles away. Sometimes actions might be going on at all points of the compass
as Vietnamese outposts and the enemy exchanged fire. In my
mind's eye remain the images of parachute flares with white
plumes of smoke descending behind the palm trees on the
riverbank in areas completely devoid of any ambient light except for distant mortar-round bursts and tracer rounds from
automatic weapons. Usually the engagements looked like
silent movies because the action was inland and perhaps a
mile or two away from our boats. If there was a sustained action that called for air support, I often switched radios to listen in to the MACV advisory net for the province where the
action was taking place. I enjoyed listening to the radio traffic.
It was usually laconic and devoid of any emotion. I, the silent
witness, wanted to know more about the violence. The pilots
always sounded like they'd just inhaled laughing gas. I suppose it was just the effect of typical FM radio modulation
heard through low-fi speakers.

Typical communications would be something like this:

"Wallop Hotel, this is Spooky 31. I am orbiting your position. I see fire coming your way from the north and west. Request you designate first target. Over."

"Spooky 31, this is Wallop Hotel. Hose down the gooks
coming from the west first. They got machine guns and rockets backing them up. They are about three hundred meters
from town. Will fire tracers now. Over."

"Wallop Hotel, this is Spooky 31. [The radio transmission
has the sound of a buzz saw in the background.] We are taking
the enemy to your west under fire. Out."

The sky would be lit up with thousands of little orange flecks of light arcing down to earth. That would usually last three minutes or less. After the firing of perhaps fifty thousand rounds of 7.62mm bullets, the gunship and the friendlies would conclude that the attack by the local Viet Cong had been defeated. Very rarely did I see enemy tracer fire going back against the C-47 gunships. Several months later I would see a Spooky being driven off the scene by superior enemy firepower from the ground.

By the end of September the rainy season had reached the Delta in full fury. Monsoon rains lasted for hours during the night. The Navy-issue ponchos did not protect a sailor from such rain. I wrote to my brother John back in Atlanta to send me proper rain gear (fisherman's rubber-coated bib overalls and a waterproof jacket that can be buttoned to the overalls).

Older brother John, who was married and with a new baby, had avoided the draft by enrolling in the U.S. Navy Reserve's Six by Six Program. Six months' active duty and six years in the reserves. John, who hated his Navy service as much as I enjoyed mine, was involved in the Vietnam War even longer than me because he had to attend monthly weekend drills at the Atlanta Naval Air Station until 1971. As an enlisted PI, photographic interpreter, he spent those weekends building mockups of targets in North Vietnam. His work was just as important as mine to the war effort, perhaps more so.

I got the rain gear within a month. Such gear would never be comfortable during the day, but at night when temperature was in the high sixties, the wind chill could make life on the boats very cold and uncomfortable. Weather conditions also produced heavy, dense ground fog on the rivers just before dawn.

It was cold and foggy around 0530 when I looked into the Raytheon scope's rubber hood and saw the little blips of surface contacts making their way to the free-fire zone on Tan Tan Island. They were less than a mile away and headed for a creek near some abandoned fish stakes near the riverbank, only a few hundred yards from where I had received my first sniper fire. I radioed the cover boat that we were going to intercept the sampans as my boat increased speed and headed for the fish stakes.

Three sampans were headed for the free-fire zone. The PBR I was on closed them to within twenty yards and came to a sudden stop. Sometimes this maneuver was called a crash turn. It was accomplished by reversing the direction of the water jets while at full speed. The boat commander and I made the boat stop exactly where I wanted it to, the forward gunner switched on the spotlights just forward of his twin .50-caliber mount, and a burst of machine gun fire was directed over the sampans. But they continued to the riverbank. The boat commander swung the PBR parallel to the riverbank and the three gunners and I opened fire. My M-79 grenade rounds were directed at the bank where I suspected a VC security squad might have automatic weapons covering the crossing. I saw someone go over the side of the nearest sampan. I also saw the two other sampans disappear into the thick nipa palm cover of the creek that was their destination. The cover boat arrived and hosed down the area with 40mm grenades and machine gun fire as my boat went alongside the twenty-foot sampan that was now adrift thirty feet from the riverbank. The sampan was low in the water, indicating that it had a heavy load. A person was crouching amidships in the sampan. With a few warning shots and a lot of shouting of encouragement, a big Vietnamese woman emerged from her crouch with her hands up. She was trembling in fear. I did not blame her.

A sailor fastened a grapnel-hooked line to the stern of the sampan near where the engine was attached, then the PBR pulled the sampan out into the middle of the river. I took a battle lantern to the stern of the PBR and examined the sampan and its occupant. The woman was now huddled between two large wicker baskets filled with what appeared to be rice. The baskets were four feet in diameter and almost four feet high. A lot of rice. Maybe enough to feed a VC company for a couple of weeks. Shouts and a couple of pistol shots in the air persuaded the woman to rise and work her way to the stern of the sampan. She was around thirty years old and a little on the heavy side. Obviously she had not been starving for food. Her Viet Cong friends on Tan Tan were probably in much more need of food than she was. We secured her hands behind her back with a nylon manacle—a superstrength garbage bag tie—and lifted her onto the PBR.

The two-boat patrol relieving my patrol arrived on the scene. I told the relieving patrol officer what had happened, and the boat I was on towed the sampan back to the YRBM-16. We took the prisoner along for interrogation by the Vietnamese national police, which had a two-man contingent aboard.

The sampan was tied up to the beer barge and the woman placed in a chair. Sailors lifted the heavy baskets of rice aboard the beer barge and probed them with metal rods, but no weapons were found. I went to the chow hall, and after a big breakfast went back to the beer barge. By then the woman prisoner was blindfolded and sitting down on the deck of the barge thirty feet from where her tormentor arrived by PBR. The Vietnamese national police chief from Ben Tre had been summoned to conduct the interrogation.

The police chief was a cheerful man in his mid-thirties. He knew some English. He knew some French, but basically, he communicated with gestures. He had an old army field telephone set in his hands. He sat in a chair and demonstrated how he would interrogate the prisoner by using two wires terminating in alligator-clipped electrodes. He mimed getting a tremendous electrical shock when he placed the two electrodes together as a young Vietnamese national policeman turned the handle on the field telephone's generator. He laughed. A lot of sailors laughed with him.

"We get *vee chee* lady to talk. We no harm her, only frighten her."

I started to get uncomfortable. I looked around to see if I was the most senior officer present at the beginning of the interrogation. Overlooking the beer barge, Jim Dykes was up on the first deck of the YRBM. I went up to him.

"Jim, I hope the police don't torture that VC female suspect I brought in. At least I hope they don't make a public spectacle of it. No sailor was injured in the engagement. Can you stop any torture?"

"Wynn, don't worry. Chief Hong is just making another show demonstration. That woman probably knows the drill. She will be back on the river with her sampan within an hour."

Chief Hong yelled at the woman as he ripped open her blouse and began to attach the electrodes to the nipples of her breasts. The woman began to wail and cry. The policeman yelled out questions as he turned the handle of the generator. She answered with screams.

After a half minute the interrogation was over. The police chief proudly announced to the assembled Americans that the woman had been pressed into the service of the Viet Cong after they had kidnapped her husband from her village two days earlier. She had been ordered to transport the rice to Tan Tan in order to secure his release. He would take her into custody to get more information concerning the VC operatives in her village who had coerced her. That was all there was.

Much later, and long since Ben Tre had been made infamous, and after I had made numerous deliveries of VC suspects to Chief Hong, I was told that Hong had been a deep-cover Viet Cong penetration. Such was the nature of the war. I figure the guy might still be alive. He was definitely a survivor to have gone so long undetected by U.S. and ARVN intelligence.

A couple of days after that incident, I kept my promise to Major Brown. At the end of a day-patrol I took my two boats up to the Ben Tre MACV boat landing to pick up the USAF FAC (forward air controller) and take him for a U.S. Navy meal in the YRBM-16 wardroom. The major was waiting at the pier in his Class A uniform. He had a Swedish K (Karl Gustav) 9mm submachine gun in his hand for the boat trip. His assistant, a USAF first lieutenant, came running from the MACV compound just as were about to get under way. Major Brown berated his assistant for not being in the proper uniform even though the USAF lieutenant had on a clean and neatly pressed green utility uniform. It was certainty more presentable than the sweaty jungle fatigues I had been wearing for at least two days out on the river. My uniform was grimy and crusted with salt in all areas not drenched in sweat. If he was coming in from a patrol, it certainly was proper attire for a river rat at the evening wardroom meal. I let Major Brown's comments pass. Both Air Force officers thoroughly enjoyed the sit-down, three-course meal served in the air-conditioned wardroom of the barge.

In early October I was pleasantly surprised when Jerry Letcher came aboard the YRBM-16. He had been transported by a YRFM (a reefer, supply ship). These little ships were just big boats. Warrant officer quartermasters usually commanded them. They sailed independently on the Mekong tributaries with cargoes of bullets and beef for the river rats. When I saw Jerry disembarking from the YFR, I ran over to him. We greeted each other like long-lost brothers. Jerry and I were on the same wavelength.

Jerry was a jay gee I had met in July, during the counterinsurgency/Vietnamese language/survival school training in Coronado. We had enjoyed a weekend in Las Vegas together before going on to Vallejo for PBR training. Our trip had been a package deal sponsored by Vegas/Catalina Airlines.

On the flight to Vegas the copilot served champagne; on the flight back he served Bloody Marys. Jerry and I stayed at the Stardust, but we tried our luck all up and down the strip. I got a kick out of watching Jimmy Durante at a dinner show. It was late Sunday morning before we had lost our gambling stakes. We were both beat from lack of sleep, but we felt that we had done the right thing—experienced the nonstop action of Las Vegas. It might be our only opportunity.

The blackjack tables in Vegas were much more honest than the tables of the sailor clip joints I had frequented in Charleston, where many a young submariner just in from a submerged deployment lost his three-months' wages within hours at notorious places such as the Merchant Seaman's Club on Meeting Street. I had visited those dens of iniquity mainly because they attracted young college girls from Converse or the College of Charleston bent on walking on the wild side, if only for a night. Losing fifty dollars within half an hour on the blackjack table at the Merchant Seaman's Club had taught me a serious lesson back in Charleston, a town steeped in Bible Belt puritanical tradition, but which closed its eyes to wide-open corruption.

I gave up the gambling tables of Charleston to concentrate on meeting girls. I soon discovered that the Wednesday night "stags and bags" night at the Charleston Naval Base Officers Club was a less expensive place to meet girls. The girls at those mixers were seldom from college. Many were divorced hairdressers or secretaries, party animals who loved to dance and drink. My kind of women at that time in my life. After

Tet, John Smock and a couple of other river rat officers who had served on ships out of Charleston before Vietnam duty compared notes while drinking beer and swapping sea stories. It was amazing that so many of us knew the same women from those Wednesday night socials back in Charleston.

Jerry was another PBR guy on loan because of the shipping delays in getting the new MK II boats. The section Jerry was ordered to had not even been commissioned. He had spent four weeks down at Binh Thuy on the Bassac as a supernumerary. He wanted more time on the river. The high command had obliged his request to go to the 522d, which was chock-full of patrol officers demanding their R & Rs before they got shipped to I Corps.

Jerry soon joined me in the 522d patrol officer rotation. We got Larsen to allow us to be on the river at the same time. If your boats step into deep yogurt, it's a big confidence builder to know that a buddy has two boats on the river just a few miles away.

Jerry soon found out about the snipers on Tan Tan Island. He made it a point to fire mortar rounds from a safe distance beyond the sniper's lair. The mortar rounds were always directed a couple of hundred meters inland from the sniper's position on the nipa-covered riverbank. Jerry figured that the Viet Cong snipers probably lived in the hamlets indicated on our charts a couple of hundred meters inland from where the fire came. Evidently this tactic pissed off the Tan Tan Viet Cong. One morning Jerry's PBR was fired on by what was probably a 75mm recoilless rifle. A recoilless projectile has a very flat trajectory and that one made a very big bang in the water twenty meters from Jerry's PBR, which was doing almost twenty knots. It had been fired from a range of over four hundred meters. It was definitely not a shoulder-fired rocket. It was an unusual occurrence.

I was on the river several miles to the south when I heard Jerry's radio report. I took my boats to Jerry's location and got him to point out exactly where the round came from. I turned on the radar and studied the image long enough to feel confident that I could recognize the area at night by using the radar.

This incident might have been the first of several in which the Viet Cong along the Ham Luong targeted individual boats during my tour. The enemy listened to our radio traffic. They recognized callsigns. Perhaps they recognized individual voices of the men on the radio. Twice, later on, English-speaking voices taunted me on our radio channels, and once there was a sniper who fired rounds only at me. Others were targeted and wounded. I became an early believer in radio security and in the fact that I was dealing with a crafty, intelligent enemy operating in familiar territory.

When off patrol, Jerry and I would spend hours preparing charts for the 534th to use when it took over the area. The charts were made from six large-scale maps of the eastern Delta. Jerry and I carefully cut up sections of the charts, cello-taped the pieces together, and taped the grid coordinates along the borders of all nine subsections. We left out the artillery fans because the guns were often moved and there were only a couple of batteries that we knew would always be available. Then we would seal the charts in clear acetate and fold them so that each chart would be compressed into a foldout of nine sections, each section ten by seven inches. The result was something like a road atlas covering the eastern Delta from My Tho to the mouth of the Ham Luong in the South China Sea. In addition to the Ham Luong, large stretches of the My Tho and Co Chien rivers were on the charts. We prepared over twenty charts, enough for every boat captain and patrol officer.

Early one late-October morning, just as Jerry and I were getting dressed for a day-patrol, a comm center messenger came into our bunk room and told us to report to the operations center for a briefing by Lieutenant Larsen. This was unusual. I never remembered Larsen being up at 0500.

Other 522 patrol officers who were off duty joined Jerry and me in the little room. Only Jerry and I had helmets and flak jackets. Larsen was sitting at one of the two desks, sipping coffee. When the last patrol officer (a bleary-eyed chief petty officer who had probably stayed up most of the night playing cards) arrived, Larsen made his presentation.

"Saigon command has ordered all sections in the Delta to 'show the flag' on VC-controlled canals. The 522 has to run the Chet Say Canal at least three times a week until further orders. We can also run the Mo Cay as a substitute for the Chet

Say. I decided that we would do our runs on the Chet Say. Let the guys on the Co Chien have the Mo Cay. You guys can pick your runs. The first runs will probably be a lot easier than the later ones. Anybody want to be the first?"

Jerry Letcher beat me. Being a Yankee, he was a faster speaker.

"XO, I'll take a run up the Chet Say this morning around 0800. I will take the boats to within a klick of the My Tho and then haul ass back to Ben Tre. That should count as a run of the Chet Say."

Lieutenant Larsen was pleased with Jerry's response. He actually got up from his desk and smiled.

"Okay, Mister Letcher has the first crack. You other patrol officers have to make sure the 522 runs that canal at least three times a week until further orders. Decide among yourselves how you pick your runs. Good luck and make sure you keep the comm center aware of your runs, and that crews always have on their flak jackets and helmets."

There was no mention of having the Seawolf gunships provide overhead cover, or plans for coordination with other units to provide reaction force assistance when the runs up the Chet Say took place.

With Larsen's pathetic little speech over, the patrol officers left the comm center. Jerry and I went back to the wardroom to catch a quick breakfast before taking our boats out on patrol. He and I discussed what would probably happen. He would take his boats up the Ben Tre at a leisurely pace through all the sampans headed for the marketplace. To any Vietnamese observer, his boats were probably going to make a routine run to get pastries for the crews. The boats would in fact land at the MACV boat landing and the sailors would get off the boats. Any enemy agent in Ben Tre in radio contact with the Viet Cong forces would probably not report anything unusual to alert the forces along the Chet Say Canal. My two-boat patrol would then shoot up the free-fire zone on Tan Tan Island after radioing our intention to take an evading sampan under fire. The radio report and the sound of our gunfire might possibly allow Jerry's boats to get under way from the Ben Tre marketplace and head past the bridge toward the Ba Lai and Chet Say Canal without setting off an early warning by Ben

Tre's spies. Jerry would make cryptic radio transmissions to me to indicate the position of his patrol. We marked some points on our charts with names such as Charlie, Whiskey, Romeo, and Alpha. My two-boat patrol would be in the middle of the Ham Luong, across from the ferryboat landing. If his boats were hit hard and needed help, my boats would come running. I would also coordinate gunship directions to the scene. We both figured that we had to do the contingency planning; Bill Larsen certainly had not given us any sort of plan.

By 0800 all the sailors on my two boats knew what was happening. The simulated firing on an evading sampan into the free-fire zone of Tan Tan Island was very brief; my sailors knew that they had to save their bullets for action up the Ben Tre/Chet Say waterway if our boats had to come to the rescue.

Over an hour later, my boat pulled alongside the PBR carrying Jerry Letcher as it exited the Ben Tre River into the Ham Luong. I had followed his patrol's progress by his short radio transmissions, noting checkpoints being passed. The sailors on the boats exiting the Ben Tre were covered with sweat. Most of them were still wearing their helmets and flak jackets. A couple of the gunners were clearing their guns.

"How did it go, Jerry?"

"This first one was a piece of cake, Wynn. We caught them by surprise. We raced by the Ba Lai and saw dozens of sampans headed for the Ben Tre. Old mamma-sans. They all froze when they saw our boats. There was nothing on the Chet Say except fresh dirt and mounds alongside that south bank. Not a single sniper round. We went in fast and got out fast. That north bank of the Chet Say looked quiet. Even around the pilings of the two blown bridges. It's that south bank you have to worry about. Beaucoup little VC flags and banners stuck on the banks near those bunkers. The VC know we were there. They are probably reinforcing the fighting holes along the Chet Say right now. Let me know when you want to make your run. My boats will be ready to assist."

As Jerry took off his flak jacket and removed his horn-rimmed eyeglasses for cleaning with a tissue from the pocket of his blouse, I decided that the second run had better take place soon.

I waited three hours for slack high water and a high sun.

With the high water, my gunners would have their weapons at the same elevation as the enemy. Straight level. No VC gunners shooting down on PBRs from the rim of the canal bank. The PBRs' bullets would bear straight down the line of fire from the enemy. And with the high sun, there would not be a problem of sunlight shining into the gunners' eyes. It was a small margin, considering that the VC on the Chet Say were probably already well aware that PBRs would be running that waterway. The American patrol boats had been ordered to show their flag in waterways controlled by the "liberation fighters." The Chet Say would be targeted. The VC would be ready.

The 522d boats I took up the Ben Tre that October day were manned by ordinary PBR sailors who got under way for an ordinary patrol. We even had a Viet cop aboard. When I told the crews that our patrol would run the Chet Say Canal, they reacted as I expected. The young gunners whooped and hollered like they were storming out of the locker room for a championship high school football game. The two first-class boat captains were a lot more reserved. They wanted to know everything I knew, and more that I did not know. What was the reason for the run? What was the intelligence situation? Would we have gunship cover? I told them what Larsen had told the patrol officers. I told them that Jerry Letcher's patrol would be the first run up the Chet Say, and that we would soon follow at the next high tide. The boat captains agreed with me that going second shortly after the first would be much safer than going third a day or so later.

Extra ammo cans were open by the guns. All loose gear such as ice chests and Coleman stoves had been secured. The sailors had done those things without orders. The sailors had been briefed on the checkpoints on the chart. Every sailor would have to know how to report the location of a firefight if the boat captains and I were unable to radio in our location. Less than half of them had been to the Ba Lai, much less run the Chet Say into the My Tho River. I had never even seen the Ba Lai. So the young sailors took much interest in the chart. I told them that as we passed checkpoints and I radioed checkpoint calls, I would yell out the location to them. They seemed to appreciate that.

We cruised up the river at a leisurely pace toward the landing at the MACV compound. There was little traffic on the river. All the sampans from the morning rush to market had departed. On our way upriver, we passed some of the larger junks carrying copra or charcoal. By then, all the Ben Tre fishermen were out on the main river in their sampans.

The water was at its highest level at slack high tide. Just what I wanted. The water was so high that we had to bend our radio antennae over as the boats passed under the Ben Tre bridge. Once we passed under the bridge, the boats kicked up to over twenty knots, leaving a five-knot reserve of speed that I hoped would not be needed. All guns were fully armed and trained on the south-bank side. We sped by the few sampans and junks on the river, our wakes raising havoc with the smaller ones. I just made sure that the boat captain on my boat did not purposely swamp a sampan.

I had been past that bridge a couple of times before. The first time was after a short liberty run for sailors to purchase things not available on the YRBM-16. I took two boats past the bridge that first time to satisfy my curiosity. I was told that the trip up to the Ba Lai could be interesting. A boat ride beyond that would be deadly. I chose to have the interesting boat ride. The first time I took the boats only four or so klicks past the bridge. The last little South Vietnamese outpost was only five hundred meters from the bridge, near a brick factory close to the water's edge. A hundred meters past that outpost, the south bank was just a green mass of nipa palms and the north bank was relatively clear. The dirt track that paralleled the river was often visible. There were no people on it. But soon we saw signs of the enemy on that north bank, literally: little, two-foot-square cardboard Viet Cong flags were stuck along the bank like crude yard sale signs. Red and blue bars with a yellow star in the center. They could have been made by five-year-olds in play school. I guess they were placed there to intimidate the undecided and boost the morale of the committed. Those signs only made PBR sailors more alert. After another half mile up the river, I saw the first enemy signs on the south bank, a ten-foot-high wall of dense, dark-green nipa palm foliage. No signs of ordinary human life but some serious Viet Cong death signs at the water's edge: skulls and crossbones and the words *Sat My* printed on them. "Death to Americans." I decided to go back to the Ham Luong. Some of the young sailors probably thought I was a chickenshit for not continuing up the river. But I knew that the time would come to make that journey and I wanted to postpone that time; I did not want to tweak the beard of some Viet Cong lion that day.

Less than two miles from the Ben Tre bridge the river widened and a straight channel appeared to the east as the main river continued south toward the South China Sea. That fork to the left was the Chet Say Canal. Dutch hydraulic engineers supervising peasant labor during the glory days of French colonial rule, at the end of the nineteenth century, had probably built it. The canal shortened the trip from My Tho to Ben Tre by over thirty miles and had probably been a wonderful accomplishment at the time. By my time it was just a narrow shooting gallery for Viet Cong in the bunkers and fighting holes erected along its banks over the previous fifteen years. The French had suffered up that canal when battling the Viet Minh and over the last year PBR sailors had bled up that canal almost every time they ventured up that straight stretch. I studied the canal with my binoculars. It had a hard turn north about a half mile up the canal. No river traffic was visible when we made our turn up the Chet Say. Jerry had reported river traffic. More little VC flags appeared along the bank.

Just as my boat was crossing the Ba Lai River to starboard, the little Vietnamese national policeman beside the after .50-caliber gun became excited and rushed up to me while grabbing my right sleeve with his left hand and pointing to the north bank.

"*Trung-uy,* Vee Chee sampan over there!"

I looked down the river. Sure enough, about fifty yards down a sampan was trying to burrow itself into the foliage of the riverbank. I ordered the boat commander to make for the sampan and radioed the cover boat to lay back as we approached a "skunk." We neared the sampan, which was empty except for two peasant women. They had cut the sampan's engine and were huddled down in an attempt to make themselves invisible. The PBR swung parallel to the sampan and a sailor attached a line to the bow while the Vietnamese policeman and I covered the women with rifles.

We pulled the sampan to the middle of the Chet Say and alongside the PBR. The little Viet cop got down on the sampan and searched the two terrified women, who had no *can couics,* the South Vietnamese identification cards. One did have a Viet Cong tax receipt concealed in her blouse. I'm sure that proper *can couic*s were concealed somewhere on the sampan.

The little Viet cop pulled his .38 Smith & Wesson Police Special revolver out of its holster, pointed it into the face of the one that had yielded the tax receipt, and began screaming questions at her. She trembled and started talking very rapidly while pointing up the Chet Say to the south bank.

The policeman returned the pistol to its holster and rapidly climbed aboard the PBR.

"*Trung-uy,* there are beaucoup Vee Chee hundred meters upriver in fighting holes to kill PBR sailors!"

With that announcement, the after .50 gunner quickly went over to the starboard side of the PBR to untie the line attached to the sampan.

Those few seconds gave the little policeman his opportunity. He swung under the .50, grabbed the handles, and proceeded to rip off about twenty rounds onto the south bank of the canal. But by the time I had reacted and pushed the little guy off the gun, the forward gunner was blasting away.

"Cease fire! Cease fire!" I yelled as loud as I could. The boat commander sounded the siren for a second or two. That was enough to get the forward gunner to stop firing. About forty rounds had been fired. I decided that our run of the Chet Say Canal was over. If in fact there were a lot of Viet Cong in their fighting holes and bunkers up that canal, they would already be at general quarters. Any element of surprise was lost.

I felt sorry for the next patrol.

The two boats turned around, headed for Ben Tre and the Ham Luong. We went back at maximum speed. Some of the young sailors were probably pissed off that we did not run the entire canal. Goldsmith was indeed a chickenshit. I felt that discretion was better than valor.

Chapter 7

I reported in person to the YRBM-16 ops center and to Lieutenant Larsen as soon as the boats exited the Ben Tre. Larsen was not impressed. He seemed pissed; he did not know if my little foray counted as a "showing the flag" mission. My boats had penetrated only one hundred meters of the canal.

I have a perverse side to my nature that sometimes unexpectedly pokes to the surface, often to my detriment. That day my mouth made it evident.

"Mister Larsen, I believe that the next patrol going up the Chet Say will be ambushed from the south bank just past the Ba Lai, if not before the Ba Lai. I think it needs a real combat leader, such as yourself, to lead that patrol."

My sarcasm hit home. Larsen's face flushed in anger. He told me to get the hell out of the ops center. I went back on the river to finish an uneventful patrol.

I slept late the next morning; I had a night-patrol coming up. I was finishing up a leisurely late breakfast in the wardroom around 0900 when someone ran in to announce that there was a major action up the Ben Tre River and two 522d boats were in trouble. One had been hit by rockets and was burning. I ran up to the helo deck with several other officers. If I had really been gung ho, I would have reported to the scrambling boats at the maintenance pontoon as a lot of 522 PBR sailors did. But I figured that what was done was done; there was nothing PBR sailors from the barge could do to save the PBR sailors on the stricken boat. Keeping a firm grasp on their lives was up to themselves, other PBRs already on patrol, and all the airpower already scrambling to their aid.

By the time I reached the helo deck I had binoculars and could see the Seawolf gunships orbiting and firing down at the column of black smoke several miles to the east. The smoke was only a mile or so upriver from the center of Ben Tre. Minutes later jet aircraft were swooping down to fire rockets and drop bombs around the smoke column. An LCM-8 boat was getting under way from the maintenance pontoon to head up the Ben Tre following three 522 PBRs already under way.

It seemed obvious that a small ambush squad of Viet Cong had hit the boats on the Ben Tre just past the bridge, before the boats had come close to the Chet Say Canal. I hoped that the PBR sailors from the two-boat patrol had survived. The second boat had probably taken a rocket in the fuel tank. The first boat with the patrol commander had probably immediately turned to cover the stricken boat and then been subjected to heavy automatic weapons fire. The sailors on the lead boat would be firing all their machine guns as it turned to help the second boat. There would be frantic calls for assistance on the radios. The survivors of the second boat would either be in the water or on the north bank; they would probably be in shock and their lives would depend on the aggressive action, tactical proficiency, and luck of the crew of the first boat. The first boat would probably take a rocket hit as it attempted to pick up survivors of its cover boat. If the crew was able to continue to fire its guns, the survivors could probably be saved by the arrival of the gunships. That was the ambush scenario we were taught back in Vallejo: call for help; take care of your buddies; fight the enemy until airpower and reinforcements come.

The training had been fairly realistic up the creeks of Suisun Slough in the east area of San Francisco Bay. The training had been hard. Combat-tested U.S. Navy special warfare experts had trained us. The guy giving the graduation speech to PBR Class 36 was a crusty old mustang (commissioned from the enlisted ranks) lieutenant commander who had fought in three wars, Lt. Cmdr. Roy Boehm, the "first SEAL" himself. Boehm's dress khakis were awash with rows of colorful campaign ribbons. The old guy (at the time he must have been nearly fifty) made an impression on me that day. He told the men assembled in the Mare Island (Vallejo, California) Naval Shipyard base theater to look around at each other.

"One in every four of you is going to be killed. Another one in four is going to spend some serious time in the hospital. Still, most of you will survive. In combat when you feel that you must have peed down your leg, you should realize that you are bleeding. Blood flowing down a guy's legs feels the same as urine. Recognize that feeling. Take care of it and take care of your wounded buddies. Good luck to each and every one of you. You men are going to be tried in combat within a few weeks. My staff and I worked hard to train you. We believe you will do your jobs well. You are all great sailors."

The 522 sailors on those two boats up the Ben Tre River that day in early November 1967 did well. Long before the LCM-8 salvage boat returned with the almost unrecognizable remains of a boat that had burned to the waterline, those of us on the YRBM-16 had heard the results. One boat had taken a rocket in the fuel tank. The other boat took a rocket in the forward cabin. The survivors of the burned boat were picked up by the less badly damaged boat. The Seawolf gunships had arrived in time to suppress enemy fire while the recovery of five sailors from the first boat was under way. A Vietnamese policeman was the only person not recovered. Four sailors had been medevacked by helicopter from Ben Tre. Army personnel had been waiting at the MACV landing with vehicles and Army medics. They took the sailors to a landing site by the Ben Tre park, where two dustoff Hueys from Dong Tam were waiting.

The burnt-out PBR was lifted aboard the maintenance barge but not because there was hope of finding anything salvageable. The job was to locate the remains of the Viet cop. Survivors said he had been hit by gunfire before the rocket found the fuel tank. After about an hour of sifting through oily, black ashes, someone discovered his badly melted pistol. Then portions of a human skull were recognized. That was all that remained of the feisty little Vietnamese cop who had been on my boat the previous day.

I knew the medevacked sailors; I'd had patrols with them on both boats. Thirty-one years later I can remember only one name: EN2 James Raimey, who had been seriously wounded, was a fellow Georgian who had been in PBR Class 36 with me. I hope he recovered and made it back to the beautiful north Georgia mountains of Rabun County. I never heard of him after he was wounded.

After the boat loss up the Ben Tre, the "show the flag" missions for the 522d were put on hold. Even young sailors full of testosterone understood that was probably a wise thing. It was back to main-river patrol as usual. And the usual snipers.

One event stands out in my mind about the rest of my time aboard YRBM-16. Sometime about the middle of November, Lieutenant Larsen called a briefing for the evening-patrol officers, of which I was one. Larsen wanted to go out on a special operation that evening. He was to be inserted in a captured sampan after dark in a known Viet Cong crossing area. The sampan would carry a sailor manning an M-60 machine gun and Larsen himself, manning a small handy-talkie for communication with other patrol boats. Two boats were always to be within a mile of his "ambush" site. The other two-boat patrol was to be in reserve within two miles. I was thinking that maybe Larsen really was a stand-up guy. I thought that he knew by intel that there was an expected Viet Cong crossing near the Mo Cay Canal in Ambush Alley. PBRs would quietly tow Larsen's sampan in the dark of night to the mid-island channel on the Ham Luong, across from the Mo Cay Canal. Larsen would alert our boats by radio when he observed enemy light signals. He would provide the positions of the enemy forces on both banks. One patrol of PBRs would run down one channel of the river to intercept the crossing body of sampans. The other would go up the other channel to blast the reception area and provide cover for the boats that intercepted the enemy main body. Larsen's sampan with its M-60 machine gun would take care of any Viet Cong sampans that made it to the mid-channel islands. A classic U.S. Navy ambush, like some of the major actions done in the southwest Pacific in 1943 and 1944. I was excited.

Then I found out exactly what Larsen had in mind. He wanted to have his sampan inserted just after dark at an uninhabited island at the widest portion of the Ham Luong between the most peaceful districts in the whole eastern Mekong

Delta. An area where no action had occurred ever. The western bank of the Ham Luong in that area was the Cho Lach capital of Vinh Luong Province, where Catholics resettled from North Vietnam. They hated the Viet Cong with a passion. The inhabitants along the eastern bank of the Ham Luong in that area were either Catholic or Cao Dai, a religious sect that hated and fought the Viet Cong more than they did the Vietnamese government. If any PBR sailor on the Ham Luong wanted to "dog" his patrol, go somewhere where there was no possibility of receiving enemy fire, that was the spot.

The situation was ripe for some river rat tricks.

At dusk my boat picked up Larsen on the maintenance barge. The sampan (the one I had captured with the rice load) was taken under tow. When we reached the three-acre island in the middle of the upper Ham Luong, Larsen and his bodyguard with the M-60 machine gun got into the sampan, which was towed to the eastern bank of the island. Just before Larsen embarked on the sampan he had a few choice words for me.

"Goldsmith, my ass is going to be on the line tonight. You had better be ready to come and help me. Don't go to sleep!"

He then handed me a tiny handy-talkie radio so that I could be in communication with him. It was an emergency radio of the kind pilots used to communicate with rescue units after being shot down. It had a range of a couple of miles or so. How Larsen got a pair of those radios I have not a clue.

Just after dusk Larsen and his sampan were deposited along the eastern bank of the mid-river island, which was out of range of small arms from both banks. It was probably like landing a boat on a tiny island in the middle of the Mississippi a hundred years ago. No ambient light on the banks. Nothing going on at all. If I'd been on that insertion that night I would have found a flat spot on the island and gone to sleep; it was probably the most secure spot of land for an American in all of Vietnam.

Larsen did not go to sleep. Every thirty minutes he conducted a radio check. On a real special operations mission these radio checks would be nothing more than one or two transmit clicks at odd, prearranged intervals. Larsen wanted more reassurance. He would call my callsign with his callsign. I would respond with a "Roger. Over." He wanted reassurance that my boats were still there to save his ass.

After a couple of these radio checks, Vietnamese voices were heard on the radio channel. The Vietnamese words were short, soft, cryptic. Professional. They might have come from local VC who had captured survival radios from shot-down American aircraft. They might have been from friendly Vietnamese forces fifty miles away, their transmissions being received due to freak atmospheric conditions. The fixed-frequency FM survival channel might have been specific for one area. In other areas the frequency might have been assigned to South Vietnamese troops. I did not know the origin of the voices. Larsen did not either. He did stop his radio checks. I'm sure he was scared shitless. I hoped that he thought crafty little VC devils with little transceivers and radio direction equipment were swimming out to cut his sorry-ass throat.

Some of the 522 PBR sailors on my boat that night really wanted to give Larsen a fright. All sorts of scenarios were discussed. One had the cover boat go around a river bend and fire a 60mm mortar flare over the island. Another ploy would be to call the other two boats on patrol to start shooting up Tan Tan Island, just a few miles downstream. Larsen would see the tracers and hear the distant gunfire. I would radio him that my patrol had to aid the other patrol and that he was on his own. Someone even suggested that we call in artillery fire on the riverbank three hundred yards from the island and correct the rounds until they were very close to Larsen's sampan. I, of course, egged on *every* idea. I even suggested having one boat creep up to the south bank and fire its .50 machine gun twenty feet over Larsen's sampan. My boat would respond by firing .50-caliber machine guns only ten feet above the sampan from a different angle from the opposite direction. All the imaginary imagery kept our sailors alert for a long night in a very peaceful area. Meanwhile a whole battalion of a Viet Cong main force regiment could have been crossing Ambush Alley that night.

A tired and mosquito-bitten Lieutenant Larsen was extracted the next morning at first light.

I greeted him with a warm welcome.

"Bill, you probably deserve a Purple Heart for enduring all those mosquito bites."

Larsen called me a wiseass. He was pissed off at my comment. At least the son of a bitch did not try to get me to put him up for a medal for his "dangerous operation." Wiseass words worked for me that day.

Chapter 8

In mid-November all ten of the 534th's MK II PBRs arrived in country and were "shaken down" in Nha Be. The boats and all their electronics and gun systems were thoroughly tested in the Rung Sat or the Saigon shipping channel, but the process was going slower than planned. Spare parts were missing. Some radars and radios were not working. That is to be expected with any new weapons system rushed to war straight from the boatyard. More troublesome were the new electrically fired forward twin fifties, which sometimes fired without the gunner's thumb being on the firing button. That could be a disaster. Ron Wolin wisely waited until every deficiency had been corrected before accepting the new boats as combat-ready. Meanwhile he sent Bill Earner and Lt. (j.g.) Pete Richards down to Ben Tre to join the fifteen other 534th sailors and myself on the YRBM-16. QM2 Robert Hunt and I drove the purloined jeep from the Ben Tre MACV compound and took advantage of a Popular Force sweep of the My Tho road to drive there and pick up the two 534th officers. Pete and Bill both appeared nervous as the jeep bounced down the mine-cratered track and little Vietnamese soldiers probed the foliage on both sides of the road. Hunt and I tried to appear nonchalant. This trip was not as interesting as my first journey down that road.

Bill Earner's mission on the YRBM-16 during that period was more administrative than operational, but it was more important than just going out on patrol; he was to make sure that the 522 river rats did not steal the 534th supplies and spare parts previously brought aboard by YFR and that they did not strip the YRBM-16 of the creature comforts allocated to the embarked river rats. Ron Wolin and Bill Earner knew how sailors acted and thought. I'm sure that if the shoe had been on the other foot—the 534th leaving a base to a new unit—the 534th would have taken anything of possible value. Over the next few weeks Bill carefully inventoried every bit of 534 equipment and spare parts and made sure it was segregated and secured in storerooms locked with the 534th's own padlocks. He even made sure that all athletic and recreational gear belonging to the YRBM-16 was secure in a Conex box and safe from the thieving hands of the departing 522 river rats.

On November 22, Bill received a radio message from Ron Wolin. The new boats were close to fully operational. Bill and I were told to return to Nha Be and prepare the section for its transit to the YRBM-16. We could enjoy the next day's Thanksgiving feast at Nha Be. I looked forward to returning to Nha Be and getting to know the new boats.

Early on Thanksgiving morning, Bill Earner, Handgrenade Hunt, and myself got under way for Nha Be. Bill had used his rank as a full lieutenant (O-3) to get the YRBM-16's LCM-8 boat to pick up our jeep at the Ben Tre ferry landing and carry us to My Tho. I appreciated that. For a squad of local Viet Cong, a heavily loaded jeep with three Americans and most of their personal gear might be an inviting target on the dirt track from Ben Tre to My Tho. The jeep had made that run unmolested too many times; I did not want to tempt fate.

We disembarked at the My Tho ferry landing and headed for Saigon. Even with Hunt driving as fast as he could up Highway 4, it was nearly noon before we arrived in Nha Be. We got there just as the Nha Be chow hall was opening for the special Thanksgiving Day dinner.

The dinner was a traditional feast of all-you-could-eat turkey, mashed potatoes, dressing, ham, salads, rolls, pies, and ice cream. There was even American football shown in a makeshift theater after the meal. Who cared if the game had taken place weeks before? A lot of bets were being placed anyway. The day made for a welcome break from the war. The Thanksgiving meal is always important to American fighting men far from home. And it was especially important to the guys who had to go back on Rung Sat patrol later that day.

After the meal I went down to the piers and saw MK II PBRs for the first time. Eight new boats were nestled two abreast from the quay down one side of the wooden pier. I could not see one chip in the dark olive green paint. The guns were masked by green canvas. A few sailors were near or on each boat. I had seen some of them in the chow hall. The ones wearing fatigues had the RivSect 534 fire-spitting dragon patch on their right shoulder, but most were bare-chested. The men were both admiring and guarding their brand-new fighting machines. They were not required to be there. Ron Wolin had officially declared the day to be a "stand down" day so NAVSUPPT Nha Be sailors were responsible for boat security on the piers. One sailor eventually recognized me as an officer with the RivSect 534 because of my patch and invited me on a tour of "his" boat.

The sailor was a giant, well over six feet and two hundred twenty pounds. He was wearing fatigue trousers and a sweat-dripping green T-shirt. The most remarkable thing about the man was that every square inch of his exposed body—his arms, his neck, his face around the ears, and even the top of his shaved head—was covered with tattoos. His neck had a dotted line of dark blue ink with the words "cut along dotted line" engraved from ear to ear. When he reached up from behind the coxswain's flat to take my hand as I went from the pier to the port engine cover, I got a better look at the tattoos on top of his head. Perfectly centered was a red, white, and blue bull's-eye target, or a replica of a Royal Air Force rondel seen on British Spitfires in World War II.

"Welcome aboard PBR 7-17, Mister Goldsmith. I'm BH1 Shadoan, the captain of this new boat. It's fast and 'bout ready for combat. I got a feeling my crew is gonna be ready pretty soon. Hope them support pukes can figure out how to keep the radar from crapping out."

My first impression of Boatswain's Mate Shadoan told me that he was the type of guy I wanted in charge of PBRs going to war. A rough-and-ready bosun fully seasoned by hard times at sea, but young and strong. A confident man, not necessarily in tune with protocol or politeness, but one who could be trusted and counted on to accomplish the mission. Our mission was independent, no-holds-barred combat against a stubborn enemy in their own backyard. Shadoan reminded me of Tony Summerlin. I smiled and shook his beefy hand.

Boatswain's Mate First Class James D. Shadoan was twenty-seven years old, young for a first class boatswain in 1967. The senior bosun on the *Fidelity,* the only first class bosun I had really known, BM1 William Bellamy, had been in World War II and Korea, and had been recommended for chief petty officer for over ten years. He could have retired after twenty years. He wanted to make chief. He was very close in 1966 but the Navy granted only a dozen or so BM1 promotions that year and Bellamy missed by a hair. Bellamy had made my life as a young ensign aboard the minesweeper bearable. He disciplined, trained, nurtured, cursed, and abused all the young sailors who underperformed until they shaped up or were shitcanned. He was a hard, profane man who could get the job done with whatever human material he was assigned.

I especially remember a sailor who was shitcanned on the *Fidelity.* A seaman recruit, let's call him "Romeo," from New York City, he was a fast-talking, fast-acting young man with a fast life. Lying, stealing, cutting, and bullying were part and parcel of that seaman's life. He was one of McNamara's Project 100,000, which authorized tens of thousands of otherwise ineligible recruits for military duty every year. The U.S. Navy had to accept its share of the boys.

Our seaman, a convicted thief, came to the ship as seaman apprentice. Evidently he did not take to military discipline. Most young sailors from basic training at least reached E-3, seaman. Romeo was assigned as a deck ape and proved very quick and alert on his feet during minesweeping details. He also stole from and intimidated young sailors in his living compartment. Since no young sailor was brave enough to bring formal charges against Romeo, who often brandished a knife, BM1 Bellamy had to suggest to me how to handle him. Bellamy's first choice was for me to set up Romeo for a court-martial for stealing government property.

I opted for court-martial. Romeo was targeted in a locker inspection. He failed, of course. As his division officer, I pulled his liberty card. Romeo got belligerent. He started a fight with his leading petty officer. He could not be busted any lower in rank in a captain's mast, but was fined and assigned to mess cook status. Romeo seethed. After five weeks of being confined to mess duties, Romeo was allowed use of his liberty card.

Once a thief, always a thief. It was a given that Romeo would steal on his first day of liberty in over a month. The honorable sailors were prepared for the event.

It was January. It was noted by the petty officer of the watch that Romeo's peacoat bulged when he went up to the quarterdeck. That night, I, as officer of the deck, was on the quarterdeck when Romeo and others were lined up for liberty call at 1800. Normally I would have been in the small wardroom watching the evening news for Vietnam War footage. BM1 Bellamy was conveniently on deck as master-at-arms, a job he never had to perform while in home port. The third class PO of the watch had an unloaded .45-caliber pistol in a holster. He was nervous. The flap of his holster cover as well as the flap of the ammo pouch on his cartridge belt—which had two loaded .45 clips—were loose. Bellamy had the master-at-arms badge on felt tied to his right shoulder. He was looking for a brawl. I had a borrowed .38 Smith & Wesson snub-nose pistol and concealed it in the left pocket of my Navy-issue foul weather jacket. I hoped Romeo would put up a fight.

We honorable men on the quarterdeck that evening were disappointed.

Romeo took the charges and resulting summary court-martial for stealing two pounds of coffee like a true New York City hoodlum. He was not concerned with being shitcanned from the military. To him, the *Fidelity* sailors, who had to go on a ten-week deployment, were suckers. He would spend a couple of months in the new Charleston Naval Base brig watching color TV in air-conditioned comfort. He would have some exercise. He would get out of the Navy before his original sentence for theft was over. A dishonorable discharge would be more like a badge of honor for him back on the block in the Big Apple.

That is one of the things the country's military had to deal with during the 1960s. During the Vietnam War, the ones who fought, bled, and died were mostly honorable young men. Most of the Marines and all of the Navy and Air Force personnel were volunteers. Of course, for many it was a case of volunteering or being drafted into the Army. The Army had to accept almost anyone for combat duty in Vietnam. The Navy did not. And thank God, the Navy did not have to go to war on the rivers and canals of Vietnam burdened with men from Project 100,000. Brown-water sailors were mostly double volunteers. Once in the Navy they asked for Vietnam combat duty. The Army took almost anybody because it needed bodies, regardless of their quality. It was the service most dependent upon the draft and the one most in need of trigger pullers.

The old salts in the Pentagon knew what was needed when the politicians decided that the U.S. Navy had to pacify the Viet Cong in the Mekong Delta waterways. Some anonymous admiral is said to have wagered that a hundred or so crusty bosuns with good shallow-water boats armed to the teeth could accomplish the mission. Secretary of Defense Robert S. McNamara bought into the idea. The Navy had already found a boat in a hasty competition. It would be a Uniflite (United Boat Company, Bellingham, Washington) thirty-one-foot sport fisherman/cabin cruiser. Within three months of the original contract the first PBRs were shipped to Vietnam. The MK I PBR was a wonderful example of what American resourcefulness can accomplish when faced with a critical challenge. Even fully loaded with government guns and electronics, those little plastic boats cost the taxpayers less than one hundred thousand dollars each.

The Navy knew how to man them. Experienced bosuns were there to captain them. A lot of those guys had cut their teeth in Korean War combat or Cold War exercises in the Med or the Taiwan Straits. They had been the coxswains at amphibious landings, the guys who made sure that the gun crews were manned. They knew responsibility. That captain's gig had better be seaworthy and spotless whenever the CO wanted to go ashore. An engineer could be at fault when the boat's engine would not start, but the bosun would get the blame. In a battle, the bosuns had to make sure that the pointers and trainers were at their stations and that ammo bearers were carrying their load. If the ship took enemy hits, the bosuns led the repair and rescue parties on the main decks.

But in 1967 bosuns were a declining breed. They were still

important to minesweeping, which in the mid-sixties was not a Navy priority as it had been early during the Korean War, when the U.S. Navy had lost control of the sea at Wonsan Harbor and two World War II–era Russian mines had sunk our minesweepers. The Russians also had a wide variety of more modern magnetic and acoustic mines that were cheap and plentiful. Some were known to be in the inventory of the North Koreans. The Navy responded by building a whole fleet of modern, wood-hull minesweepers that entered service in the late 1950s. The old bosuns gravitated to minesweeping. It was, for many of them, their last chance to make chief. Rapid-fire automatic guns, missiles, fewer wooden decks, and fewer ships' small boats had almost rendered bosuns obsolescent. Technology and, to some extent, touchy-feely leadership styles had also diminished the need for the jack-of-all-seaman skills that the bosun embodied.

But the brown-water navy of Vietnam needed bosuns even more than the minesweepers. When the urgent need for some type of shallow-draft river patrol boat was first recognized, the rapid availability of such craft was a problem. However, manning them was not a problem. The Navy wisely turned to its abundance of experienced bosuns. The planners, human resource allocators, and operational types all agreed that the ideal PBR commander would be an E-6 bosun, a BM1. A man with at least six years of hard-earned experience in handling young sailors and Navy boats. The men of the boat crews would mostly be young gunners, sailors fresh out of boot camp. Give them a few weeks of training in weapons and they could fire the guns. They would respond to the orders of the boat commander. All young seamen knew that E-6s were almost chief petty officers, godlike figures for young recruits, and that E-6 bosuns were often more intimidating than Navy CPOs of other ratings.

It was an E-6 bosun who had accomplished the most extraordinary achievement of any one man in the entire war. A burly, gruff first class boatswain's mate from South Carolina by the name of James Elliot Williams had led a two-boat PBR patrol that destroyed over sixty VC and NVA junks and sampans and killed over seven hundred well-armed enemy on canals ten miles west of Dong Tam just over a year before.

October 31, 1966, a day and night memorialized as the "Halloween Massacre" by the brown-water navy. Every river rat knew the story. At the time I thought the details of the contact were examples of hyperbolic Pentagon propaganda. Navy PBRs and Seawolf gunships followed by fixed-wing air strikes killed maybe a hundred enemy soldiers and six hundred VC "civilians." Much later I came to the conclusion that the PBRs and gunships had really done what has been told about that day. PBRs had shown the world that the little fiberglass boats were a formidable weapons system in the hands of smart and courageous U.S. Navy sailors. I was glad that the first 534th boat captain I had met besides Tony Summerlin was a big, brassy bosun from the same mold as James Elliot Williams. They were the guys I wanted to be with in combat.

The other boat captains I met that day also exhibited a lot of pride and professionalism as they checked over their boats. Most were bosuns, like Tony Summerlin and Williams from South Carolina, or they were from the other "deck ape" ratings—quartermaster and gunner's mate. Some of them had the familiar southern drawl. QM1 Carl Evans was from Georgia. RD1 (radarman first class) Robert Wenzel was from Alabama. GM1 Ned Caldwell was from North Carolina. BM1 Irvine Burney had the right drawl but said he was from California. Burney stood out because he was small and black. In my limited Navy experience I had seen a lot of Afro-American petty officers but never a black E-6 boatswain's mate. In fact, I had never known a slight and white E-6 bosun. The Navy at that time was still over 90 percent white. The only black E-6s I had known in the Navy were steward's mates on their fourth hitch or college-educated technicians in fire control of missiles, finishing out their first four-year hitch. After only a brief chat, Burney impressed me as a squared-away sailor. A man fully in control. The fact that he made E-6 bosun in those days really impressed me. I felt good that in combat commands the Navy was selecting the best-qualified personnel for boat captains. Burney might have been small and quiet, not built in the traditional bosun's mold, but he was one of the best. He was also a guy I would depend on many times in the future.

I was also impressed by the brand-new boats and the eager confidence of their crews. Many of the young gunners had already seen more action than me in other river sections. These faster, quieter boats manned by exuberant but competent crews would surely make my life easier in the months ahead. I felt like I was part of a fresh team.

Chapter 9

The lone swimmer slipped from the covering nipa and silently entered the water. He had a face mask, snorkel, wristwatch with compass, rubber fins, and a knife in a sheath attached to the belt around his waist above his swimming trunks. He might have had a small, red-lensed, waterproof flashlight attached to his belt. A thin, insulated wire was tied around his ankle. The other end of the wire was on a big spool left on the bank at the water's edge.

The first leg of his mission was an easy swim, in slack water after an ebb tide. He had been trained well and was in excellent condition. His target was visible and only a hundred fifty meters from the riverbank—a big, steel mooring buoy that rose over four feet from the surface of the river. He had timed his entry into the water just as the roving security boat had passed the buoy and went back upriver. He knew that another fifteen minutes would pass before the security boat would again come near the buoy. That was enough time for him to reach the buoy, tie the end of the wire to the anchor chain underneath it, and return to shore.

For the next few minutes he secured flotation gear around the charge of explosives. He also made sure that vegetation was tied to the tops of the partially inflated automobile tire inner tubes. As the security boat made another pass, the swimmer made his most difficult swim. He had to use all his strength to drag the heavy gear completely into the water. His calculations had been good. Once in the water the flotation gear gave the heavy container a slight negative buoyancy. He followed the wire out to the buoy, pulling the load behind him. By the time the security boat made another run near the mooring buoy, three hundred pounds of high explosives were secure underneath the buoy and only an inch of black rubber tube from the sapper's snorkel was above the surface. The young swimmer rested and waited the two hours it would take before the flood tide would be right for him to complete his mission.

That mission was a spectacular success for the Viet Cong. Around 0200 on the morning of November 25, the blast virtually destroyed the YRBM-16. The explosives had been placed expertly at the waterline opposite the bunkers containing thousands of gallons of diesel fuel and adjacent to the sleeping quarters of River Section 522 sailors. A fire followed the massive explosion, a fire that could well have totally destroyed the barge.

River Section 522 PBR sailors came back from patrol and helped save the mother ship. For hours there was a shuttle of boats from the burning base to the Ben Tre ferryboat landing. Jeeps and the one Ben Tre ambulance raced the wounded to the Ben Tre airfield for evacuation. Trucks moved firefighting equipment that had been rapidly airlifted to the Ben Tre airfield to the ferry landing. MACV U.S. Army personnel took the supplies (fire pumps and foam cans) to the ferry landing for sailors on PBRs ferrying wounded Navy sailors to the landing. The boat sailors went back to the burning barge to receive more wounded. Other sailors on the barge worked feverishly to dump tons of ammunition into the river before the fire reached the munitions storerooms. Lt. Jim Dykes, the easygoing 522 River Section commander, took charge of the firefighting efforts that saved the base. Some said that if not for the work of Jim Dykes, the YRBM-16 would have been totally destroyed.

The fire burned out a day and a half later. By that time seven sailors had died and thirty-five were medevacked with serious burns. Many more suffered minor burns and smoke inhalation. The base finally settled to the muddy bottom of the Ham Luong. It is a tribute to the U.S. Navy brown-water sailors that they managed to save all the boats except for one battle-damaged boat from River Section 521. It had been up on skids on the second deck and was totally destroyed by fire. Most of the weapons from the armory were saved as well, so the disaster was not total. The blackened, three-quarters-sunken hulk was fully refloated at Dong Tam, temporarily patched, then towed to Japan. Within six months the old girl was back in the combat zone serving the brown-water sailors once again. The U.S. Navy should be proud of the divers, tugboat crews, salvage boat crews, and ordinary sailors by the hundreds who got the burnt-out hulk of the YRBM-16 off the bottom of the Ham Luong River in a combat zone.

Enemy swimmer sappers like the one who hit the YRBM-16 and sunk the *Jamaica Bay* (the dredge sunk earlier at Dong Tam) would strike again with even more deadly results. Some to this day claim that the frogmen sappers in the Mekong Delta were probably deep-cover communist agents unknowingly trained in UDT operations by the U.S. Navy in 1965. An entire class of eight South Vietnamese UDT trainees had defected to the Viet Cong underground upon their return to South Vietnam. I and a lot of others had heard that rumor back in Coronado. Some of the rumors even alleged that Roy Boehm had received letters from the former students praising him for his training and thanking him for his kindness. Supposedly, the letters had caused that hard-bitten warrior a lot of grief. The VC sappers definitely did not acquire their skills off the wind.

I heard the news about YRBM-16 in the chow hall around 0700. First reports indicated some dead, a lot of wounded, and others missing. I lost my appetite. I thought at the time that the disaster had been compounded by the arrogance of commanders who refused to credit the enemy with capabilities they had already shown. That was a long day for me and the rest of the men of the 534th, all of whom wanted to know what had happened to the 534th contingent on the barge and what the loss of the base meant to us. I figured we would still be assigned the Ham Luong but be stationed in Dong Tam. Not all bad. At least Dong Tam had Red Cross girls.

The next day Ron Wolin assembled the 534th sailors. Jerry Letcher had survived the attack and only one 534th sailor had been medevacked of the nine stationed aboard the barge at the time. This was great news. The bad news was that the 534th had suffered severe materiel damages. Most of the spare parts for the new MK II boats had recently been shipped down to the YRBM-16. All those parts had been destroyed in the barge's storerooms. That would delay commencement of combat operations. We had to be resupplied with critical spare parts and then we would transit to My Tho and operate from there until replacement for the YRBM-16 was available. I looked forward to getting out of Nha Be, where the 534th was regarded as a supernumerary, as was the 535th, which had also just about received its complement of new MK II PBRs.

I remember little about the next eighteen days. I believe they were busy with making admin runs into Saigon in pickup trucks or on PBRs to receive high-priority airlifted parts lost on the YRBM-16. I do remember our new PBRs showing off in front of the older MK I PBRs on the Saigon River. We would pass them, cut across their bows, swing behind them, and then pass them again. Those little show-off admin runs probably contributed to the long-lasting, friendly friction between MK I PBR sailors and MK II PBR sailors. Those older boats had proud crews. They did not enjoy our antics. But the more pissed off they were at our showboating, the more we rubbed it in.

Early on the morning of December 9, 1967, a twelve-boat flotilla of small craft (ten MK II RivSect 534 PBRs and two LCM-8s) left Nha Be, transited down the Soi Rap, and entered the South China Sea. Each boat was loaded with men and materiel. All the personal possessions of the sailors and officers were crammed into seabags and AWOL bags aboard the PBRs. The Mike boats carried ammunition and spare parts. Because the roster of the 534th that day comprised six officers and fifty-six enlisted, each PBR probably had at least six sailors aboard. Even though the guns were loaded and sailors were at the ready, we were really just cruising up the river. The little armada was limited to the twelve knots of the Mike 8 boats. I was on the first boat as a passenger. Bill Earner was the navigator and he had assembled a team of quartermasters and signalmen on the boat to make the transit. Using our Raytheon radar and old charts, we made the mouth of the My Tho River transit in good formation with no radio communications. It was a damn good feat of seamanship because we passed mudbars and shallows that could have stopped the Mike 8s as we hugged the coastline. I was glad I was not in charge of the navigation.

The trip up the My Tho, the deepwater branch of the mighty Mekong, was uneventful. We overtook some oceangoing junks headed upriver and saw patrol aircraft overhead. Mostly we saw nothing except Vietnamese sampans hugging the riverbanks.

Viet Cong observers all along both banks probably figured that a mighty American offensive operation was going to take place. A few miles south of My Tho we saw villages and signs of human life along the banks. I looked at the chart and realized that the My Tho end of the Chet Say Canal was approaching to port. I took a pair of binoculars and studied the left bank. A large cleared area came into view. In the middle was a large South Vietnamese outpost. As our boats passed the outpost I got a good look down the Chet Say, which was straight as an arrow as far as I could see. Those Dutch engineers had done a good job but all their work had been to support commerce. The waterway had become a free-fire zone for gunships during the day and a communications route for Viet Cong at night. I doubted that the Vietnamese fort was much of a threat to enemy sampans sneaking out onto the My Tho River on dark nights. The machine guns in the gun towers probably could not even be brought to bear against sampans hugging the south bank. The River Section 532 PBRs out of My Tho probably regarded that canal a major fishing hole at night, the same way the PBRs on the Ham Luong regarded Ambush Alley and the Mo Cay.

Between the eastern end of the Chet Say and the city of My Tho our little armada passed the wreckage of a Japanese destroyer that had grounded on a mud bar after being nearly destroyed by U.S. Navy fighter-bombers early in 1945. An enlisted veteran on my boat was familiar with the area. He told me that the Jap destroyer was a great radar point of reference at night and a good object for target practice during the day. I studied the Jap wreck in my binoculars. Sure enough, a lot of .50-caliber bullets had torn through the thin, rusted, outer skin of the wreck along all of its two hundred feet exposed above the waterline.

The 534th's arrival at My Tho caused some little inconveniences to the daily life of the river rats from the 532 and 533 River Sections; we had to crowd into their hotel billets. We took the place of the 522 sailors who had crowded into My Tho facilities after the mining of the YRBM-16. The River Section 522 boats and men had been shipped off to I Corps by LST ten days before we arrived. Some support troop survivors from the YRBM-16 had remained at My Tho. A hotel room that normally housed four now had at least six occupants. Some sailors had to hot bunk. Some complained loudly if not sincerely. We knew that the living conditions were a hell of a lot better than those of the tens of thousands of troops bivouacked out in the boonies. But being the sailors we were, we bitched and moaned.

On the third floor of the Victory Hotel, Pete Richards, Frank Walker, and I shared a room with three junior officers from the 532 River Section. At least the room had a window and an overhead fan. The double bunks had mosquito netting. We had coolers to ice down beer and a table for playing cards. Life was good.

The next day all the sailors who had lost personal possessions on the YRBM-16 were assembled on the quay wall of the My Tho naval base. We were given forms on which to itemize our lost property. Cash losses were limited to one hundred dollars. The form was easy for me; I had lost several khaki uniforms, a set of tropical whites, a pair of shoes, a pair of boots, a few skivvies, and a cheap camera. I was one of the first to turn in the form. I was promptly given about a hundred dollars in MPC by a young lieutenant (j.g.) supply corps officer. The men at the end of the line saw what was going down and rapidly revised their forms. Sailors started claiming losses of two-hundred-dollar Nikon cameras, three-hundred-dollar Rolex watches, and so forth. All claims were paid without qualms until a third class commissary man known as Preacher on the barge (for his cheerful "Praise the Lord" greetings when he served troops in the chow line) claimed an expensive watch, a high-priced camera, and two diamond engagement rings valued at five hundred dollars each.

The supply corps officer felt that he had to question that claim.

"Do you expect me to believe that someone earning only

two hundred fifty dollars a month could afford one five-hundred-buck engagement ring, much less two? This is a bullshit claim!"

The little cook was evidently prepared for such a challenge.

"Sir, I have been in the Navy for over four years. I don't spend my money on liquor or whores. I don't own any property except what was in that locker. What money I do not give to the church was invested in the items lost. Those rings were purchased in Hong Kong last year with my shipping-over (reenlistment) bonus. I got two rings because I got two different lady friends. The rings were different because the ladies are different. The one who writes me most will be the one getting the first ring. I planned to sell the other ring before I got married. That's the honest truth."

The cook got his claim. He certainly made out better than the gamblers and loan sharks who had probably lost hundreds of dollars in cash over the hundred-dollar limit. He became somewhat of a local hero for the rest of the sailors. Another brown-water legend was born. I really believe that the Navy command bent the rules in favor of the claimants because it realized that the survivors had been recklessly exposed to an enemy swimmer attack. I did not believe the cook's claims, but I admired him for seeking some sort of personal justice.

The 534th enjoyed a short two days of settling in. The sailors learned their way around My Tho. The boat captains and the patrol officers went on unofficial cruises to get them familiar with the rivers that were new to a lot of them. I was regarded as an old hand on the Ham Luong and spent a lot of time on the water taking boats down it at cruising speed while I pointed out known enemy crossing areas and likely sniper-firing positions. We soon found out that the MK I PBRs from My Tho's 532 River Section and the River Section 531 boats from the *Harnett County* had provided only sporadic patrol coverage on the upper Ham Luong after the 522d had been transported up north to the Cua Viet. That was understandable; their coverage had been stretched thin in the previous two weeks. They were very appreciative that our new MK IIs had finally arrived to take up the slack.

On December 11, 1967, I led a three-boat night patrol on

the Ham Luong. The boats were the 7-15, 7-17, and 7-13 with boat captains BM1 Tony Summerlin, RD1 Robert Wenzel, and BM1 Irvine Burney. Because our base was at My Tho, it was a long patrol. Fourteen hours long for me, longer for the boat sailors, who had to square away the boat after the patrol—all lines flaked down, all guns covered, all boats fully fueled, and so on.

The patrol was routine. Its only significance was that it was the first MK II PBR combat patrol. The first of thousands of patrols made by MK II PBRs in Vietnam's Mekong Delta, the rivers along the Cambodian border west and north of Saigon, and the waterways of Cambodia, Panama, and even the Persian Gulf many years later. The first combat operation for a great little boat that served the Navy very well. My claim to fame is documentary evidence that I took them out for combat first.

The only MK II operational PBRs today belong to brown-water veteran associations. The Vietnamese might have a few of the old boats still floating; we left behind over two hundred. Some of them went down fighting even after NVA tanks captured Saigon. It took months before the NVA "pacified" the Mekong Delta in 1975. The South Vietnamese sailors manning those boats will forever be unsung heroes; they fought the good fight until they ran out of fuel and ammo. Some Vietnamese sailors attempted to reach Thailand in their little PBRs.

Two days later, a 534th PBR received its first enemy fire from the free-fire zone on Tan Tan Island at 1300. This heavy automatic weapons fire was suppressed only by the fire of three PBRs. Enemy fire was so heavy that Seawolf gunships were called on to make some firing runs. The next day, December 14, 1967, two patrols of 534th boats were subject to light automatic weapons fire from Tan Tan Island and from the west bank of the Ham Luong, near the Mo Cay Canal. Our boats' fire suppressed the enemy's fire. Half the 534th PBRs had been under fire within three days of our first operational patrol.

The attitude of the 534th during those first days was gung ho to the max. The 534th was the new kid on the block. We had the new toys. We had engaged the enemy while sustaining no friendly casualties. Even though many of our boat captains and senior enlisted were veterans of MK I PBR sections, we were basically an untried unit whose officers had little brown-water experience. The senior enlisted made all the difference.

We had a lot of spirit and unit pride. Ron Wolin and Bill Earner, in their respective roles of OinC and XO, made us that way. Wolin was the visionary. He saw potential and opportunity. An aggressive commander, he expected his sailors to be the same. He told us to seek out the enemy. Without notifying the operations center, we could go into any canal to intercept evading sampans. At the discretion of the patrol officer, we could split up a two-boat patrol. We did not have to wear flak jackets and helmets, but they had better be ready when needed. We were encouraged to go into other patrol areas without orders if a major firefight occurred. We were told to contact the local MACV advisers and visit their outposts, visit the marketplaces. Swap things with the local forces. Give them pop flares and grenades in exchange for fresh vegetables and fish. Get to know the little guys on the ground who we had to give fire support at night. We would not be required to carry Vietnamese maritime policemen. If we saw a good opportunity to capture an enemy soldier, we could get off the boats and run him down.

Sailors were permitted to openly carry personal weapons, including formerly proscribed sawed-off shotguns. Sailors started to walk around with all sorts of personal weapons. I saw everything from .22 derringers to single-barrel sawed-off 12-gauge shotguns and sawed-off M-2 (automatic) carbines. One guy even carried an old .45 Colt revolver on a pistol belt that looked like a prop from a John Wayne shitkicker.

Searching sampans and junks was secondary to seeking and destroying the enemy. At night only two men had to be awake during normal patrol—the boat captain (or a surrogate) and the forward gunner. The others could sleep by their guns until they were relieved. E-3 gunner's mates could take over the throttles to give the boat captain some shut-eye. These procedures ran 180 degrees counter to the scanty, official PBR patrol directives—sailors to be awake at all times and in full battle dress and the like. Our sailors loved these departures from the stringent rules; they could do their thing without feeling guilty. It was a happy medium between the middle-of-the-river, by-the-book, sampan searching of Jim Dykes's River Section 522 and the macho MACE team concepts of the "Bassac Interdictor," Don Sheppard. Basically we were telling the troops to go forth using their common sense and do the best things in their ability to hurt the enemy without being foolish.

Bill Earner was placed in the difficult role of hard-nosed XO (short for "executive officer"; the official Navy title at the time for second in command was "operations officer," but all sailors knew that the OinC was the CO and his second was the XO). Someone had to preach and enforce all the Navy regulations that were necessary to maintain discipline and military bearing even in a combat situation. That was Bill's role, and why he wrote the first of his many "Getting the Word" missives to the troops. Bill dictated those pronouncements to Bruce Burns, our third class yeoman. Burns carefully typed the missives on a stencil, mimeographed them, and distributed them to all the troops.

Bill noted the corrosive influence of the My Tho SEALs on ordinary sailors: sailors were no longer giving courtesy salutes to their officers; some PBR sailors started going on patrol in tiger-stripe jungle fatigues. Bill quickly put a stop to such practices. Young gunners were pissed off but the boat commanders and the patrol officers loved his message. We (the boat commanders and patrol officers) told the troops that, like it or not, they were part of the U.S. Navy. If they got out of line they were in for some major shit. We told them that Earner was an Annapolis man: "He would send you to the brig as soon as look at you." We told them that they had signed up for the Navy and now they had to live with it. It was the Navy way, and it sure as hell beat the shit out of being a trigger-puller in the Army.

As senior patrol officer, I had to make up the patrol schedule: pairing boats and assigning patrol officers a week in advance for around-the-clock coverage of our river area. It was a simple job, but I made sure that in the rotation all boats were on an equal schedule of day- and night-patrols and alternating patrol areas—Area 1 (from the My Tho River to a mile north of the Ben Tre ferryboat landing) and Area 2 (from the Ben

Tre ferryboat landing south until our patrol area reached the River Section 531 area). I attempted to pair boats. The two boats would have three consecutive day- (or night-) patrols followed by a day off and then three night- (or day-) patrols. The next week the boats could be paired with other boats, but stay on the same day-and-night rotation.

I tried to have one of the three commissioned patrol officers—myself, Pete Richards, or Frank Walker—on patrol at all times. The result was that we three roommates seldom were in sync for evening meals or our precious liberty time or even on patrol at the same time. My primary reason for scheduling the officers this way was that I wanted to make sure that we all had a chance to be tested. I knew that some fights were bound to occur that would require more than two boats, and that people would be hurt, boats possibly would be sunk, and so forth. I wanted to make sure that I and my two other junior officer buddies were prepared. Whenever our boats went on patrol, it was expected that the senior man on the river at the time was to take charge. I felt an obligation that that first senior man be a commissioned officer, not because I felt that commissioned officers were better qualified than the first class or chiefs to take command but because I felt it was our duty to assume the command role. That is what the whole structure of the military is about. If Pete, Frank, or I fucked up in some fur ball of a firefight, we knew that we could be shitcanned in disgrace. However heroic or incompetent an enlisted man in charge of those little plastic boats was in some battle, it was an officer who would receive the glory or the disgrace. Even if the officer was miles away. I just wanted an officer around to shoulder the load. If stupidity or cowardly actions killed sailors, the guy who got the blame should be wearing gold stripes, an officer near the scene or who had ordered the operation. I knew that I would give credit to the men. I did not know if I would be able to make the right decisions; I did not know if I could possibly contribute; I did know that leadership was my job. The boat sailors would have to be on patrol for at least six fourteen-hour patrols each week. The patrol officers had to be on the river for at least five fourteen-hour patrols each week. We junior officers did enjoy some privileges of our rank. But then again, we had to do a lot of the admin work ordinary boat sailors hated with a greater passion than long hours on patrol. Drafting procedures, performing inventories, writing up action reports, writing up citations, performing locker inspections, and on and on.

Early on the morning of December 15, as I was preparing for a patrol, Ron Wolin informed me that my two boats were to leave our patrol area and return to My Tho at 0830 for a "special mission." My two boats would join Ron and two other boats for a run through the Chet Say Canal, leaving only two boats on Ham Luong patrol. Our run would be all the way from the My Tho River to the Ham Luong. A pair of Seawolf gunships would be overhead flying air cover.

I was apprehensive but not surprised. Sooner or later the 534th would have to start going down enemy-controlled waterways. Ron Wolin's leadership style made it a preordained conclusion, and the Chet Say was the big bad wolf in our patrol patch. I knew that our boats would be running enemy canals long before the Saigon warriors ordered us to "show the flag" on them. I was comforted by the facts that our OinC was going to be with the boats on this first run and that we had air cover. Ron had also made a good choice of running the canal from east to west with the sun behind us and at a time when the water would be high. In a way, I was looking forward to the mission. The spirit of the men was high and it was a good time to test us. Weeks of long patrols and the tedium of searching thousands of sampans would surely take their toll on us in the coming weeks. If we had to get into a fight, at least we were in good shape to take on a fight, especially one of our own choosing.

The four boats going on morning patrol that day got under way before dawn and made a routine patrol exchange down on the Ham Luong. I did a couple of things to make the time pass before heading back to My Tho. I got the four boats on patrol together to make a high-speed sweep down Ambush Alley at dawn. I then split the boats up, three boats drifting at various points across from Tan Tan Island and one running the length of our northern patrol area. We even searched a few sampans that morning. The Viet Cong could not see any pattern.

When my two-boat patrol (PBR 7-20, boat captain QM1 Earle Milliken, and PBR 7-14, boat captain GM2 Ned Caldwell) arrived at the My Tho base at 0830, Ron Wolin and two boats were just casting off from the pier. Ron's boat came alongside my boat. Ron was grinning. He was wearing his standard uniform: heavyweight green fatigues and a green Marine Corps–style utility cap.

"Okay, Wynn! Right on schedule. The Seawolves will be airborne in ten minutes. They should be over us at a thousand feet when we are entering the Chet Say. Since you are familiar with the Chet Say, your boats will lead the way. You set the speed with Milliken's boat in the canal. Keep a couple of knots in reserve. Slow down if Caldwell's boat gets more than fifty yards behind you. I will be on Engle's boat, just behind Caldwell's. When you see the Seawolves behind us, go to speed for the canal. Their callsign is Seawolf 44. Give them a radio check right after I give them a radio check. After that you should be close to entering the canal. Take care, and good luck!"

Ron had not told me how he wanted the guns trained. That was good. I did not want to have the guns staggered from one bank to the other on the four boats. In fact, I preferred to have all guns trained on the south (port) bank. The south bank was completely under Viet Cong control. The north bank was occasionally contested by South Vietnamese troops. As a precaution I reluctantly told Caldwell and Milliken to have the forward fifties and the M-60 trained on the south bank. The after gunner on each boat was to have his .50 trained on the starboard bank. Better safe than sorry.

I took the boats down the My Tho River. A river full of junks and sampans headed to and from market. If enemy watchers saw our new boats headed east, they had no clue of where we were going. Nothing about this "special" had been radioed ahead. During the trip I got a close look at the half-sunken Jap destroyer as my boat passed it fifty yards to port. A fifty-foot salvage barge alongside the warship was flying the South Vietnamese yellow flag with its red horizontal stripes and a smaller Japanese flag with its big red disk in a field of white. Milliken told me that he had heard in My Tho that a Japanese company was trying to recover materiel from the ship. Our old enemy had eliminated a great practice target for our guns. The Japanese would likely take such things as anchors, chains, and bells back to the homeland as memorials to their war dead. The rest of the wreck would be converted to new steel to be sold at a high price to the Americans. The fortunes of war.

As the entrance to the Chet Say approached, I looked back to the west. The air cover was there as expected. The Seawolf gunships came flying directly overhead at about five hundred feet, banked left, and gained a little altitude.

"Seawolf 44, this is Pineapple Bowl Zulu. Radio check. Over."

"Pineapple Bowl Zulu, this is Seawolf 44. I have you loud and clear. Over."

"Seawolf 44, this is Pineapple Bowl Zulu. This unit is the third Papa Bravo Romeo. Pineapple Bowl Charlie is lead Papa Bravo Romeo. Break. Pineapple Bowl Charlie, do you copy?"

That was my cue.

"Pineapple Bowl Zulu, Seawolf 44. This is Pineapple Bowl Charlie. I read you both loud and clear. Over." I was surprised at how calmly the words came out of my mouth; my right hand, holding the mike, was twitching.

"This is Pineapple Bowl Zulu. Roger. Out."

"This is Seawolf 44. Roger. Out."

"This is Pineapple Bowl Charlie. Out." At least I knew we had good communications.

As we entered the canal the Seawolves climbed several hundred feet a half mile behind us, flying slow and aligned on the straight axis of the Chet Say. I was standing behind the rear armor plate of the coxswain's flat, directly behind Milliken. I was buttoned-up, my steel helmet's chin strap buckled and all snaps and the zipper of my flak jacket snapped and zipped. I held an M-79 grenade launcher in my left hand. I had four M-79 rounds in the side pockets of my fatigue blouse, just below the flak jacket. Another dozen rounds for the weapon were in front of me at chest-high level in a .50-caliber ammo can attached to the armor plate. I was as ready as I could be. The gunners were similarly buttoned-up and ready for battle. There were no rah-rah cheers or profane exclamations either from me or Milliken. Most of the young gunners had been in firefights. They knew what was expected of them.

We went into the canal at about twenty-four knots—about twenty-seven miles an hour. We still had another 10 percent increase in speed available if the throttles were pushed to the stops. We went up in mid-channel, about thirty yards from either bank. The first mile and three or so minutes, vegetation on the banks was sparse. Fallow rice paddies. Then we passed the pylons of a destroyed bridge. The vegetation changed. The south bank was covered with the same dense nipa palm and six-foot shrub trees familiar along the Ham Luong. The foliage on the north bank was not as dense but still had some stretches of heavy nipa palms. My eyes concentrated on the south bank, looking for mounds, fresh dirt, and cleared lanes of fire, but all I saw was a blanket of green vegetation to the water's edge. That bank was a dark abyss to me. I knew that things very dangerous to me were hidden by the dense green cover on that bank.

I heard the staccato bark of fire up front and to the left. Twenty fast rounds. At least three weapons. I fired my M-79 into the south bank. Even before I discharged my weapon the forward fifties had started blasting away. As I broke the breech of the M-79 to reload, the M-60 gunner behind me was firing. And the after .50 gunner had swiveled his gun around and was firing at the south bank. All that in less than two seconds. Milliken pushed the throttles to the max. We had had no idea if we were at the beginning or the end of an ambush site. We did know that we had at least three miles to go before we were out of enemy-controlled waters.

Just about every PBR sailor suffered from hearing loss during the Vietnam War. Mostly it was from the roar of three 50-caliber machine guns firing almost nonstop for sustained periods on a small platform in the close confines of a canal. Usually the hearing loss and ear pain were temporary. The eardrums would be healed with minimal hearing loss. But there are more than a few old PBR gunner survivors today who depend on hearing aids because of their PBR service. All PBR sailors were issued rubber ear protectors packed in a small plastic cylinder the size of a 35mm film container that could be easily attached to their flak jackets. Like most PBR sailors, I never used them. That day I regretted not wearing my ear protectors. The roar was deafening and painful.

As I reloaded the grenade launcher a third time, I glanced at the FM radio console in the coxswain's flat to the right of Milliken. The RECEIVE light flashed on and off. Mostly on, with a millisecond or two off. Radio communications were useless to me. The gunships saw what was going on and reacted. They swooped down to two hundred feet and blasted that south bank with machine guns and a couple of rockets, their fire directed at the south bank astern of my boat. They did not fire more rockets because our boats were moving so fast and no boat had been disabled. If a boat had been disabled the gunships would have poured in the rockets to get some time for the boat to get out of harm's way or for other boats to retrieve survivors. The Seawolf pilots' main concern had to be all the .50-caliber bullets we were firing, which hit the water and riverbank and then were deflected hundreds of feet into the air.

The forward gunner on Milliken's boat—the one I was in—set the tempo for my boat, the first in line. He had been the first to see the enemy fire and first to fire back. When he stopped firing, the after gunners and I stopped firing. During one of those brief intervals, I looked ahead. Bullets were being fired from the south bank into the middle of the river. The forward gunner resumed firing. The after .50 gunner realized that he was down to the last fifty rounds in his ready tray so he swung up the M-18 Honeywell grenade launcher and cranked off slow shots timed to land and explode just before our boat reached the point of impact. The M-60 gunner was slapping another two hundred rounds into the ready box on the port engine cover gun stanchion. I looked back at Caldwell's boat, which was firing nonstop into the south bank. Then I noticed all the incoming bullet splashes between the two boats. I turned my head forward again and fired an M-79 round in front of my boat. In that instant I finally saw the red muzzle flashes of enemy guns. Little twinkling lights right at the riverbank. The Viet Cong guns were right at the high water's edge, not five yards away from the bank in the nipa palm, as I had assumed. The enemy bullets were not purposely directed. They were hitting the water in front of the boat and skipping off to who knows where. I realized that those Viet Cong guys were just hunkered down in spider holes and sticking their AK-47s or belt-fed machine guns over their heads and firing across the canal, hoping for lucky hits. They were probably more scared than we were. Our firepower had them cowering in their holes. Thank God for good old American firepower! An American infantry company advancing on these positions would have been decimated at close quarters. All we had to do was keep the enemy hunkered down as we passed them.

If you did not see the flashes you could not recognize a firing position; the only tracers in the air that day were the orange-red tracers from U.S. Navy PBRs and Seawolf gunships. The Viet Cong had scooped holes in the bank at low tide, dug into the bank horizontally six feet or so, and then dug up to the surface, which they covered with a matting of bamboo and palm fronds. At high tide they could pop out of their watery holes, take some shots, and then disappear below the surface. At low tide they could shoot out of muddy holes from twelve-inch apertures in the riverbank, then disappear back into their muddy caves. The enemy's positions were well camouflaged from both the air and the river. Some were perhaps the same holes that the Viet Minh had used against the French twenty years before. The enemy troops in them were not zealots like the Japanese soldiers American Marines faced in World War II. Or, thinking back, maybe they were. They just had much more patience than the Japanese. We did not have to root them out of their holes with MACE teams armed with flamethrowers and satchel charges. We just had to withstand their fire in a live shooting gallery in which we were the ducks for a few minutes. Thank God we were well-armed ducks, and the shooters in the blinds basically closed their eyes when firing on us. The Viet Cong just wanted to stay alive to fight another day. They knew that our boats were only passing through. They knew they would have many more days. If a MACE team or infantry squad had stormed their positions, they would have fought to the death and taken a lot of their enemies with them. That was the nature of war. We were "showing the flag." The Viet Cong were unprepared that day. Nobody told them that some PBRs were going to invade their territory. The stalwart VC troopers who manned those fighting holes were probably satisfied with just showing they had fire-power and grit.

Those VC regular force guys were just like the U.S. Marine grunts who fired M-16s blindly over walls during the battle for Hue and had their actions captured forever on film for just about every Vietnam documentary shown on television. Not necessarily an image of fearless fighters, but an image of tired warriors trying to stay alive and make the enemy retreat so they could fight another day on more favorable terms.

One Viet Cong with a recoilless rocket or B-40 rocket almost got lucky. His round hit just astern of QM1 Fred Engle's PBR 7-12, the boat Ron Wolin was riding in. The after .50 gunner got a piece of shrapnel in the face. Engineman Keenbeck got a slight wound. He was the first 534th sailor to be wounded. The first of many.

Most of the Viet Cong firing on our boats that day along a mile stretch of the Chet Say Canal were probably not scratched. Thousands of bullets had been fired very close to them. Our boats and the Seawolf gunships probably shot off forty thousand rounds. Nobody could accurately count the number of Viet Cong fighters there or their volume of rounds fired. I just remember almost a mile run of PBR guns being fired and seeing gun flashes and bullets hitting between my boat and the boat astern. The firing on "my" boat (Milliken's boat) had set the pace. The forward gunner controlled the firing. After the initial enemy shooting positions had been passed, the forward gunner fired short bursts in front of the boat. Three or so rounds into the bank. When he saw muzzle flashes and bullets hitting the water, he went full automatic with his machine guns. The after gunners followed suit, i.e., recon by fire followed by fire suppression. Not the standard procedure, but it seemed to work.

Our tactics worked that day simply because the enemy was not expecting us, and only a skeleton crew was manning the Chet Say fighting holes. Most of the enemy soldiers in those holes had close calls during those minutes of the running battle. And most of those Viet Cong would be killed before the war ended, their younger brothers taking their places. They were in the war for the duration. We were not. If they had advance warning that American patrol boats were to transit the canal that day, some Viet Cong commander would have had a detailed plan to nail us. He would have concentrated his forces and targeted the last boat. And he would have a small force on the opposite bank to destroy other boats coming to the aid of the survivors of the fired-on boat. A few dozen well-armed Viet Cong could have accomplished that job if they had been prepared.

All firing stopped within a half mile of the Ba Lai River. Our sailors started to shout and yell and move away from their guns when we passed the Ba Lai. They thought they had cheated sudden death and won. They were right. We had cheated death. The new guys, like me, knew that they had survived a firefight. They could get the little silk tabs at the back of their black berets cut. The old hands, with only a couple of months to go on their tour, thought they maybe had a good chance to survive Vietnam. Maybe Ron Wolin would see the danger of running enemy canals and settle down to patrolling the wide rivers the way the 522d had done for so long.

The Ba Lai passed close to port and we were in the upper Ben Tre River, heading for Ben Tre and the Ham Luong. It was near the part of the river where the 522d boat had been destroyed back in October. The sailors were not concerned. A boat getting waxed there seemed unlikely. I was not so confident. I had seen the charred hulk of the 522d boat, ambushed just east of the Ben Tre bridge. I told the gunners to get back to their guns. We could celebrate once we reached the Ham Luong. The Ben Tre River was no place for sailors to be off guard.

Once the boats reached the wide river, everyone removed their flak jackets and helmets. The thousands of brass cases from spent bullets were scooped up and dumped over the side of each boat. We looked around for battle damage. No bullet holes were visible. Just some shrapnel nicks on the stern of Engle's 7-12 boat. Keenbeck, the wounded gunner, had a small strip of gauze taped to his right cheek. He had a shallow half-inch crease beside his nose. He was lucky. A little higher and that little bit of thin rocket warhead casing could have taken out his eye.

Just as everyone was getting comfortable as the four boats drifted together, Ron Wolin decided to get the juices flowing again.

"I think now is the time to run the Cai Cam. The enemy will soon know that we have arrived. Maybe they are not prepared. If we got through the Chet Say today, we can get through the Cai Cam. I want to see what the backside of that sniper-infested Tan Tan Island is like."

The sailors were happy at the prospect. I was concerned. The Cai Cam was only fifty feet wide in some stretches. Viet Cong, flat on their stomachs at the water's edge, could hurt PBRs by throwing grenades. And on that trip we would have no Seawolf air cover. It was an operation that Ron had dreamed up on the spur of the moment. At the time I was nervous but feeling lucky. I was concerned that I would be responsible for killing civilians if any were on the small tributary and our gunners opened up on them. Many a time I had let sampans evading into the Cai Cam go unharmed after determining to the best of my ability that they were civilian craft. The water on the tributary was not considered a free-fire zone. Even helo gunships did not blast sampans traveling down the waterway. What would happen if a sampan saw a PBR racing toward it and went for the east bank, the free-fire zone? Would I order my gunners to blast away—possibly killing old women and children? Would I lead the PBRs into a Viet Cong death trap by chasing down the sampan to search it?

Ron Wolin took a lot of anxiety from me when he told me he was going in first with PBRs 7-12 and 7-16. I was to stay back on the Ham Luong with the other two boats as a ready reaction force.

The two boats entered the wide end of the tributary. I watched as they followed the curve of the little river to the left. Less than five seconds after the boats were out of sight I heard an eruption of gunfire. Short and violent. Ron was on the radio.

"Zulu One, this is Zulu. We took a rocket hit in the bow. Let's get the hell out of here!"

My two boats were entering the Cai Cam when we saw Ron's two boats speeding toward us. A fist-size hole showed in the bow of QM1 Carl Evans's 7-16 boat. The hole was on both sides of the bow just above the waterline. I told Milliken to move alongside the speeding 7-12 boat. Ron was just shaking his head and grinning. QM1 Engle was not grinning. His right hand was trying to push the throttles through the stops as he steered with only his left hand on the wheel. I saw why Engle was disturbed. There was a bullet hole in the Plexiglas windscreen just to the right of where Engle's face probably was during that brief encounter. Ron and the forward gunner jumped over to Milliken's boat from Evans's boat. I grabbed Ron's hand as he swung himself aboard.

"Boy, did they surprise us. A burst of automatic fire and a rocket in only a second or two. The damn rocket went through the bow from port to starboard before it exploded on the right bank. I figured we had to get out because if we had to slow down we would take enough water to sink." Ron was still grinning.

Even with two people off the 7-16 boat, it had difficulty keeping its wounded bow up out of the water. Cans of ammo from the damaged boat were passed over to Milliken's boat. Even after these measures, the weight of water in the bow had slowed the boat to a mere twenty knots, just high enough for the holes in the bow to be above the waterline. Just enough speed so that we did not have to attempt a tow or beach the boat on an uninhabited island in the middle of the river. Just enough speed for the boat to reach the maintenance pier of the My Tho base. This was at about 1030.

Before we resumed our patrol on the Ham Luong, my boats began to top off fuel and replace the ammo we had expended up the Chet Say. Ron went over to Lt. John Smith and the maintenance sailors who were at work lifting the 7-16 boat onto skids. As portable cranes were hoisting the boat, I noticed Ron talking to a couple of SEALs. Just as my boats were getting under way, Ron shouted to me to hold up. The two SEALs accompanied Ron. They were carrying M-16s and ammo pouches.

"Wynn, I don't believe you have had enough excitement for today. These two guys want to go out with you and do a little recon on Tan Tan Island. Maybe they can nail those gooks that shot up the 7-16 boat. Would you take them with you? I would love to go with you, but I have to make reports and make sure we have everything we need to patch up the holes to 7-16 boat."

Ron was grinning again. I smiled back and told him, "You bet I would."

I could lie like a streetwise New Yorker when my boss wanted only to hear confirmation. His question was like the onerous things my mother would often ask me to do, prefacing the bad news with, "Would you like to do . . . ?" Of course I would like to play bridge with some old biddies or go shopping all over town for some elusive item. Of course I wanted to go on a spider-hole hunt with overeager SEALs.

What the hell, I'd been lucky so far that day. I was always a dutiful child. I wanted to please my mother. I wanted to please Ron. I hoped the SEALs were lucky. The SEALs were in their basic My Tho attire: green T-shirts and cutoff knee-length camo fatigue trousers, sunglasses, jungle boots, and soft bush hats. They were young and strong. One was almost a platinum blonde. The other had sandy-colored hair. I never got their names. They were from SEAL Team 2 and had just arrived in country. Neither had ever been down the Ham Luong, much less set foot on Tan Tan Island. They figured that the two of them were more than equal to the task. They had volunteered for the mission on their own. Their officers were never informed. It was just another way Ron Wolin did business: see an opportunity and take it. He saw some eager SEALs and conned them. I guess I became an "operator" myself. I was conned. But at the same time I really believed this little op might work. I was ready to try something new. I conned myself and two boat crews into doing something foolish.

On the way downriver I showed the SEALs the chart of Tan Tan Island and indicated the firing positions the Viet Cong had used that morning alongside the east bank of the Cai Cam as well as every sniper position on the island's Ham Luong side that I was aware of. The three of us devised a plan. The two boats would make a moderate-speed run up the Cai Cam, turn around just before the bend to the left, and exit at full speed. The hope was that some Viet Cong would see us coming and run for their firing holes farther downstream. As soon as the boats exited the little stream, my boat would run down

Left to right: Ron Wolin, Pete Richards, Bill Earner, Frank Walker, and John Smith. The original 534th officers (besides me who was TAD to the 522d), going to Vung Tau from Nha Be to pick up the first MK II PBRs. Walker and Smith would both be wounded seriously enough to be disabled long before their tours ended.

BMSN Wayne Forbes with a new AK-47 he earned in combat. Twelve VC were surprised when a 534th PBR caught them crossing a bamboo foot bridge over a thirty-foot-wide creek. Twelve VC were KIA. Eight brand-new Chicom AK-47s were captured. It could have been courts-martial for the guys in charge. Forbes was in the thick of things for over a year.

Hulk of a 522d PBR destroyed on the Ben Tre River.

Wynn Goldsmith receiving his first Navy Commendation Medal from Comdr. Sayre A. Swartzrauber, Commander River Squadron Five. March 1968.

Wynn Goldsmith on a 534th PBR. March 1968.

Jack Harrell in the "purloined" Boston whaler.

Father Charles "Chuck" McCoy—formerly a USMC staff sergeant in Korea, now a USN chaplain— leads a memorial service for Ensign Third Class Webb. This was one of many services for brown-water sailors that he had to conduct.

Jerry Letcher with an AK-47.

The Ben Tre marketplace burning during combat.
January 31, 1968.

A 534th boat after being carelessly handled the day
before the 1968 Tet Offensive. Exhausted sailors
worked for hours before the tide refloated the boat.
They were read the riot act for their negligence. The
next day they were heroes.

Pete Richards.

Tony Summerlin and Ned Caldwell.
Two tough sailor heroes.

Burned-out hulk of the YRBM-16 after salvage ops.
This base was virtually destroyed by an enemy
swimmer. Seven river rats died in the attack, something never reported in the press at the time.
November 1967.

Captured Viet Cong.

View of the after gun on a 534th PBR.

534th PBRs, with accompanying U.S. Navy river assault craft, getting ready to sortie from Tan An on the first day of Operation Giant Slingshot. Within days, the brown-water navy saw its fiercest combat ever. River Section/Division 534 was at the tip of the sword. December 1968.

Shot of the Bloody Alley stretch of the Vam Co Dong during Giant Slingshot. December 1968.

Ron Wolin with a plaque bearing the emblem he designed for the 534th.

Lt. Bill Dennis attending to captured VC suspects. Dennis was killed just days after this photo was taken.

Ron Wolin, Wynn Goldsmith, and Frank Alla at the Ben Tre ferryboat landing the day of Jack Harrell's party.

Wynn Goldsmith now only goes boating to fish.

the Ham Luong for a hundred meters and insert the two SEALs on the west bank of Tan Tan. Then the SEALs would walk through the waist-high grass of the fallow rice field on a line toward the rocket firing position. They would kill the rocket shooters and come back safely to the boats.

The first part of our dumb-ass plan worked. The two PBRs made a successful feint up the Cai Cam, reversed course, and went south for a hundred meters or so.

The SEALs jumped off the boat's bow and spread about ten yards apart. The one to the south walked ten feet ahead of the one on his right. It was near high tide and I could follow their movements in my binoculars. They looked like guys walking a field in pursuit of quail. Suddenly they froze in a crouch. The blond kid on the left gave a hand signal to his buddy. Then they split farther apart and started trotting at a crouch, disappearing from sight. I grabbed the radio mike and was prepared to call in a "scramble one"—meaning sailors in desperate straits needed Seawolf help fast. I had not really thought this action through. There was no radio communication between the two SEALs and my boats! The SEALs were out of sight. What would happen if an eruption of gunfire was followed by a minute of silence? Would I not have to send armed sailors ashore with smoke grenades to locate them before I called in the gunships? I was in over my head. I was the senior guy. How did I let myself get into this situation?

Fortunately within a few minutes the SEALs reappeared at the water's edge. The blond kid stood up and waved his M-16 in the air. The other guy was right behind him. My boat went into the bank to pick them up. They were a little more dirty and sweaty than they'd been ten minutes before. They said that a Viet Cong sentry was at the edge of the tree line they were walking toward. Evidently he saw them just as they saw him and he disappeared into the foliage. The SEALs had no clear shots and had to evade through the grass back to the river in case an alerted automatic weapons squad in the tree line took them under fire.

"Lieutenant, show us some sniper holes. We still have a chance to fuck Charlie." The blond kid was grinning as he wiped down his weapon. I guess he was still on a high from his successful evasion through the grass.

Finding sniper holes was easy. The two PBRs raced down the middle of Ham Luong. Just as the fallow rice fields on Tan Tan abruptly changed to heavy vegetation I had Milliken turn the 7-19 boat into the bank. I knew of several sniper incidents from approximately that location. Caldwell's boat stayed twenty yards away as our PBR's bow settled into the bank. The two SEALs gingerly stepped off the bow into the chest-high bushes at the water's edge. They went out of sight as the 7-19 boat reversed off the bank. Within twenty seconds they were on the bank, signaling our PBR to come to them.

The blond kid yelled out, "We got beaucoup fighting holes right here. There must be at least twenty of them less than five meters apart. You PBR sailors must have pissed off some gooks. They went to a lot of trouble digging out these holes."

The SEALs wanted concussion grenades. They said that the TNT in a concussion grenade could punch out the river sidewall of the spider holes and that the tidal action of the river would then collapse the holes. It was all theory of course, but concussion grenades are cheap compared to sailors' lives. We gave the SEALs twelve concussion grenades, all we had on both PBRs. The SEALs buried the grenades in the mud walls of the holes, pulled the pins, and stood back. The holes were close together along a twenty-meter stretch of riverbank. After the explosions a whole stretch of riverbank seemed to collapse. One side of me hoped that the Viet Cong snipers would get discouraged when they saw what had happened to their holes. Another side figured that the enemy would just get pissed off enough to make stronger holes with better camouflage and booby traps set around them. I also was discouraged with the thought that there were many more holes on the island, perhaps hundreds of them.

As the 7-19 boat backed off the bank with the SEALs safely aboard, I believed that my excitement for the day was over. I would take the SEALs back to My Tho and return to normal patrol.

I was wrong.

The SEALs wanted to see some more holes.

"I told you guys we don't have any more concussion grenades. We only have some M-26 fragmentation grenades.

You said concussion grenades do a much better job on the holes than fragmentation grenades. Come out with us tomorrow. I will get you cases of concussion grenades. You can spend the whole fucking day setting off charges in spider holes."

I thought they'd see the point, that there were *hundreds* of fighting holes on the riverbank. Enough holes to occupy a platoon of EOD specialists for weeks.

They did not see my point.

"Hey, Lieutenant, lighten up. We're just trying to help out you boat sailors. Fragmentation grenades are perfect. This time we will booby-trap the holes. A dead gook in a spider hole is worth ten collapsed holes. Hell, we've been taught to booby-trap VC bodies so we can get at least another one of the fuckers. Don't you agree?"

Again it was the blond kid talking. He was as big a wiseass as I was.

"How are you going to make sure the fragmentation grenade kills a sniper? Suppose some little kid falls into a hole and sets off the grenade?"

"Well, Lieutenant, then we got a VC dead before his prime. What the hell, this is war. We got to do unto them before they do unto us. Anybody checking out spider holes on the riverbank will be at risk. If old mamma-san and her kids get wasted, so much the better. There will be fewer fighting holes being built."

A young PBR sailor heard these SEAL words and contributed a few of his own.

"Fucking A. Fuck up every firing hole and every dead gook body with grenades. That will teach them not to fuck with us!"

I was impressed and disheartened. The troops doing the fighting should go after the enemy. Let the dead enemy and their unarmed families be. Let the Air Force bomb the hell out of Hanoi from thirty thousand. The bomber crews could do their technical thing while knowing that they could be shot out of the sky at any moment without the slightest pang of conscience about the results of their bombs. They did not have to see carnage close up. They did not have to target people up close and personal.

I realized that I was part of a "dirty war." That bothered me. Then I did a real dumb-ass thing. My big mouth again.

"Maybe we should save our fragmentation grenades for those fighting holes we experienced this morning up the Chet Say. At least we know that armed men stay around those holes and the area is not full of innocent peasants."

A chorus of "Fucking A's" was the response to my words.

I soon found myself back in the Chet Say Canal.

Chapter 10

The SEALs carefully deposited a half-dozen grenades with their pins removed in some holes on the south bank of the Chet Say almost a mile west of the firing positions we had encountered earlier and very close to the mouth of the Ba Lai River. Very close to where the little Vietnamese maritime cop had grabbed the after .50 and started firing, over a month ago. But it was two miles past the point where rockets had hit the 522 boats and the little Viet cop had been killed. I figured that the Viet Cong did not man that part of the Chet Say. They would be expecting PBRs to come from the My Tho side as we had done two hours earlier. The survivors of our earlier incursion would be back at base camp going over lessons learned.

The SEALs and PBR sailors did not see a soul on the western fringes of the Chet Say that day as the SEALs demolished several fighting holes. The spider holes were well camouflaged and well maintained, and Viet Cong could have manned them with a few minutes' warning. We were lucky. Especially me. If sailors had been hurt, I was the one whose ass would be in the sling. Rightfully, of course; I was the senior man. I had let myself get talked into doing something foolhardy. Nobody back at the My Tho base or at the Ben Tre MACV compound had been informed of where we were. A couple of well-placed rockets could have turned the situation into an uncontrolled disaster. It would have taken a half hour for gunships to come to our aid, longer for other PBRs to arrive.

Two hours later, after we had taken the SEALs back to My Tho, my two-boat patrol received a dozen rounds of sniper fire from the west bank of Tan Tan Island less than half a mile south of where the SEALs had blown the spider holes. Evidently the local VC had gotten the word that we had destroyed some of their holes and wanted to indicate their displeasure. I just marveled at what might have been. What would have happened if I had chosen that stretch to go spider-hole hunting, and a sniper or two with a rocketeer or two had actually been in the holes when my PBR went up to the bank in front of them?

I had been double lucky that day. I knew it. I resolved not to squander my luck. I resolved that I would never again lead SEALs on any ad hoc sniper-hole hunts. I resolved never to go up the Chet Say Canal unless ordered. I resolved to take my chances at random with everyone else. I resolved not to tempt fate by bearding the lion in his den. Like so many of my resolutions over the years, those fell by the wayside. At least I had some of the real fear of God put into me that day.

The last two weeks of 1967 saw a lot of combat for the 534th river rats. But not for me. None of the combat-action summaries I retained all these years strike a resonant chord in my memory bank. Altogether there were sixteen instances of enemy fire received and returned. Every one of our ten boats received fire in those two weeks. Some had been under fire seven times. Three 534th sailors in addition to Keenbeck were wounded. GM3 Wayne Murray, a forward gunner, and BMC James A. Raymond, a patrol officer, had to be medevacked. Both returned to duty within a few weeks.

Four Purple Hearts in half a month by a sixty-man complement. That ratio of wounds would increase, decrease, and increase again over the next year and a half. On the whole that ratio was just average for PBR river rats. In a numbers game, one could argue that there were almost as many wound awards as there were PBR sailors. That was certainly true for the 534th. But there are wounds and there are wounds. Some guys got a couple of Bronze Stars on their original Purple Heart for scratches. Some guys were disabled for life when they earned their first.

Most of the combat actions involved sniper or heavy automatic weapons fire from Ambush Alley or the south bank of Tan Tan Island. One action had four boats returning from Ham Luong duty coming to the aid of a River Section 533 boat on the evening of December 28. The 533 boat had taken a recoilless rocket from the north bank of the My Tho River three miles west of Dong Tam. Five 533 sailors were seriously wounded. A 75mm recoilless round packs a lot of energy and several pounds of hard steel casing that turns into thousands of bits of white-hot shrapnel when it explodes. This was why the sailors on the 533d boat were so torn up. Only supporting fire allowed the boat to get away. The firepower of five PBRs and two Seawolf gunships was insufficient to suppress the enemy's fire, so fixed-wing air strikes had to be called in to silence the enemy's guns. That incident should have been a warning.

I vaguely remember it; I was off the river at the time. It was just another story of violence and destruction. I, and many more like me, regarded it and all the increasingly violent attacks on PBRs in the eastern Delta as a temporary thing. That was my hope and belief at the time: the attack had been an isolated incident, some dedicated Viet Cong unit bent on doing one big thing at least once. I dismissed the fact that fixed-winged fighter-bombers had to be used. Maybe those PBR guys had overreacted. I could not believe that the Viet Cong were that strong and that bold. The incident took place within range of at least twenty tubes of Dong Tam artillery. The river was wide. PBRs could run out of range of enemy fire. Why didn't they use the fifties to suppress the fire at a range of five hundred yards? I put the episode out of my mind. I never talked to the sailors involved. We were too busy doing our day-to-day jobs. That action was not even a pin on 534th charts. It was out of our area.

I had my own agenda. I had to go out on the Ham Luong River day in and night in for fourteen-hour patrols until I finally got twenty-four hours off. Five patrols a week at the minimum was standard for patrol officers. The boat crews did not have it so lucky. They went for two weeks at a time before they got a full day off.

What I remember most about those last two weeks of December 1967 are little things. Frank Walker and I finally got a daytime liberty together. We went to a waterfront restaurant and enjoyed a great meal in a Chinese restaurant. Taking in a movie followed—a flick at the local My Tho movie emporium. The theater reminded me of the old movie house that I had first known when I was five years old. My mother would give me and my brother John a quarter each on Saturday mornings. That would pay for a movie ticket to double-feature shitkickers, a Coke, two candy bars, or a bag of popcorn to be shared. The My Tho movie house had cheap tickets. It had Cokes. It had popcorn. It had the same old wooden seats of those old American small town movie houses. The same erratic projector handled by the same doofus operator. But the theater also had the smell of the Orient. Local dishes were served in the lobby.

The movie was an action film starring Anthony Quinn, *The Lost Command*. The only movie I ever saw with Vietnamese-dubbed audio and French-written subtitles. The first ten minutes of the movie were very interesting to me at that time and place. Anthony Quinn and his brave Foreign Legionnaires getting overrun by the Viet Minh at the battle of Dien Bien Phu. Holy shit. I had watched that battle unfold on black-and-white TV when I was eleven years old. I had rooted for the French in that lost cause. Each redoubt—all named after women— was overrun, one after the other, until the whole base was overwhelmed. And I was in Vietnam fighting the war left over from that defeat of the French. I was surprised that the audience did not stand up and cheer when the French survivors were finally rooted out of their bunkers and sent off to POW camps. The audience never cheered during that long war movie, one that, primarily, depicted atrocities in the French-Algerian war of the late 1950s. There was none of the gung ho, rah-rah cheering that I had participated in during the old movies that I watched in a similar theater. I guess that was because young Vietnamese kids were absent from the movie house. The audience consisted of sophisticated folks who knew war well. I bet more than a few of them were dedicated Viet Cong. Like most Viet Cong agents in towns and cities, they pretended to be passive where war was concerned.

We had a stand-down at Christmas. There were no action reports for December 24 through 26. On Christmas Eve, I took the purloined jeep with a few other sailors on liberty down the three-mile dirt track from My Tho to Dong Tam to purchase sundry things at the Dog Town post exchange. About a mile from Dong Tam an Army truck nearly ran us off the road while overtaking us from the rear. I was driving the jeep and was pissed off about being run off the road by the Army truck until I saw the two screaming, wounded soldiers lying in the back. Blood was flowing from the truck's tailgate. Land mines and booby traps don't respect any stand-down. What a way to experience Christmas for a couple of draftees who probably figured they had only a few hours of routine patrol sweeps around friendly villages before they went back to a dry rack in the barracks and got ready for a festive meal and music at their base in the morning. I hope those 9th Division soldiers survived the day.

That night Pete Richards, Frank Walker, and I celebrated Christmas in our mosquito-infested hotel room. That was probably the first and only night we were all together. We had a lot of goodies. The cookies I had received from my Aunt Irene were mostly crumbles; they still were delicious. The cheese, hard salami, crackers, olives, and sure to God, Beefeaters gin that Pete had received from Mary Brown, his sister-in-law in Boston, were a real treat. Of course, Mary had put the gin in a plastic quart Lux soap container and our cocktails were a little soapy. Hell, they were awfully soapy; we drank them anyway.

I also remember the staged suicide of a long-tailed monkey during this My Tho period. The monkey was a mascot of a recently arrived SEAL platoon. The monkey was not unusual. It seems that every SEAL platoon finishing up jungle war training at Subic Bay in the Philippines before its Vietnam tour had at least one monkey as a pet. Every SEAL platoon wanted its own pet monkey with them when they went into combat. They got their monkeys into Vietnam the same way they got their weapons into country, in sealed, classified containers— off limits to all inspectors.

This little monkey was like most SEAL monkeys. Hell, they were just like the monkeys in other areas of Vietnam— untrainable. It bit and spit and was a nuisance. Finally the monkey managed to learn how to pull the pins out of practice grenades. It took only a few seconds for that little monkey to pull the pin of a live grenade he found in a rusted-out shipping container into which he had been thrown. Like me, most of the guys witnessing the event just laughed. Some of the old-hand SEALs regretted that they had not been able to rig up a little parachute for the monkey the way they had for other monkeys, which had been dropped out of helicopters over jungle areas.

My two-boat patrol had a leg on the escort of a ten-thousand-ton Chinese merchant ship being taken up the Mekong River. PBRs were on both sides of a ship, which flew the communist red flag. The 532d had two boats running with my two 534th boats accompanying that little ship. That ship was laden with munitions to kill Americans but it had safe passage because the Mekong was an international waterway. We could only make sure that the munitions it carried were not dropped off to the Viet Cong before the ship reached Cambodia and its cargo was sent back across the border to Vietnam in small loads. What a farce! The ordinary sailors were even more pissed off by the situation than the officers. One gunner on my boat asked permission to get the attention of the gooks in the pilothouse. He told me what he had in mind, and I agreed. The sailor brought up an M-76 LAW and pointed the rocket launcher directly at the pilothouse of the Chinese freighter. The gooks in the pilothouse ducked out of sight for ten seconds or so and the ship veered off course. I was hoping the son of a bitch would run aground. But the gooks eventually figured out that we were just bluffing and the ship righted its course. The Chicom captain and his Viet-namese pilot went back to the ship's control and the ship sailed into Cambodia later that day.

I hoped they got a good scare before going on to Cambodia and unloading all their munitions. I hoped they felt that some-day the Americans would get serious about Cambodia. The Viet Cong and Red Chinese on that ship that day probably felt lucky. They were. Any sign of firing from that little freighter would have resulted in the firepower of our four PBRs being brought to bear. We had them surrounded; we were locked and loaded; and I was looking for an excuse to go to war with the suppliers of weapons against us. The rules of engagement would have allowed me to take action against a foreign-flag ship if I felt my crew's lives were in danger from it. I was will-ing to face a bunch of sea lawyers in any inquiry. I knew the sailors would back me up even if some of their buddies were killed. I figured we could have wasted that sucker in less than a minute by ourselves. Forty or so LAWs. Eight thousand rounds of fifty caliber at point-blank range. If necessary we could have called in airpower. Helo gunships and fighter-bombers would have been there within minutes. In a real war that ship would have been sunk. It would have been a great Navy sea story. Thirty-one-foot plastic gunboats destroy ten-thousand-ton enemy ship upriver. It could have happened.

On December 30, 1967, the river rats from the 534th got a belated Christmas present from Admiral Veth. It was in the form of the APL-55 (auxiliary, personnel, living), another floating base quite similar to the YRBM-16. The "Apple Five Fiver" was anchored on the wide My Tho River about a half mile west of the Dong Tam base. It was almost exactly like the YRBM-16. And it had a beer barge. It lacked only the ammi pontoons (twenty-by-forty-foot shallow-draft steel barges with flat decks) lashed astern with the repair sheds that had been attached to the YRBM-16. Those would soon come.

The APL-55 had been a CTF-115 (coastal patrol force) support base for PCF (patrol, coastal, fast) Swift boats off the southwest coast near Rach Gia. When the Swifties were put ashore at a newly constructed South Vietnamese naval base on the coast, the APL-55 had been turned over to CTF-116. Somebody at the high echelon (probably Admiral Veth) had made a good choice. The overcrowded My Tho hotels and the long commutes to our patrol areas had started to drag down the morale of the 534th. After sailors had nestled those boats not on patrol and all our gear had been stored, some sort of ceremony was to take place aboard the top deck of the APL-55. Ron Wolin and Bill Earner had received the word that CTF-116 himself, Capt. Paul Gray, USN, was coming aboard by helicopter to look over his new base, Earner called for an assembly in our best uniforms. He made it sound like a personnel inspection, a drill that is usually dreaded and takes a lot of preparation time. The rest of us scrambled to the top deck, wearing our best uniforms and spit-shined boots, just before the helicopter landed with the VIPs.

There was no inspection. Just some pithy comments from

two real characters. The first were from Father Charles (Chuck) McCoy, the CTF-116 chaplain. Father McCoy was a lieutenant commander in the Chaplain Corps. He was also a former Marine staff sergeant with Korean War combat experience. He said a little prayer for our new base and told us, "Put your faith in the Almighty, fight the enemy, take care of your wounded shipmates, treat the Vietnamese civilians as you would want to have your mothers and fathers treated, and resist the temptation to exact vengeance on defenseless people who maybe supported the enemy."

Father McCoy was always there when we needed him over the tough months to come. He realized the stress and trauma young American warriors had to endure in that often crazy war. He helped us get over our grief and right our moral compass so we endured honorably.

Capt. Paul Gray's little speech was of a different kind. He told us we were "some of the best fighting men the U.S. Navy has ever assembled—you are on the 'cutting edge of the sword of American imperialism.' "

I almost doubled over with laughter at Gray. He reminded me of the deranged Air Force general in the movie *Doctor Strangelove*. At least Gray gave a good parody of George C. Scott doing his thing on the screen. But Gray was no movie character. He was in charge of virtually all the PBRs, SEALs, and Seawolves in Vietnam. I now realized why he had bought Don Sheppard's MACE team concept. He was completely out of touch. Megalomaniac, glory hound, power crazed, whatever the words used to describe him, Paul Gray was a character, and a bad actor for the troops under him.

1968—what a year! A turbulent year, filled with some unforgettable events that will remain forever in the minds of my generation. It started as a usual day for the river rats of the 534th. We went back to our business on the Ham Luong, searching sampans and dodging sniper rounds.

The first big action occurred early one morning. Probably around January 3, 1968. A large portion of the ammunition stocks at Dong Tam went up in a fireworks display that lasted hours. Some smart and crafty Viet Cong had done a great job. They had sneaked a large sampan with a 75mm recoilless rocket launcher to within three hundred yards of the Army base and fired their rounds, only a few, with maximum effectiveness. The Dong Tam ammo stores were bermed north and south against enemy mortar attacks from that axis. The 9th Division had sent hundreds of grunts north of Dong Tam to secure the north in boring, lackadaisical, nighttime ambush positions. The Army commanders must have had great confidence in the wide My Tho River and Navy patrol boats to secure its southern flank. That confidence was misplaced; the river rats had never been tasked with Dong Tam security. We just cruised past Dong Tam. We never set up a blockade. We figured the base could defend itself from snipers on sampans. The American military once again underestimated the enemy.

The Viet Cong struck fast and with precision. They knew exactly where to fire. Their rounds hit stacked pallets of powder charges for the big guns, all lined up in a neat thirty-foot-wide row, in the middle of a long trench filled with shells and bullets. The resulting fire and explosions destroyed millions of dollars' worth of ammunition. Another U.S. military fiasco unreported in the press, like the destruction of the YRBM-16.

It was a great show. My boat and two others from the 534th were called on to go downriver and help the My Tho boats find and eliminate the enemy shooters. By the time I arrived with two 534th boats there was nothing on the river other than PBR sailors watching a memorable fireworks show.

Two RivSect 534 river rats were wounded on the fourth of January in the first of many combined actions with the Popular Force irregulars from Kien Hoa district outposts during my tour. Ron Wolin and Jack Harrell at the MACV compound coordinated that little operation and many more to come. Our little speedboats would each take on about fifteen South Vietnamese troops from the Ben Tre ferry landing or the ramshackle wooden piers of their outposts. We would take them a mile or so up or down the river and land them so they could go out and make contact with the enemy. This first one was a success. Eleven Viet Cong killed, one captured by the locals. The two recorded 534th wounded were SN John A. Wisecup and EN3 T. C. Jones, both M-60 gunners superficially wounded by enemy bullets hitting their splinter shields when three RivSect 534 PBRs fired on the flanks of the enemy platoon being assaulted by the South Vietnamese Popular Force guys. The Cong shooting back must have been firing high, but not high enough. The M-60 gunners were the high targets on our boats. Only the splinter shields protected their lower bodies, and the bullets hitting those shields had fragmented and sprayed their arms with little bits of shrapnel.

Jerry Letcher reentered my life. Jerry had been bounced around from river section to river section after the YRBM-16 mining. He had spent time on boats out of Binh Thuy, Vinh Long, and Nha Be. TAD to one unit after another. Since he was familiar with the Ham Luong from his 522 experiences, he figured the 534th could use his services. We were glad to have another hand.

Over the next week, 534th boats came under fire five more times. Typical interruptions of normal patrols. Nobody was wounded nor were there any known enemy casualties except for a couple of shot-up sampans that had to be destroyed after the occupants took to shore. Enemy casualties unknown—a typical ending to the thousands of exchanges of fire between PBRs and Viet Cong. Often the enemy sampans were used as decoys to lure one of our boats into the bank. They were manned (womened) or unmanned bait.

The Viet Cong learned that the 534th sailors were wise to their game and not greenhorn suckers. We approached all evading or suspicious sampans with caution. Except for the few Viet Cong who were highly trained and had been provided with telescopic sights, the average Viet Cong were not good shooters at a distance of a hundred meters or more. Our boats' constant movement made it difficult for the ordinary Viet Cong to score hits on the first volley of small arms even at ranges of less than a hundred meters. We had to be within fifty meters before Viet Cong riflemen could score with a first shot. But we seldom got that close to obvious enemy traps on the Ham Luong. The Cong would get impatient. We would tempt them by coming in at oblique angles to within their normal firing range in such situations. They would open fire. Their rounds would usually be long or short. After that first volley our PBRs went into motion with guns roaring. The bait sampans were then wasted by .50-caliber machine gun fire from two hundred meters' range. Typical PBR action on wide rivers with typical results.

The things that were never recorded are what I remember most about Vietnam. We were still basically in the Dong Tam area. Support troops were working mightily to get the APL-55 fully ready for our job. The big thing was to get a freshwater system operational. Evidently the barge had been provided fresh, potable water from a shore facility when it was part of CTF-115 on the coast; the Navy had not considered installing a self-contained freshwater system for the barge. The base was floating on salt water and had no steam evaporators to generate fresh water. The barge had gotten its fresh water from nearby shore bases. Now based on the Mekong it had only the river as a source of water, and the APL-55 had not been equipped with a water purification system like the YRBM-16. The Mekong's water was safe enough for showers for the troops and hosing down equipment, but it was not fit for American drinking water, even though all the Vietnamese used it for everything—cooking, drinking, bathing, urinating, defecating. Only old hands with several months of Vietnam duty could get away with drinking Mekong River water without suffering a bad case of diarrhea. Of course, those old hands would suffer when they went back to the States and their bodies had to get reacclimated to the "pure" water from municipal water systems. The support troops constructed big settling tanks on the rear of the maintenance ammi pontoons. Alum was dumped in to settle the muck, and bags of some chlorine compound were periodically dumped into the tanks, supposedly killing the bad bugs. Standard fire hoses were used to charge the freshwater system of the APL-55 and pump up the water. Nobody complained about that water system. We all knew that 9th Division Army grunts in the field for days at a time often drank from the water in rice paddies that had been fertilized with human and water buffalo waste when they could not safely be resupplied with fresh water. The settling of solids and a good dose of chlorine made that Mekong water a hell of a lot better for us than rice paddy water.

One monsoon night my boats were racing down the Ham Luong to join another patrol for a sweep of Ambush Alley. It was dark and the rain was torrential. We could navigate only by radar. The radar detected a couple of sampans near the free-fire zone of Tan Tan. We ran up to within fifty yards of them but still could not see them through the sheets of water. I grabbed a pop flare and fired it. Just as the flare's rocket ignited the flare tube slipped from my right hand. The burning projectile hit me in the forehead just over my right eye. Another example of dumb mistakes and good luck on my part. The sampans were also lucky. They got away clean.

One morning I had eaten a big breakfast after my patrol and was looking forward to some sleep. Sleep I did for an hour or so until being rudely awakened by a sailor around 0900. Some sort of crisis. I was needed at once. I put on my uniform, flak jacket, and pistol belt in a matter of seconds. I felt that I had been ordered to save the lives of some buddies. I soon discovered that I had been tasked by Ron Wolin to escort an eighteen-foot Boston Whaler down to Ben Tre. It was one of two U.S. Army boats the 534th river rats had stolen from Dong Tam just a few days before. My mission was to get it down to Jack Harrell before the Army CID (criminal investigation guys) discovered it. The cops were coming. I had only a few minutes to get away.

Once again I felt part of a criminal conspiracy. I readily agreed to participate this time. The whalers were used only for admin runs by 9th Division lieutenant colonel (paygrade O-5, the equivalent of Navy commander), battalion commanders assigned to the Mobile Riverine Force. With their twenty-horsepower outboards, the whalers were neat lit+le boats: fast, nimble, rugged. The Navy could put those assets to better work than as personal transports for Army officers who did not want to rub elbows with their troops to get from here to there. The same crack team of 534th river rats that had stolen and covered up the theft of the Air Force jeep back in Nha Be had struck the Army. Two PBRs had performed a wonderfully executed clandestine mission in the Dong Tam harbor around midnight. Diversion and coordination had succeeded. The Navy and the APL-55 had two new boats that were quickly repainted and given new numbers. We intended to mount M-60 machine guns on them and go trolling for Viet Cong at night in conjunction with the PBRs.

Unfortunately, the second class quartermaster who led the raid was a little too brazen. He took one of the disguised whalers back to Dong Tam for a liberty run on the Dong Tam

PX. The Army had wisely figured out what had happened and they were waiting for the thieves to return to the scene of the crime. They were caught.

QM2 Hunt and two other sailors were nabbed. Hunt fessed up to taking a boat that somebody (maybe a CPO, name unknown) must have given him permission to take from the APL-55. He claimed that the other two sailors with him were just innocent joyriders. If something was wrong about the boat, he would take responsibility. Hunt was a stand-up Navy petty officer in the fine tradition. He was taken to the Dong Tam stockade. The two others were sent free.

QM2 Hunt had admitted to knowing only about the boat he was on. He even lied about it. "Some My Tho base sailors must have left it parked on the APL-55. Didn't know shit about another whaler." The Army radioed ahead to the APL-55 that Hunt was in the stockade and that they had criminal investigators on the way to talk to the river rat command. That's when I was awakened to remove the second stolen boat.

Two 534th sailors cranked up the whaler. Another two off-duty 534th sailors started a PBR. I got on the PBR and got the thing going. The PBR masked the sight of the whaler from astern. We went at full speed to escape the law. In my binoculars I saw boats from Dog Town approaching the Apple.

The whaler was successfully delivered to Jack Harrell in Ben Tre. Ron Wolin somehow got Hunt out of the Dog Town jail. I'm sure Ron promised the CID guys that Hunt would get a Navy court-martial and be severely punished. Ron's story was that both whalers must have been stolen by My Tho–based river rats. That out-of-control Hunt, a new guy from some other unit, had a lot of buddies in My Tho. Maybe one of his lowlife buddies lent him a whaler for a day. Even if Hunt was involved with those liars and thieves from My Tho RivSects, they probably put Hunt up to the escapade. A thorough Navy inquiry would follow. Heads would roll. Amazingly, the Army guys bought Ron's story and they looked toward My Tho for the other missing whaler. I guess the battles during Tet quashed their investigations. No black marks on any Navy personnel records, just higher marks on "resourcefulness" for Robert Hunt.

Ron Wolin gave Hunt his own PBR as a reward. The young

second class quartermaster became a boat commander. Bill Earner, the USNA-trained XO and a very straight arrow, must have had severe heartburn. I just got a wink and a nod from Ron Wolin. I had done my part. In any official investigation the sea lawyers would have had a difficult time with me; I had no firsthand knowledge. I had executed a proper order, or at least an implied order; I believed the sailor waking me up had received orders from my commanding officer, blah blah. Another bullet successfully dodged.

Within a week that little Boston Whaler took my buddies Jack Harrell and Rusty Redding (a detached young SEAL officer who had found a kindred spirit in Jack) up the Ben Tre River and down the Ba Lai River all the way to the South China Sea. This was like a couple of GIs taking a twenty-mile boat ride down the Rhine River in early 1945 before the 3d Army had gotten fifty miles within the west bank—something only young, foolhardy adventurers could accomplish. Jack and Rusty really were guys who did not give a damn for conventional wisdom. They got away with that jaunt with no shots fired. The next trips down the Ba Lai by Americans on boats were on slow MRF boats with artillery and air cover or by SEALs in the dead of night. The 9th Infantry soldiers attached to the MRF referred to the intersection of the Ba Lai River and the Chet Say Canal as the "crossroads." The "crossroads" is the scene of a lot of bad memories for 9th Division veterans who had been assigned to the MRF. Every one of the subsequent forays there for the next five years resulted in Americans killed. God does indeed care for the stupid as He cares for the brave.

The water system and maintenance facilities of the barge got up to snuff in mid-January. The APL-55 and RivSect 534 moved eight miles closer to our patrol patch, and eight miles farther away from the brass around Dong Tam and My Tho. The APL-55 anchored at the My Tho/Ham Luong junction.

We continued to do our thing. We chased down evading sampans in the waters around Tan Tan Island and Ambush Alley. We destroyed the sampans when the occupants fled into those "specified strike zones." We destroyed a bunch of sampans. GM2 Ned Caldwell, boat commander of PBR 7-14, was wounded in the nose by shrapnel from a rifle grenade. Caldwell was medevacked but returned to duty within five weeks. Typical PBR wound and results in a scrap where PBRs fought the enemy near the banks, in water where the boats could maneuver to get out of range if they came under heavy return fire.

I got my chance to run the whole Cai Cam tributary on the west side of Tan Tan Island. The first time I went from the north side. A couple of other boats had done that earlier. They had reported clusters of bunkers on the south bank just past the big turn to the south; just foliage on the north bank. Since the first two hundred meters of that narrow channel had only foliage on the north bank, and I had been that far at least twice, I chose to have the guns on my boat (first of two) staggered. The twin fifties forward were to be to port, where the expected threat was. I had an M-16, safety off, selector switched to auto. I and the after gunners would cover the right flank until we passed that turn to port, where the gun emplacements had put a rocket into Engle's boat several weeks before.

Just after the turn to the left, as the gunners redirected their weapons, I caught a glimpse of a small sampan in the thick foliage to the right. Forty feet away. A man stood up and began to jump from the sampan. An image frozen in time in my mind. No weapon, just fear in his eyes. He saw my weapon aimed at him. He just looked at my rifle and me. I had a great shot, but all I saw was a frightened, unarmed man trying to leap from an empty sampan. I waved him off with a sweep of my hand. If he had been carrying a weapon, or if I had seen any materiel in the sampan, the man would have been killed. Not even a New York second for me to cut him in half. He might have been some important VC courier. He might have been just a farmer taking a shortcut to Ben Tre. He got a lucky break that day, mostly because I figured that if I fired on him every Viet Cong within hearing range would run to the prepared fighting holes farther down the channel. My job was to run the Cai Cam from one end to the other. That day was as good as any to make my first run. Shooting some unarmed Viet Cong at the start would just make the trip more hazardous.

I made that trip with no incidents. I saw the fresh dirt of

recently constructed fighting holes on the east bank after the
turn to the left. I finally relaxed when my boat approached
the bamboo footbridge guarded by a South Vietnamese near
the end of the channel. The wide Ham Luong and safety were
only a minute away. We got there and took off our helmets and
flak jackets and went back to routine sampan searches.

Sometime between that run of the Cai Cam and my next
run a week or so later, 534th sailors started carrying brand-
new Chinese AK-47 rifles as personal weapons on our boats.
First one or two. Then a half dozen more. The sailors said they
had bought them from ARVNs in My Tho while on liberty.
The officers bought this line. I for one was skeptical that those
sailors had the money to buy such weapons. Fifty dollars (the
going rate at the time) was steep. I fired a couple of the AKs.
They were good. They did not ride up on full auto like an M-
16. They had a little more backward kick. Much more rugged
than the M-16, a weapon often disparaged as a "made by Mat-
tel plastic toy." The AK-47 was simply constructed of wood
and steel—not the nylon and lightweight stamped metal that
made up a large part of an M-16. I already knew that the enemy had good weapons. Now I believed they had a better rifle
than we had.

When researching material for this book I discovered the
truth about those eight new AK-47s the 534th sailors were
carrying on the boats. During a phone conversation, Tony
Summerlin, Master Chief Boatswain, USN, Retired, admitted
to me that he had taken a boat up a twenty-foot-wide creek between the Cai Cam and the Ham Luong, with the boat brush-
ing the banks as it inched its way up the creek. The boat
rounded a turn to the left. A twelve-man squad of Viet Cong
were on a monkey bridge or waiting to cross from the river
side. They had a bigger surprise than the river rats on Tony's
boat. Their weapons were slung over their shoulders. All
twelve were killed in a brief, violent engagement, mostly from
the M-60, M-16s, and shotgun blasts from sailors on Tony's
boat. The big fifties were useless at point-blank range. The
river rats had reacted a lot faster and better than the enemy by
reaching for the weapons the situation required. Eight new
AK-47s were recovered in the one-minute body search that
followed. Tony's boat backed up and made eight-point turns to

get out of the creek. He never reported the incident at the time; he remembered a 522d boat commander who was relieved of his boat command by Lt. Jim Dykes when the boat captain sent a sailor ashore near the Ben Tre ferryboat landing to rip down a Viet Cong flag flying from an abandoned building on the bank of the wide river. Of course, if Summerlin had fessed up to Ron Wolin about the incident, Ron would probably have made Tony a patrol officer on the spot, after getting a brand-new AK-47 to add to his collection of firearms. Bill Earner would have gotten just a case of heartburn.

Tony, like all boat commanders and patrol officers, was well informed of the intel we had on the enemy forces on Tan Tan Island. The Viet Cong fighters lived in hamlets in the middle of the island and were protected by heavy foliage from above and wide clear fields of fire on the fallow rice paddies from the river side. They had bunkers to hide in when air strikes or artillery rained down on those hamlets. Now when 534th PBRs went down their western flank on the Cai Cam, the Viet Cong started building firing positions on the Cai Cam. They built them on the bank nearest to their homes. Tony knew where to hit them. Right in the middle, where they least expected a riverboat to venture up a narrow creek. Tony never told me what 534th patrol officer he was operating under that day. It must have been RD1 Robert Wenzel. Wenzel was bold almost to the point of recklessness. He was also a seasoned PBR boat captain just ordained as patrol officer. He could have even conceived the foray up that creek to impress the other boat captains temporarily under his command. Or, it could have been Tony alone with one PBR. Both guys were big gamblers, and gamblers' luck held that day. From my memories of Summerlin and Wenzel, I guess they let the three or so gunners who did the killing keep an AK each. The rest were put on sale. Wenzel probably even loaned money to the guys who could not afford the fifty-dollar price. Wenzel was one of the biggest "brown-water operators" who ever served. Tony Summerlin was not far behind.

Late in January, I took four boats up the Cai Cam from the south end. I chose high, slack tide so our guns would be above the fighting holes. The tide was so high that we had to partially disassemble our radar and light recognition masts to get under the bamboo footbridge. The drill was: pull out pins in the pipes, bend over the last sections, secure them, and re- verse the procedure once under the bridge. It took several minutes, the sailors away from their guns, and contributed to the stress of the mission.

QM2 Robert Hunt was the commander on my first boat. "Handgrenade" Hunt had recently been given his own boat, presumably as a reward for stealing jeeps and Boston Whalers. Hunt was very proud of his little command. So proud that he rammed the throttles of the PBR to the max be- fore the last two boats had cleared the bridge.

I grabbed for the throttles to pull them back. Hunt's grip would not give. I shouted in his ear.

"Hunt, get this fucking boat back to the bridge! We got three other boats. We have to stay together!"

"Mister Goldsmith, this is my boat, and I don't want it blasted like a sitting duck in the water waiting for the other boats!"

Hunt would not obey my order and he continued to strug- gle with me; the semicocked .45 I pulled from my holster and pushed at the bridge of Hunt's nose got his attention. He turned the boat around.

Hugging the starboard bank, all four boats proceeded up the Cai Cam at cruising speed. A mile up the channel we went around a bend and surprised four Vietnamese women with picks and shovels who were digging fighting holes. When they saw us they dropped their tools and lay flat at the water's edge. We closed to touching range but the only weapons we saw were their digging tools. Some young sailors were surely disappointed that we did not waste them because those old women were the people who built the holes from which they received fire.

But the fact that I was ready to blow away Robert Hunt for disobeying an order must have gotten their attention. Sailors could see that some young, dumb-ass junior officer was pissed, and that he was ready to blow the brains out of a boat commander for dereliction of duty. They restrained them- selves; it was a no-brainer. The pissant junior officer (me) had the power. I called the shots. In other wars an officer would have possibly blown Hunt's brains out and ordered some other enlisted to toss his body over the side. Most likely there would be no official report. The enlisted would expect that. The officers were the law. I knew that this war was different from other wars. A war in which drugged-out draftees felt they had a right to "frag" officers they did not like and often got away with their crimes. I also knew that Hunt was a favorite son of Ron Wolin. Down deep I liked and admired Hunt, but disobeying orders in a combat situation was a serious offense, and his action that day really pissed me off.

I did the right thing. I reported Hunt to Bill Earner. Bill did the right thing. He relieved Handgrenade Hunt of his short-lived boat command with no adverse remarks in his file. I figured that if I reported Hunt to Ron Wolin, Ron would probably have *me* transferred. Hunt went on to retire as a well-decorated, deep-sea-diver-qualified, Navy chief petty officer, a colorful man who endured so much stuff in his twenty-plus years of active service that his memoirs would be much more interesting than mine. Bob, I salute you. I also salute your bride, Marilyn, for being strong enough to put up with you for so many years.

Without Bob Hunt's dedication to old shipmates this book could not have been written with any degree of accuracy. Bob kept up with shipmates. I, like most, did not. He and I remember shared experiences with no regrets, anger, or remorse. We were both young guys doing unusual things under great stress.

More important, there was no slaughter of unarmed Vietnamese that day. If I had done a William Calley on those Vietnamese that day, I probably would have gotten away clean except for a conscience that would have plagued me for life.

One other little incident caught my attention during the last week of January 1968. Jack Harrell was blown off a RivSect 531 boat minutes after being picked up at the MACV boat landing. The MK I PBR from the *Harnett County* was to take Jack downriver to meet with some Army advisers, but a rocket hit the boat and Jack was blown overboard. Jack survived with minor (considered by the medics and Jack at the time) wounds and a five-minute swim in the Ben Tre River while the 531 sailors suppressed the enemy fire from the south bank.

That was an unusual incident and River Section 534 officers, including myself, figured that Jack had been targeted.

We all thought that Ben Tre was still safe for river rats, at least from the Ham Luong to a mile or so past the bridge. But Jack had drawn attention by his aggressive spirit. He and the 531 boats had probably grown lax in their radio procedures, perhaps inadvertently giving away the time and location of the pickup.

Chapter 11

The night-patrol of January 30, 1968, began as any routine night-patrol for me and PBRs 7-20 and 7-21. General Westmoreland had called off the much discussed "Tet cease-fire" because of numerous communist aggressive actions up north in I Corps. There was no special alert for the forces in IV Corps.

I had Patrol Area 2, from two miles north of the Ben Tre River and south through Ambush Alley. By that time the PBR crews knew the drill. We would make random passes south through Ambush Alley with all guns manned; we would split the boats up for a mile or so to keep radar coverage for several miles near the Ben Tre River—time for catnaps for half the crews. An hour or so at max. Our first sweeps that night were made one right after the other. My choice of random order that night. Maybe the Viet Cong attempting a crossing would feel safe after our boats had passed them and would be bold enough to cross after we went back north. The high water early on that night favored crossings before midnight. We saw nothing in those sweeps. I decided that the boats would spend the next hours near the Vietnamese outposts around the Ben Tre/Ham Luong junctions. The boats cruised. I catnapped between 2400 and 0100. Then I decided to have the boats go slowly upriver and drop sea anchors close to the old favorite crossing area near the abandoned fish stakes on Tan Tan Island. It was a dry fishing hole that night.

At about 0300 my self-imposed biological clock awakened me from almost a half hour's sleep on the boat deck outside the coxswain's flat. The muted chatter on the radios had not disturbed my sleep. Somehow I had trained myself to sleep even during a rainstorm, but always to awaken myself if I

heard my callsign on a muted radio. That night was clear. No
calls for Pineapple Bowl Charlie interrupted my nap. I woke
up refreshed and decided another run down Ambush Alley
was in order. The river was still running to the sea. In another
two hours it would be low and slack. One last chance for sampans sneaking through Ambush Alley before daylight. I told
QM1 Howard Stevens, PBR 7-21's boat commander, who had
been on watch for my nap, to get his crew to the guns. I then
radioed QM1 Earle Milliken's boat, PBR 7-20.

"Charlie One, this is Charlie. Let's take a trip south."

"Charlie, this is Charlie One. Roger. Out."

Our boats cruised down the wide channel of the river at
twenty knots until we saw the 531 boats on our radars at the
northern end of their patrol area. We exchanged radio checks
to acknowledge each other's presence. The two 534th boats
turned around and headed north down the narrow channel of
Ambush Alley at near maximum speed. Every gun fully
manned. Nothing going on at all. Another peaceful night on
the river.

At the Ben Tre river junction the crews relaxed, cleared
their guns, took off helmets and flak jackets, and got ready for
more relaxed conditions.

I took over the controls of the 7-21 boat so Stevens could
catnap. Our boat was idling in the middle of the Ham Luong.
Milliken's boat was sent a mile to the north. To the east the
streetlights in Ben Tre cast an amber glow. We were settling in
on the last hours of an uneventful patrol. In another few hours
we would have great food, air-conditioned comfort, and nine
hours of uninterrupted sleep, or at least some sleep after we
wrote letters home. Maybe one or two would have the whole
day off to go on liberty. The young gunners traded their liberty time like riverboat gamblers. Some were rich. Many others were poor.

An hour later we heard gunfire. The tattoo of rapid-firing
guns from a distance over water. I turned my eyes in the direction of the muffled noise. To the east, from both banks of the
Ben Tre River, flecks of fire sparked in the night. Red flecks
and green flecks crisscrossing. I got the binoculars and trained
them to the east. Bright orange and white bursts soon joined

the picture. For a moment I believed that the South Vietnamese in Ben Tre were wasting their ammo loads in some sort of Tet celebration.

I soon realized that something big was going down. There were too many green flecks from that south bank. I called Milliken's boat to join my boat (Stevens's boat) at the mouth of the Ben Tre River. The boats came together a few minutes later.

As the boats idled a foot apart I made a little speech, primarily for Milliken's boat crew. The PBR crew of the boat I was on (Stevens's 7-21 boat) were already breaking out cases of ammo from the forward compartment and were in battle dress. Stevens was motivated; his common-law Vietnamese wife, pregnant with his child, was in an apartment in Ben Tre. Stevens would do anything in his power to go up the Ben Tre. The young gunners would come along as a matter of course. I was there only to get the cover boat to follow us.

"The gooks are shooting up a lot of ammo up the Ben Tre. A lot of that fire appears to be Cong fire. We got to go up there to see what's going on. Get your boat at GQ. We are going up the Ben Tre."

Milliken responded in his usual manner. No wasted words. No profanity. Just a professional sailor doing his job.

"Aye, aye, Mister Goldsmith. My boat will be battle ready and right behind you."

That was it. I led the two little plastic gunboats up the Ben Tre River. The tide was low. Any enemy gunner on the bank could shoot down on us if he saw us. The boats went upriver for a little over a mile, around the turn to the right. Then I saw what was happening in the dim light. Six South Vietnamese LCVPs (landing craft, vehicle, personnel) were strung along the north bank of the river approximately five hundred yards in front of us. The crews were firing their machine guns (four to a boat) almost nonstop at the south bank. The red tracers from the Popular Force sailors were being answered in spades by green tracers from the south bank. Occasional bright orange flashes on the north bank were followed by explosive noises. A scene from World War II at some important road junction in the early hours of the Battle of the Bulge.

I eased the boats to within a hundred meters of the Vietnamese boats. We idled in midstream. I radioed the MACV compound.

"Willow Rule, this is Pineapple Bowl Charlie. All hell is going on west of you on the river, over!"

"Pineapple Bowl Charlie, this is Willow Rule. What is the situation? Over."

The voice coming back to me over the radio was an excited, alert voice, not at all like the laconic, disinterested MACV radio operator voices I usually heard.

"This is Pineapple Bowl Charlie. My unit is a klick and a half west of your position. The Ruff Puff Papa boats are fully engaged with at least a company of Victor Charlie on the south bank. The gooks are hitting the north bank with a lot of machine guns, rockets, and mortars. Over."

"Roger, Pineapple Bowl Charlie. We are taking fire ourselves. Over."

"Willow Rule, this is Charlie. Everybody in your compound better be at general quarters. Over!"

"Charlie, Willow Rule. What are your intentions? Over."

"Willow Rule, this is Charlie. My units will stand by. Got to report to my command. Over!"

"Charlie, this is Willow Rule. Stay close. We might need you. Out."

I grabbed the other FM radio mike and called the ops center on the APL-55. I told the radio watch where my boats were and asked them to alert Pineapple Alpha and Pineapple Zulu (Ron Wolin and Bill Earner). I figured that the two-man radio watch at the APL-55 ops center had monitored the MACV transmissions between the boat I was on and the Ben Tre compound, and would immediately rouse the CO and XO from their bunks and tell them that hell was loose up the Ben Tre River and that my little two plastic boats might have to go to the aid of the MACV compound in a tremendous crossfire of bullets. I was mistaken.

For another ten minutes we watched the battle. I inched the boats upriver until we were only fifty meters from the South Vietnamese LCVPs. Their machine gun fire was unrelenting, as was the fire of the Viet Cong. I then saw the outline of the MACV compound past the friendly boats on the north bank.

The compound was being hammered. I ran back to the after gunner and told him to be ready to crank out M79 grenades at the source of the green tracers if we had to go past their firing positions.

The noise of the firing was so loud that it made radio monitoring impossible. When the little red lights of both FM receivers both blinked on and off in rapid succession, I entered the control flat, put my left index finger into my left ear, turned up the gain on the MACV channel, put my right ear by the speaker, and answered the phone.

I received a message that I dreaded.

"Charlie, this is Willow Rule. Request your units to come to my posit for fire support, over!"

"This is Charlie, we are on our way. Out!"

I had Stevens turn on all lights on the recognition-light mast, turn on the sirens, and get as close as possible to the Viet boats' starboard sides as we went upriver at about fifteen knots. Soon we were abreast of the first LCVP. The little Popular Force sailor gunners in their underwear stopped firing and cheered us on as we passed them within a foot. Passing those guys was a memorable sight. They had the discipline to let our little boats enter the fray without blindly shooting across the river as we passed them. The LCVPs in front of us also stopped firing to allow us to pass.

I had had my doubts about those South Vietnamese home guard sailors; my doubts were over. I told the gunners to fire at will at the source of enemy fire. They did. Not blindly, but in short bursts.

Green tracers now were directed at my PBRs. A steady stream of green tracers from many guns passed over our heads. Thank God those tracers were high. By the time Stevens's boat was past the second LCVP, both boats were in the middle of the river, at good speed, and firing all guns at the enemy's suspected positions. As our guns fired, I felt a relief. My boats were in the game. I knew that the sailors had been champing at the bit for over an hour. I thought that most of them, not like me, were unafraid. I believed that they would hose down that south bank with no end until their gun barrels melted or the ammo was exhausted. I had been frightened witless until the gunners finally opened up. Their fire control was calculated and professional. The bullets appeared to shut down enemy machine guns one after another. It seemed too easy. Those lines of green tracers came to an abrupt halt as the HEIT (high explosive, incendiary, tracer) rounds from the fifties went to their source. The effects of the explosive rounds of the fifties were impressive. Maybe the explosions and fires, the trees being knocked down over their heads, and other mayhem put the fear of God into those Cong gunners. More likely their commanders, whose plans had not considered our heavy counterfire, ordered them to stop firing.

I was firing and reloading my grenade launcher as fast as I could. I was also cringing at the effect those .50-caliber bullets were having on the hootches on the south bank. Those HEIT bullets (old Air Force ordnance with 1952 Korean War markings) that Ron Wolin had stockpiled were doing a job on the dwellings on the south bank. The Viet Cong could have fired down on us. Our heavy guns were firing over their heads as theirs were firing over our heads. The tide was low and the enemy gunners had sighted their weapons on structures on the north bank. But our .50 fire was knocking down treetops and roofs of buildings fifty meters behind the enemy guns. Only the M-79 grenades and M-60 bullets from gunners standing on the engine covers found their mark. Their fire was right into the teeth of the enemy guns.

Each and every enemy belt-fed weapon firing tracer rounds was targeted. Structures were set on fire, most by the .50 rounds that went over the enemy gun positions and impacted on dwellings behind them. Some tracer and HEIT rounds started fires. I hoped that innocent civilians were not killed, that they had been inside the defensive bunker the Vietnamese government allowed each family to build by their home. Mostly I hoped that the firepower of our boats scared the VC enough for them to run back to their "secret zones."

Less than a minute and approximately fifteen hundred rounds later, the 7-20 and 7-21 boats were abeam and twenty yards from the MACV compound. We stopped. The enemy fire had stopped. Our guns went silent. The PBRs idled in front of the compound. We had silenced the enemy fire. The gunners replenished the depleted ready trays. In the dim light

I could make out figures manning machine guns in sand-bagged positions in front of the block-long brick and masonry structure as our boats performed slow lazy eights in front of the compound. (Later I learned that Jack Harrell, my Navy buddy, was intrepidly manning one of those machine guns.) Ten minutes of tension followed. We saw no more green tracers, but there were some blasts of mortar rounds hitting the north bank fifty yards to the east. I had no clue of the enemy's size or intentions. I was just like everyone else.

After those long minutes of silence, when every combatant was catching his breath and trying to figure out the next move, the FM radio blared out a familiar drawl.

"Pineapple Bowl Charlie, this is Pineapple Bowl Delta. I'm at checkpoint Zulu. Where you want me? Over."

Frank Walker's two-boat patrol had arrived at the mouth of the Ben Tre. The relief of my two-boat patrol had arrived a half hour early. It was 0630. Still dark. Enough time for the VC to let loose another final barrage before they scurried to the secret zones. I was elated. My boats were not alone. Four PBRs in a tight situation were ten times better than two PBRs in a tight situation. If one boat on a two-boat patrol was disabled, the other boat would come alongside on a rescue mission but also be vulnerable. Both boats could easily be destroyed. Two additional boats could mean successful enemy fire suppression and survival for everyone.

"Pineapple Bowl Delta, this is Charlie. You come upriver and I'll meet you. Willow Rule needs our units. All guns to starboard. Beaucoup Viet Cong on the south bank. Over."

"Charlie, this is Delta. We're on our way. Out."

My two PBRs sped west. When we rounded the bend to the south, we could make out Frank Walker's two boats racing up from the Ben Tre River in the light of the approaching dawn. The 7-20 and 7-21 boats quickly reversed course and let the first of the other boats close us. Frank was on the leading 7-14 boat. I could barely make out his stocky features at twenty yards.

I shouted to him, "Frank! We're going to the compound to run a slow racetrack up and down its length. It was taking a lot of fire from the south bank!"

Frank responded with a quick "Got it." Then all four boats

sped upriver to the "racetrack." At the eastern end of the block-long MACV compound, Milliken slowed and turned the 7-20 boat around. The three other boats followed suit with an interval of fifteen yards. We began our racetrack outrider covering formation. Small fires and a lot of smoke were on the south bank. No sign of the enemy. No small arms, no rockets, and no mortars. It was an eerie silence compared to the earlier fireworks.

When I heard a few seconds of silence on the MACV radio channel, I grabbed the mike and turned up the gain. "Willow Rule, this is Pineapple Bowl Charlie. I have four Papa Bravo Romeos at your location. Over."

"Pineapple Bowl Charlie, this is Willow Rule. We appreciate your help. Out."

For a minute or two we continued to patrol up and down the river in front of the MACV compound. Then there was a sputtering of automatic weapons fire a quarter of a mile to the east on the east bank. The MACV TOC (tactical operation center) requested me to investigate activity at the Ben Tre bridge. The four boats went in a slow, loose line formation toward the bridge. As the 7-21 boat went under the bridge I looked over on the south bank where a small Vietnamese guard post was burning at the end of the bridge. I saw what appeared to be two bodies sprawled out on the ground. We continued east another fifty yards. Sampans and an occasional junk were tied up to banks of the river, as expected, near the marketplace. What was different was that there were no lights or cooking fires on the Vietnamese craft. It was nearly 0730, well after the end of curfew.

As the 7-21 turned around to head west, what appeared to be two mortar rounds hit in the middle of the river opposite the MACV compound. The rounds impacted right where our PBRs' "racetrack" had been, adding a new dimension to the situation. I believed that whatever size Viet Cong force had hit Ben Tre that morning, they were up to their usual modus operandi: they would beat feet back to their secret zones just before daylight, leaving behind a rear-guard security group to cover their escape. I thought that group was targeting our PBRs. My feeling was that daylight would soon sort out the situation and that an unseen enemy now targeted our boats.

"Delta, this is Charlie. Let's clear the area."

"Charlie, this is Delta. Roger. Out."

"Willow Rule, this is Pineapple Bowl Charlie. Over."

"Pineapple Bowl Charlie, this is Willow Rule. Roger. Over."

"Willow Rule, this is Charlie. We saw no signs of enemy at the bridge other than a couple of bodies by the outpost at the south end. A couple of rockets or mortar rounds hit in the river just south of your location. My units are clearing the area and will stand by at Pineapple Bowl. Over."

"This is Willow Rule. Roger. Out."

Our four boats sped west to the safety of the Ham Luong. By the time we reached the wide river, there was enough daylight for the MACV compound to assess the situation. Frank Walker's boat, PBR 7-14, commanded by BM1 Charles Carvander (temporary replacement for the medevacked GM1 Ned Caldwell), came alongside Milliken's boat.

Frank shouted over to me, "Two guys on this boat say they saw some Viet Cong swimming just past the bridge near the north bank. I want to go back and capture them."

What the hell is this about? I thought. I sure did not see any swimmers. Nobody on Milliken's or Stevens's boat had seen any swimmers. Of course, I had only momentarily glanced at that north bank. All of my attention had been on the south bank.

"Frank, I'm not going back up that river until the MACV compound tells us we are needed. As far as I am concerned it's your patrol now. Radio Willow Rule that you are going back to the bridge to investigate swimmers. My boats will stand by here if you run into major shit. Don't be a hero; try to stay out of trouble."

Frank took the 7-14 and 7-13 boats back up the Ben Tre. I really did figure that the situation was under control. I could see some South Vietnamese LCVPs had already started to make their way back up the Ben Tre, and two MK I PBRs from River Section 531 stationed aboard the *Harnett County* had radioed that they were on the way to Ben Tre.

We idled around the ferryboat landing for about fifteen minutes. The crews were still in battle dress. I was monitoring both radios. The MACV network reported enemy contact at several outposts near Ben Tre. Not a good sign.

It was nearly 0815. Normally at this time after a night patrol I would have been in the rack asleep after eating a big Navy breakfast. I wished Frank had radioed me that everything was under control. He had had more than enough time to reach the bridge.

The sound of heavy machine gun fire up the Ben Tre River came fast and furious. I recognized the sound of eight fifties at rapid fire. Our boats went into the Ben Tre River. We saw red tracers bouncing into the air.

A frantic radio message followed. "Pineapple, this is Pineapple Bowl Echo! We got wounded men!" The excited voice did not belong to Frank Walker. The naval operation center acknowledged and requested further information. None came. I got on the radio and told the NOC (naval operation center) to get Pineapple Bowl Zulu (Ron Wolin) on the radio. I also told the NOC that the 7-13 and 7-14 boats had been hit at the Ben Tre bridge and that my units were proceeding there. My guts were wrenching as the 7-20 and 7-21 boats headed back up the river. Just as we approached the south bend in the river, the 7-13 and 7-14 boats came speeding down. My boat turned around and closed the 7-14 boat. Nobody on the 7-14 was manning a gun. Two bloody figures were on the engine covers with two sailors attending them. Both wounded were apparently conscious. One of them was Frank Walker. He and the after gunner, GMSA David Copenhaver, had bloody leg and shoulder wounds. Thank God there were no sucking chest wounds, head wounds, or gut wounds. I shouted to Carvander to take both boats down to the LST to evacuate the wounded, then got back on the radio.

This time the familiar voice of Ron Wolin answered. I told Ron as much as I knew, and that the 7-13 and 7-14 boats were under way to the *Harnett County* with the two wounded men. Ron ordered me to stand by at the mouth of the Ben Tre. Other 534 units would arrive as soon as possible. I was happy to obey that order.

About ten minutes later a couple of River Section 531

PBRs came speeding by us, headed for the ferryboat landing. I looked back at the ferryboat landing and could see the tall, familiar figure of Jack Harrell waiting for them. Evidently, while I was on the radio with our NOC, Jack Harrell had made contact with the River Section 531 boats headed for Ben Tre. Jack had requested a boat ride and the 531 sailors had obliged. More power to them, I thought, as the 531 boats headed up the Ben Tre. Let Jack and those old MK I PBRs figure out what had happened. The 534th boats had already done their duty.

The 531 boat's mission was to get Jack Harrell past the bridge to describe the situation on the south bank to the Vietnamese and American command at the MACV operations center. They had lost all radio contact with the outposts on the south bank east of the bridge. The PBRs went at full speed past the bridge for a hundred yards when they saw approximately one hundred armed men snaking along a path through the underbrush fifty feet from the south riverbank. When the MACV TOC confirmed that there were no friendlies in the area, the PBRs opened fire into the bushes. This was akin to kicking an anthill. It greatly agitated the enemy soldiers, who immediately started firing back. The PBRs made a hasty retreat to the MACV compound as Jack Harrell reported to the TOC. The report was simple—a large body of Viet Cong was approaching the south end of the bridge. There were no friendlies anywhere near the bridge. Within minutes the PBRs and the MACV compound came under heavy automatic weapons fire from positions almost directly across from the compound.

While the 531 boats were engaged up the Ben Tre, the 7-13 boat came speeding back from the *Harnett County* and pulled alongside the 7-20 boat. BM1 Carvander, boat captain of the 7-14 boat, and GMSN Wayne Forbes, forward gunner on the 7-14 boat, were aboard BM1 Irvine Burney's boat. They explained that the 7-14 boat was being checked out for battle damage aboard the LST and that Frank Walker and Copenhaver had been medevacked by helicopter from the helo deck of the LST.

Every sailor seemed eager and excited to get back into action. I first made them describe what happened under the bridge. They all seemed to talk at once, each guy wanting to describe what he experienced. Some talked of getting fire from the second and third floor of buildings in the marketplace. That seemed ridiculous to me. Some said they captured some VC swimmers. Others said they rescued South Vietnamese sailors. Machine gun fire, AK-47 fire, rockets, and mortars had hit them all at once. They all agreed on that.

From Burney and Carvander I got a good description. The boats had raced immediately to the bridge, where they saw three Vietnamese men in uniform, in the water, clutching the concrete pilings of the nearby concrete jetty that ran out into the river from the marketplace on the north bank. Smoke and haze still obscured visibility on the riverbanks. The 7-14 boat recovered the men in the water at gunpoint while the 7-13 boat provided cover. The boats went back to the MACV compound, a hundred meters to the west. There Frank Walker shouted to the soldiers manning a machine gun at the water's edge that he had some prisoners. This got an immediate response from the MACV soldiers. Within seconds the MACV guard gate was opened and a Vietnamese officer and an American came running out. They ran to the small boat dock in front of the compound and motioned Frank's PBR alongside. There it was determined that the "Viet Cong prisoners" were actually survivors of a South Vietnamese LCVP sunk hours earlier while tied up to the marketplace jetty. The Vietnamese sailors said there might be more survivors in the water. Since the tide was still low, there was no way they could get to the top of the steep bank. Eight sailors had been aboard when their boat was hit by rockets. Frank took the Vietnamese sailors downriver, where they met the first of the Vietnamese LCVPs returning upriver from the Ham Luong. Frank turned the three sailors over to their shipmates and went back to rescue the other survivors.

But as soon as the two PBRs got to the bridge, they were taken under heavy fire from the south bank. Even Viet Cong in sampans upriver opened up on them. As the PBR gunners blasted away on the south bank, they got blindsided by fire from the north bank. A rocket or mortar round hit near the stern of the 7-14 boat, and a long burst of machine gun fire from the south bank cut down Frank Walker and Copenhaver.

As the boats retreated under the bridge, most of the gunners were blazing away at the south bank. One young gunner, GM3 James Hurt, the M-60 gunner on Burney's boat, momentarily looked up as the boat sped under the bridge. He saw a Vietnamese woman running across the bridge with a heavily laden *chogi* pole on her shoulders, the baskets at each end filled with RPG rounds. Hurt swiveled his gun around and up and cut her down with a long burst. Blood for blood. The first Viet Cong killed by PBRs that day was a woman.

The sailors on the 7-13 boat were eager for more blood. Definitely more eager than me.

It was about 0915. As I was digesting all this for a situation report back to the 534th NOC, Ron Wolin and PBR 7-18 came speeding up to us. My thoughts were, "Thank you, God!" I did not relish being in charge of boats in that situation. I had not talked to the two 531 boats that had gone up the Ben Tre twenty minutes ago. I could see and hear that they were engaged. Who was supposed to take the lead? Was I the senior Navy river rat? The Ben Tre River was the 534th patrol patch. When those 531 boats came on the scene, I was happy. Now that I knew what we were up against, the thought of command responsibility weighed down on me. I wanted help in the worst way.

Lieutenant Ron Wolin was his calm, confident self. He was wearing his utility cap and a crisp set of utilities. (For some reason Ron always favored the heavy cotton fatigues over the thin tropical uniforms.) Evidently he had plans of cumshawing or politicking that day—definitely not fighting the war on plastic boats. He had been shaving when Bill Earner rushed into his stateroom with the news that Frank's boats had been hit at the bridge. He had immediately ordered that a boat and crew get ready for him while he rushed to the NOC to get briefed on what happened. Ron Wolin did not hesitate.

"Wynn, tell me about this little mess that ruined my plans for the day."

I told him everything I knew; Ron knew most of it already. He had been in contact with the 531 River Section and the *Harnett County*. He had more boats coming and had requested the *Harnett County* to get under way for Ben Tre. More than anyone else in the entire eastern Mekong Delta brown-water navy, Ron Wolin realized that Ben Tre needed a maximum effort. When the 531 boats came running back down the Ben Tre to the Ham Luong a few minutes later, Ron told me to take the 7-20 and 7-21 boats back to the APL-55.

"Wynn, go and get some sleep. Jerry Letcher's patrol is on the way. More 531 boats are coming. We'll play out this hand with what we have. I want you and your boat crews ready this afternoon. I don't need boats with little fuel and tired crews now."

I was officially relieved. My personal sense of relief was greater than my sense of obligation to my country or my unit. I knew in my bones that I was not prepared to do more battle at the time.

As the 7-20 and 7-21 boats sped back to the APL-55, the two-boat patrol of Jerry Letcher (PBRs 7-16 and 7-17) came running downriver. The radio traffic was so full that I did not get a chance to say hello to Jerry. We just waved to each other.

Part of me had wanted to stay with Ron and see what could be done at Ben Tre. I definitely wanted to punish the troops who had wounded Frank Walker. I also knew that the combat effectiveness of my patrol was diminished. We were down to a quarter tank of gas (diesel fuel), the crews were dog-tired, and we had shot up over a quarter of our ammo. I also thought that the enemy force at Ben Tre was only the rear guard of a company or two. The local militia with the Army advisers could certainly clear any Viet Cong snipers remaining in the marketplace. It would be dicey for PBRs to suppress enemy fire from the south bank at the bridge with the Vietnamese outposts near the bridge overrun, but in daylight it could be done with the force already assembled. I felt relief and confidence that outweighed my feelings of anger and regret. Most of all, I was exhausted.

Upon arrival at the APL-55, I grabbed some food in the chow line and rushed to the NOC. It was 1000 in the morning. The comm center was crowded. The four radios were going nonstop. Bill Earner told me that all hell was taking place. River rats were engaged all over the Delta—at My Tho, Vinh Long, Chou Doc, as well as Ben Tre. The 534th boats under Ron were going up the Ben Tre to support the MACV compound. I no longer wanted to hear the action on the radio. I had hoped for some sort of victorious conclusion. I definitely did not want to hear of more wounded 534th sailors. I wanted to go to sleep with the hope it would all be over by the time I awakened. If it was not over by the afternoon, I knew I would need that sleep.

While I was eating breakfast, Ron Wolin and Jack Harrell were making ad hoc war plans at the Ben Tre ferryboat landing. Wolin had established a command presence with four 534th PBRs. The two 531 boats went downriver to rearm. Harrell was alternating between a PRC-25 radio on the purloined jeep tuned to South Vietnamese frequencies and the MACV frequency on the 534th 7-18 boat. Ron Wolin was on the Navy frequencies demanding air cover. Both officers were frustrated. The radios were jammed with transmissions from all over. Chaos ruled. Gunships were not available. The TOC at Ben Tre said that the compound was taking direct fire from heavy weapons directly across the river and that a hastily assembled company of South Vietnamese infantry was being pushed back from the Ben Tre marketplace by a superior force of Viet Cong. Something had to be done to take pressure off the MACV compound until airpower arrived. Harrell and Wolin decided that the 534th PBRs had to go back upriver.

Ron Wolin led the four 534 PBRs up the river. After a turn to the right a mile upriver, they saw the province chief's home and the nearby MACV compound being pummeled by fire. Any PBR going up to the compound would be hit with all the stuff that was blasting the fortified compound. Ron chose a standoff weapon. The 7-18 boat had a 60mm mortar. It fired all of the thirty rounds of high explosive and white phosphorous munitions on the boat at the enemy positions across from the compound, safely and from a range and angle that the enemy could not hit. The Viet Cong fire slowed down when the mortar rounds hit their positions. Ron called Jerry Letcher to come up and fire the mortar on his boat. That is when Jerry informed Ron that he did not have a mortar. Jerry and I had both neglected to transfer a mortar and rounds from my patrol when we had been speeding past each other earlier. The Viet Cong barrage on the compound started up again. Ron Wolin was pissed. Maybe another dose of mortar fire from PBRs would have stabilized the situation. He took the boats back to the Ham Luong. He knew what was coming, and it was not going to be fun.

At the ferryboat landing Jack Harrell confirmed to Ron Wolin what Ron had felt. The Viet Cong controlled the south end of the bridge and were massing for a full-scale attack. The defenders at the compound had all their attention turned to squads of infiltrators who had broken through from the marketplace and were attacking the north side of the compound. The Cong fire from the east bank was now even three hundred meters west of the compound. South Vietnamese outposts on the east were being overrun. The compound with its three hundred or so South Vietnamese Ruff Puffs and support troops and one hundred American advisers was in mortal danger. A major defeat was at hand.

Both Wolin and Harrell knew what was needed. Calls for air support, additional PBRs, anything and everything were again requested. Jack Harrell was to coordinate the radio communications as Ron Wolin's 534th boats went into the breach.

Ron Wolin made BM1 Carvander the boat commander of the 7-18 boat. GMSN Wayne Forbes was to man the 7-18's forward twin fifties. These guys were both eager and had been in combat under the bridge earlier when their 7-14 boat had been hit. The two guys they replaced became extra guns on the 7-13 and 7-16 boats. With Lt. (j.g.) Jerry Letcher on the 7-17 boat, each boat had five men. Those not manning machine guns or driving the boats had M-79 grenade launchers and M-16 rifles. The boat commanders had rifles and shotguns with them in the coxswain's flats and had their .38 pistols in their laps. The after gunners carefully arranged open cans of bullets at their feet. They then quickly broke out more 40mm grenades from ammo cases in the forward cabins and made up spare belts for the M-18 grenade launchers. Then they placed M-72 LAWs within easy reach. Some sailors even removed the plastic caps and extended the bails on these rockets. The rockets could be grabbed, aimed, and fired within seconds. Within a few minutes the four boats and crews were as ready as sailors could possibly be in their situation.

The four boats sped up the Ben Tre River, racing to the sound of increasingly violent gunfire. Rounding the bend to the south, they saw that the MACV compound was being hit hard from the south bank. Little figures of soldiers were firing at each other on the bridge beyond. Explosions, smoke, and tracers were getting closer and closer. Within three hundred yards of the compound, the boats were hit by fire from scores of Viet Cong riflemen who had taken over hootches at the water's edge on the south bank. The boats' guns responded. Structures were set ablaze. The enemy fire stopped in seconds.

The high-explosive, incendiary tracer bullets leveled and burnt the flimsy hootches on the south bank. The boats did not even slow down. The gunners did not waste their bullets. The big fight was yet to come. Within a minute the boats passed the MACV compound. South Vietnamese soldiers and American advisers were firing across the river from sandbagged positions on the street and from the top of the masonry walls. The 534th boats paid little attention. They had to defend the bridge.

The bridge now got bigger and bigger. South Vietnamese troopers on the north approaches were battling a group of Viet Cong storming across from the south bank. Jerry Letcher remembers a little South Vietnamese trooper kneeling down near the center of the bridge. He was firing a Browning automatic rifle at Viet Cong riflemen who were ducking and firing AK-47s as they ran across the bridge toward him less than forty yards away from his exposed position. The forward fifties of the 7-18 boat sprayed the enemy on the bridge and then concentrated on a mass of Viet Cong firing from kneeling positions at the south end of the bridge. GMSN Wayne Forbes saw some get cut down by his fire. It was payback time for the Viet Cong. Before Forbes could think about what was happening, he noticed bullets hitting in front of the boat from the north side. A rocket went over the bow of the boat and exploded on the south bank. He swung his guns around. By now the 7-18 boat was directly opposite the Ben Tre marketplace—the very center of the town of over thirty-five thousand inhabitants. Those two- and three-story stucco buildings were filled with Cong riflemen and B-40 rocketeers. They were in the windows, on the balconies, even on top of the

roofs. Unlike the enemy on the south bank, who were primarily dressed in black pajamas or dark bluish-green uniforms
and wearing web gear full of ammo or supplies and floppy
cloth hats or conical straw hats, the enemy in the marketplace
looked like young men going to school. They all wore long-
sleeve white shirts, black trousers, and no hats. Each had a
two-inch-wide band of red cloth tied around his left arm between the elbow and shoulder. This was the battle attire of
hundreds of Viet Cong who had infiltrated (or come out of
hiding in) the center of town over the last seven hours. These
were no schoolboys. They were dedicated fighters, well armed
and well positioned.

Each boat in the column received fire from both sides
when it reached the marketplace. The gunners quickly shifted
their fire to the most immediate threat—the town center.
Twenty or so rockets were aimed at the PBRs during that first
run. Perhaps ten thousands of rifle and machine gun bullets
also. Most of the rockets being fired at them were coming
from the two- and three-story buildings at the marketplace.
The rounds were long or short but usually on line. Our gunners identified rocket firing positions either by direct visual
contact or by following the contrails of rocket smoke back to
the source. The boats turned around about a hundred meters
from the marketplace when the enemy fire slackened. The
boats reentered the gauntlet of fire at the marketplace and
bridge. By then the after fifty gunners had exhausted their
ready trays so they swung up the M-18 grenade launchers into
firing positions and started cranking out streams of 40mm
grenades. The unprotected enemy infantry firing from prone
or kneeling positions on the south bank were being punished
by the carpet bomb effect of these rounds. M-60 gunners
grabbed M-72 LAWs when their trays went empty. Ron
Wolin, Jerry Letcher, and RD1 Robert Wenzel (a supernumerary on the 7-16 boat) were firing all the small arms available
to them. Jerry preferred the M-16. Ron Wolin and Wenzel
switched back and forth from M-16s to M-79 grenade launchers to LAWs. Whatever weapon was handy. Everybody was
firing as fast as he could and there was no time to scrounge for
new rounds for just-emptied weapons. The number of targets
and the volume of enemy fire demanded nothing less. Just as

the boats raced under the bridge again, an enemy rocket sailed inches over the coxswain's flat of the 7-13 boat and impacted on a forty-foot junk beached on the south bank. The junk exploded in a tremendous fireball. Apparently the enemy on the north bank had inadvertently destroyed one of its own ammunition stockpiles.

The four boats regrouped near the MACV compound. River Section 531 boats were on the scene by then, leveling the hamlets across from the MACV compound. The whole south bank was burning trees and hootches. The 534th boats rearmed their machine guns and small arms and prepared for another run up past the bridge. Ron Wolin's intention on that run was to have the boats go a little slower and not as far upriver, and to have two boats concentrate fire on the marketplace while two more blasted the area near the eastern end of the bridge where the massed enemy force had been in full view near the riverbank. Ron Wolin also wanted to nail a Viet Cong rifleman who had fired on him from the window of a wooden building east of the bridge on that first trip. As the boats went back toward the bridge, Wolin manned the M-60 machine gun on the 7-18 boat. The rising tide would make his task easier. By standing on the engine covers he could have a level view of that particular sniper's lair.

As the 7-18 boat raced under the bridge and the forward machine gunner sprayed the marketplace ahead to the left, Ron Wolin again saw AK-47 muzzle flashes coming from the window of the targeted Vietnamese home on the other bank, just past the burning Viet Cong junk. He fired at least one hundred rounds into that structure. He briefly noted a china cabinet with a full mirror disintegrated by his bullets as the boat went by the doorway. It reminded Wolin of an old western movie scene where the bad guys shot up the back of the bar. He did not know if his fire had hit his adversary but it had relieved some stress. By then the bulk of enemy fire was coming from the opposite bank. Most of the enemy on the south bank were cowering in the bushes. The main business at hand was the town center. Bullets and rockets were streaming over the port side of the boat. Ron Wolin shifted his attention to the marketplace, the place all the sailors had relished on their infrequent liberty, the friendly place they had enjoyed.

As the boats reached a point in the river directly across from the center of the marketplace, the 7-18 boat made a fast 180-degree turn. The other boats followed this maneuver in line formation. Most guns were now directed toward the marketplace. As well they should: another thirty B-40 rockets and thousands of bullets would be shot at them within ten minutes from the windows and balconies of those buildings. Little, circular, white-smoke contrails from the rockets laced the air above the PBRs. Again the rockets missed their mark. The rooftop snipers had disappeared. The Viet Cong riflemen would fire a magazine of AK-47 bullets or a B-40 rocket and retreat into the recesses of the buildings. Their aim was off the mark because thousands of heavy .50-caliber and .30-caliber bullets and many M-72 LAW rounds were tearing up their protection, and the marketplace was set on fire by the HEIT rounds of the fifties. One PBR sailor fired an LAW into an enemy rocketeer's position in the second story of a marketplace building. This set off a big secondary explosion that tore off the roof. The destruction of the marketplace was going down like the special effects of a Hollywood movie.

Just as the four River Section PBRs were almost out of bullets and headed back west under the bridge, a Viet Cong rocketeer got lucky. A B-40 rocket smashed into the starboard cowling of the 7-18 boat inches above the head of the forward gunner, GMSN Wayne Forbes. The rocket exploded directly in front of the coxswain's flat at an angle that fortunately directed most of the force of the explosion out the port side of the boat. The blast did blow out the controls of the boat and knocked BM1 Carvander and Ron Wolin off their feet. Both were sprayed with shrapnel. By the time they got to their feet, the boat was out of control and heading toward the south bank.

Wayne Forbes's forward fifties were out of commission; the blast had knocked out the electrical firing system of his guns. But the gunner did not panic. He quickly abandoned his useless guns and crawled aft through the smoking forward cabin to the starboard deck, where he knew he could find a weapon. He grabbed an M-16 and several magazines of ammo and commenced firing on the south bank, which was now only ten meters away and full of enemy troops getting up from the bushes to finish off a wounded PBR. Forbes did not realize that the boat was out of control. He just wanted to fire at the enemy. He had a lot of targets.

Ron Wolin and BM1 Carvander struggled to their feet. They both realized the situation. The whole control console was blown out. No steering wheel, no throttles, no radios. Just a smoking mess of wires and cables. The boat was about to beach on the south bank where hundreds of Viet Cong were hunkered down in the bushes. The enemy gunners near the east end of the bridge saw an easy target and fired their weapons.

Wolin and Carvander struggled with the cables controlling the water pumps to attempt some steering as PBRs 7-16 and 7-17 rushed to the aid of the wounded 7-18 boat. The 7-16 boat shielded the 7-18 boat from the south bank as the 7-17 (boat captain BM1 James Shadoan) boat attached a line to the bow of the 7-18 boat. All boats were hit by automatic weapons fire as they limped back under the Ben Tre bridge. The 7-18 boat took over forty bullets in its fiberglass hull. Hundreds more enemy rounds must have sailed over the boat during its ordeal. Numerous small arms and rocket fragments had hit all the other boats. The PBRs had expended almost every round from their machine guns. Most gunners had only M-16s or shotguns in their hands when the boats passed underneath the bridge. But no more sailors were wounded.

Just as the four 534th PBRs reached the relative safety of the MACV compound that was being protected by the 531 boats, airpower finally arrived in the form of a Navy Seawolf light fire team (two ships) from the HAL-3 (helicopter, attack, light) detachment of the *Harnett County*. Those naval aviators arrived just as the Viet Cong on the south bank started to re-group after the punishment the 534th sailors had dealt them.

It was all a matter of timing. The *Harnett County* Sea-wolves had been busy all day down the lower Ham Luong and assisting their Dong Tam brethren on the My Tho River. Then Ben Tre finally got some command attention from the flyboys. It was their fourth combat sortie of the day. They were fully rearmed and refueled from the helo pad of the *Harnett County,* which was at anchor on the Ham Luong opposite the mouth of the Ben Tre River, only two miles away. Jack Harrell from the MACV TOC was directing the Seawolves. Their first priority was to blast away the infiltrators who had been pressing an attack on the east wall of the MACV compound. That was successfully done. Then it was taking on targets of opportunity. The Viet Cong in buildings on fire at the marketplace and their comrades across the river near the south end of the bridge presented many targets. Seawolf fire teams from both the *Harnett County* detachment and the Dong Tam attachment rotated missions for many hours that day. Tens of thousands of bullets and hundreds of rockets were poured into the enemy positions. The 534th boats went to the Ham Luong and the *Harnett County,* where Ron Wolin and Carvander were treated for wounds. The four PBRs rearmed and prepared for yet another run past the bridge with replacements.

The PBR sailors of the 534th and 531st returned up that river time and time again as the Seawolves from the Dong Tam detachment alternated with the fire team from the *Harnett County*. The PBRs secured the river up to the steel bridge while the gunships reduced the enemy in the marketplace and on the east side of the bridge.

By 1400 the gunships had beaten back most of the enemy around the bridge. Lieutenant Bill Earner was by then the senior river rat on the scene. He took four 534th PBRs past the bridge for a couple of hours of high anxiety.

Bill's first run past the bridge was on TM1 Malcolm Fullam's boat, the lead boat. By then the center of town was in flames and the area around the south end of the bridge had been reduced to smoking rubble. When clearing the bridge, the forward .50 gunner cut loose with a long burst into the burning marketplace. The after gunners took the cue and fired their guns on the marks of the forward gunner. Bill Earner, who thought the enemy was only on the south bank, went ballistic. He screamed, "Cease fire! Cease fire! Don't fire into the town!"

Our gunners stopped firing but the Viet Cong machine gunner on the second floor of some burning building continued to fire at the PBRs. Bill Earner soon countermanded his order with a "Belay my last! Continue firing!" Some pissed-off sailors on the PBR went back to work. They soon eliminated the machine gun position and every other Viet Cong position giving them fire. One run up and down suppressed the automatic weapons fire. The boats slowed down. The gunners looked for targets amidst the smoke and fire. Snipers were still firing on the boats. The occasional enemy round was answered in large and deadly volume by PBR machine guns. Mostly the sailors just watched the town center burn itself out and listened to the explosions around the north end of the MACV compound. The gunships still had some targets out of sight from the river and continued to blast the enemy forces attempting to regroup on the south bank.

For two hours the sailors were on their guns in a small river with both banks looking like hell itself; at any moment an opening in the flames and smoke would give the enemy a clear shot. These enemy rounds were answered by overwhelming fire on our part.

Meanwhile, suicide squads of VC sappers were doing their damnedest from the buildings adjacent to the north wall of the MACV compound. Those guys exposed themselves only when the gunships were far away. Finally the South Vietnamese commanders in the compound made an anguishing decision. They called in artillery fire onto buildings infested by Viet Cong less than fifty meters from the compound. They called that fire down on their own homes and families. The first weapons to fire were from a battery of 155mm guns located at the soccer field less than a mile away—a point-blank fire mission. Those guns had been seized by the Viet Cong early in the morning, then recaptured by South Vietnamese soldiers in the afternoon. With heavy artillery in the air, the Seawolves had to clear the scene. Without air cover, the 534th PBRs withdrew to the Ham Luong.

The action up the Ben Tre River that day at high noon would be the high-water mark for two of the best Viet Cong battalions in the Mekong Delta during the 1968 Tet Offensive. The Main Force 516th and 518th on the south bank of the Ben Tre were at a combat strength of about fifteen hundred experienced fighters supported by the labor of hundreds of sympathizers, who carried their supplies. They had meticulously planned an attack. With the hundreds of Viet Cong infiltrators, guided by deep-cover agents in place in the marketplace, and with elements of the 520th Reserve Battalion secreted southwest of Ben Tre, the communist commanders must have felt confident. Their force outnumbered the American advisers and South Vietnamese troops in and around Ben Tre by a six-to-one margin. Most of the South Vietnamese soldiers around Ben Tre were peasant part-timers. Many of South Vietnam's regular army guys in charge of the locals would be off visiting family during Tet. Most of those in the city itself were just support troops, the guys who ran the motor pools, repaired the weapons, supplied the food and ammo, and did all the admin work for the South Vietnamese citizen-soldiers, under the tutelage of American advisers, for the whole province. The Viet Cong commanders must have also believed the stuff that the political cadre had told them: "The puppet forces will collapse and the people will rise up to help our cause."

The Viet Cong forces at Ben Tre were tied to a rigid timetable set months in advance. The attack was to begin at 0430 to coincide with other attacks all over the country. Mortars and machine gunners would first eliminate the South Vietnamese Popular Force boats and contain any American boats coming upriver. Then there would be a coordinated attack on the MACV compound by sapper infiltrators as two companies of infantry stormed across the Ben Tre bridge supported by a heavy barrage of 82mm mortars, 75mm recoilless rockets, and .51-caliber machine guns in place across from the MACV compound. Big miscalculations of timing and estimation of the fighting spirit and resourcefulness of the enemy was rampant during the Tet Offensive. The low tide had prevented the Viet Cong's getting to the north bank of the river at the marketplace in force. The low tide had also fooled the machine gunners, who had set their guns' sights at the water's edge on the north bank at high tide. So the heavy stuff that was supposed to be in position at daybreak was pinned down for hours by PBR fire as the Viet Cong infantry failed to cross that damned bridge and secure the north bank. The PBRs and Seawolves took the starch out of the Viet Cong around Ben Tre the first day of that battle. But the biggest Viet Cong miscalculation was the civilian population; it did not rally to their cause. Those few who did not hunker down during the battle usually helped the defenders of the town by running to friendly lines and reporting Viet Cong infiltrators in their neighborhoods.

It was only after many days of continued hard fighting that we recognized that the U.S. Navy prevented Ben Tre from becoming front-page news on the first day of Tet, 1968. And that was because PBR sailors and Seawolf crews kept coming back time and time again to battle the enemy. Without the brown-water navy the Viet Cong could have overrun the entire town, and the cost to recapture it could have surpassed the number of American casualties at Hue. This is not hype for my little book. This is what happened and what could have happened. Every available sailor from the 534th and 531st River Sections was engaged in combat up the Ben Tre River that day. Repeatedly, crews were augmented, changed, and rotated by officers on the scene. The U.S. Navy's brown-water sailors saved Ben Tre.

I was back on the river that evening and stayed the night and a good portion of the next day. From 2100 to after midnight we viewed the battle as spectators. The Viet Cong would not yield their toehold on the south bank. It appeared that their gunfire was even closer to the Ham Luong. Their heavy fire from a dozen or so .51-caliber machine guns actually drove off a C-47 Spooky gunship. The thousands of little red tracers coming down in a steady stream from the air were matched by thousands of bigger greenish bullets being fired all along that south bank. The *Harnett County* was at anchor in the middle of the Ham Luong and was firing its 81mm mortars and 40mm cannons. Around midnight, after the Spooky was driven off, a Seawolf fire team had to make an emergency scramble to spray the north wall of the MACV compound as yet another squad of determined sappers attacked. (Later one of the pilots told me that Jack Harrell, who had called the gunships, said that the personnel inside the compound were prepared to evacuate into their bombproof bunker and have the gunships fire their rockets into the compound. Jack and those inside the compound truly had a very long and terrifying day. For me and the other river rats of eight or so everready 531 and 534 boats cruising up and down the Ham Luong, it was just a great pyrotechnic show across the water.)

At 0800 on the morning of February 1, 1968, we received an urgent call from Jack Harrell. The South Vietnamese outpost on the east bank of the Ham Luong just south of the mouth of the Ben Tre needed assistance. It was a rinky-dink outpost but it had command of the mouth of the Ben Tre River. Fifty meters of cleared brush surrounded the little outpost on the sides not facing the wide river or the Ben Tre. The clearing was for fire lanes for the defenders. In normal times, duty for the outpost was probably like manning a lighthouse outside Hampton Roads. Rivers surrounded it on two sides and friendly forces on the other two sides. But not that day. The outpost was receiving heavy automatic weapons and rocket fire from the rear. Viet Cong infantry were coming out of the tree line behind the outpost and it was in danger of being overrun. A company of Viet Cong with 75mm recoilless rifles and .51-caliber machine guns could play havoc with boats trying to go up the Ben Tre from that position.

The *Harnett County* was a mile up the Ham Luong, shelling a brick factory suspected of hiding a reserve Viet Cong battalion. The gunships were busy at My Tho and Vinh Long. Eight 534th boats were on the river. Ron Wolin had three supporting the *Harnett County*. Only five 534th PBRs were close at hand at the Ben Tre. I had three and BMC James Raymond had two. Chief Raymond and I made a hasty plan. I would take the 7-13, 7-14, and 7-21 boats up the Ben Tre a quarter mile and he would close the outpost from the Ham Luong side, then we would blast the tree line behind the outpost from two angles. The plan and a couple of thousand rounds of .50-caliber bullets and a belt or two of 40mm grenades seemed to work. The Cong broke off their attack.

I dispersed the boats after we reached the Ham Luong. Any watercraft on the river that morning needed to be searched. A couple of hours later (1030) one of the boats picked up a couple of Viet Cong suspects in a sampan that was attempting to cross the Ham Luong to Tan Tan Island. The suspects, young men in peasant attire but with no identification, were turned over to me, I guess because I was the senior guy around. It was my job to turn them over to the Vietnamese national police. But that police station was more than a half mile up the Ben Tre and I had my doubts about going that far upriver. I radioed the MACV compound and asked if the area around the police station was secure. When the answer came back "affirmative," I made another dumb decision; I took the suspects up the Ben Tre River. At least I took three boats for a job normally tasked to two. I just wanted to get rid of the VC baby-sitting job as soon as possible. (Later I would discover that other PBRs picked up suspects that morning and did things the right way—which was also the easy way. They turned them over to the *Harnett County*, which had a secure brig and lots of sailors to feed and guard prisoners.)

I was on the 7-13 boat, captained by BM1 Burney, with the two prisoners. The two other boats (7-14 and 7-21) were to be at battle stations with all guns aimed at the south bank when the 7-13 boat dropped off the prisoners. As the boats approached the police station, located in a small building fifteen feet above water level, I glanced over to the south bank. There was something strange about the little outpost diagonally opposite the police station to the west. The tattered and sun-bleached little yellow flag with its horizontal red lines was still flying from the flagpole, but there was not a soul in sight. I expected at least some of the fifteen or so South Viets manning that outpost to be visible. Just after the 7-13 boat docked at the rickety boat landing of bamboo scaffolding, I jumped off with the two suspects. A little policeman came running out to meet us with a drawn .38 pistol. He was not the familiar portly Viet police chief I knew. He was shouting and waving his pistol at the south bank, then fired a couple of shots at the south bank. That was all the warning I needed. I jumped back on the boat. Burney and the other two boat captains (QM1 Howard Stevens and QM1 James Radford) were getting the boats turned back to the Ham Luong. That's when I noticed that the abandoned South Vietnamese outpost was sporting new colors: a six-foot-by-four-foot flag, blue bar over red bar with a yellow star in the center, had risen on the flagpole. It was the biggest and brightest enemy flag I had ever seen. Automatic rifle fire was coming from the outpost, and the fire was directed at us. Our boats responded with the fire of a dozen machine guns. Within seconds the boats were racing past the outpost and back to the Ham Luong. Within a few more seconds three rockets landed in quick succession in the water thirty feet from the boats. The first round was abreast of the 7-13 boat. The two others were between the 7-13 boat and Radford's boat. Luck, poor Kentucky windage on the part of three rocketeers, and the warning provided by the little Viet cop saved my ass and the three boats. I had fully intended to take the suspect up all those steps to the police station and tell the cops where he'd been apprehended. That could have taken minutes. Time for the Viet Cong rocket guys to carefully pick out individual boat targets and make good hits. My dumb luck again.

Once back at the Ham Luong, I got on the radio and sarcastically told the MACV radio watch that their intel was behind the times. The sailors replenished the ready trays of the guns. The boats then watched the *Harnett County* sortie south down the Ham Luong. Nothing was said over the radio telling me why. I told the other boats to monitor the MACV channel for me. Then I switched off the Kien Hoa advisory frequency on my boat and channel-surfed. I knew most of the freqs for the eastern Delta by heart.

Boy, was I in for a shock. Amid all the frantic radio transmissions, I determined that the PBR base at Vinh Long had been abandoned and that the river rat base at My Tho was still under attack from both the river and the city. I asked a sailor to turn on his AM transistor radio so I could hear what the official USMACV organ in Saigon had to tell. The news was not encouraging. The U.S. embassy grounds in Saigon had been infiltrated. The Cholon section of Saigon was being contested in heavy fighting. Holy shit, the battle was much bigger than I had ever imagined. I was beginning to think that Ben Tre was a lost cause, maybe the whole damn war was lost. Maybe the CO of the *Harnett County* had seen the writing on the wall and bugged out while the getting was good. I knew that Ron Wolin (just upriver and doing his thing against VC around Tan Tan Island) would expect every sailor to fight until the bitter end. I was not prepared to die. I mentally calculated how far out in the South China Sea my PBRs could go on existing fuel. The boats could reach the sea. I would conserve fuel and food. I would lash the boats together in the ocean. The sailors would rig sails. We would all survive. I really felt that the world was tumbling down. I had to save the people under my command. It was 1145 in the morning. The lowest point I experienced in my one year in Vietnam.

Minutes later the U.S. Air Force arrived on the scene in force. Flights of F-100 (Super Sabre) fighter-bombers began to bomb and strafe the south bank of the Ben Tre. Judging by the fireballs, I assumed they were dropping napalm. Then I saw a deployed parachute a mile up the Ben Tre, drifting over the south bank. The Viet Cong were getting their licks in. For over two hours those fighter-bombers came in waves. Some began to drop their loads on the north bank behind the MACV compound. The pretty little river town was being blown apart. I listened to Chet Brown in the air in his little O-19, directing the destruction when he switched to the common Kien Hoa frequency and asked for targets. Chet must have had a lot of mixed feelings. He must have known some of the inhabitants of the buildings that were being destroyed.

Around 1345 the *Harnett County* came back to the mouth of the Ben Tre. The fighter-bombers were still doing their job. I got Burney to take the 7-13 boat alongside a 531 boat cruising around the LST as the ship dropped anchor. I found out that the *Harnett County* had not bugged out that morning; it had gone only five miles down the Ham Luong, where it delivered heroic and yeoman fire support to the Mo Cay district town (not the proper district town of Mo Cay, which was firmly in control of the enemy at the time) and outposts that were being hard pressed. That old ship and its sailors (who went ashore in landing craft to aid the burning towns after the VC had been beaten back) had done the U.S. Navy proud. I was a little bit ashamed that I had thought that the ship might have abandoned Ben Tre. The 534th boats went back to our ready positions at the mouth of the Ben Tre River a little more determined.

We watched the burning town get dose after dose of explosives and napalm.

I had read a lot of books about combat operations in World War II. I had listened to all the stories about combat from the teachers I had had in high school. I had watched the newsreels on the Korean War. I had seen *Victory at Sea* and other war documentaries on television. As the jets continued to bomb Ben Tre, I knew that their efforts were only a stopgap measure. Sooner or later and in spite of all the bombs, hardened VC light infantry would breach the MACV compound walls. This enemy was willing to sacrifice many lives to reach its objectives.

I thought Ben Tre was going to be a miniature Dien Bien Phu. A superior force on the ground would get its way. The rubble around the compound would only give those enemy fighters who survived the air onslaught a lot of cover for another night assault. Their persistence would eventually pay off. River rats and airedales in fragile helicopters or fast jets could not prevent the numerically superior enemy from capturing its objectives. Especially when that enemy was fighting in its own backyard. Only infantry could root out the Viet Cong. Where the hell was the fucking U.S. Army? I mentally saw what would happen in the early hours of the next morning—PBRs under heavy fire evacuating the survivors of the MACV compound. A miniature Dunkirk. Dead and wounded all being brought out through some nightmarish inferno. I knew that the Navy would perform that mission. I was resigned to doing my part. Judging from the demeanor of the sailors on the boats, I believe that they all shared my pessimism. There was little of the usual grab-ass and wisecracking that sailors normally did on patrol. Everybody was serious, almost solemn. We were preparing ourselves for sacrifice.

The U.S. Army finally arrived unannounced. I could see dozens of "slicks" in tight formation approaching Ben Tre from the north. The troop-carrying choppers were flying at about five hundred feet. Air Force jets were high above them. The helicopters landed somewhere between the airstrip and the center of town. Probably on the soccer field. The cavalry had finally arrived to save the wagons. The hundred or so hot, tired, hungry, angry, scared, brown-water sailors on PBRs or the *Harnett County* who witnessed the arrival of those helicopters cheered. It was a reaffirmation of faith in Old Glory and in the U.S. military, our chosen profession. I did my version of the rebel yell at the top of my lungs. Perhaps the battle would even end in a victory. Every boat guy seemed to have the same feelings. They shouted a lot of profane expletives, joyous expletives. The sailors began to talk to each other.

They got off their guns and placed cans of C rations on the engine manifolds. Hunger had replaced fear. We all felt that the worst was over.

For the first hour after the choppers landed, the 534th river rats saw thousands of tracers (all red) and explosions from the vicinity of the landing zones. The F-100s were back to dropping bombs in that area. We all thought that the 9th Division doggies and the U.S. Air Force was kicking ass and taking names. After that first hour of violence we saw only a few bursts of tracers and the fighter-bombers flew away. I began to see (through binoculars) sampans crossing the Ben Tre River from the north bank to the south bank. Hot damn! The Cong were on the run to that little outpost opposite the police station. I believed that a battalion of 9th Division grunts was sweeping from north to south. In my mind's eye I saw the soldiers capturing or killing every Viet Cong in their path with a textbook execution of maneuver and firepower. American arms doing their best as they had been trained. The Cong infiltrators inside the town were being driven across the Ben Tre River. The battle was won. I was beside myself in confidence and relief.

Around 1430 all three boats were idling at the mouth of the Ben Tre, several hundred yards in front of the LST. All the sailors had witnessed sampans crossing to that south bank. Enemy soldiers escaping the wrath of the U.S. Army. This time I saw another small motorized sampan ease out from the north bank of the Ben Tre. There were two people in the sampan. They seemed tentative. They were waving their arms in the direction of the Cong-controlled outpost on the south bank. Maybe the Viet Cong had abandoned that captured outpost.

The sampan was only a half mile from my PBRs. The opportunity was too much for me to resist. I gave a loud declaration. It was not exactly an order, much less a proper military command. But it sure did have consequences.

"Let's go nail that sampan!"

The boat commanders rammed the throttles and the three PBRs started up the Ben Tre. The race to get to the sampan before it reached the south bank had started. The 7-14 and 7-21 boats had been first at the starting gate. Burney's boat was right behind them. I had lost control from the beginning. I wanted a quick trip upriver while hugging the left bank. The boats could stop fifty yards from the sampan and blast the two Viet Cong just as they reached the south bank with our boats out of the line of sight of Cong gunners in the outpost. I just wanted to see some enemy fall to our guns. My personal payback for Frank Walker. I never expected the other two boats to lead me in a direct line to intercept the sampan before it reached that south bank. That sampan was now closing that south bank fast with Stevens's 7-21 boat on a line to intercept at the water's edge. I scrambled to get extra magazines for the M-16 I had just grabbed. Within a few seconds the first boat (QM1 Stevens's 7-21 boat) started firing. Not at the sampan but at the south bank. Radford's 7-14's guns came on line next. Again the guns were all toward the south bank. I could not see what was so interesting on the south bank. I just saw two Viet Cong in a sampan. Then the forward gunner on the 7-13 boat opened up. By now the little sampan had reached the south bank. It was surrounded by splashes of hits from PBR machine guns. I fired two magazines from the M-16 at the two young men scrambing up the riverbank as the 7-13 boat raced to them at a range of thirty feet. They were unarmed but wearing the signature attire of the infiltrators who had been in the marketplace. They both wore black trousers and white long-sleeve shirts with red armbands on their left arms. The 7-13 boat was bouncing up and down in the wakes of the other PBRs. All my M-16 shots went over the two Viet Cong. They momentarily got up from all fours at the top of the bank before they were bowled over, knocked up in the air, and torn apart by machine gun fire from the after gunners on Burney's boat. I momentarily took my eyes off the bank and looked beyond. I saw the big Cong flag atop the outpost. I also saw the rapid winking of automatic weapons being fired directly at me. I ducked down, scrambled inside the coxswain's flat, grabbed the radio mike, and yelled orders to the other boats.

"Charlie One, Charlie Two, this is Charlie! Turn around, exit to the Ham Luong!"

The two other boats had already turned around and were just about to pass Burney's boat as I looked up from the console. Burney swung the 7-13 boat around in a crash turn. We followed the other boats in a firing run at the outpost. One of the most memorable visions of my whole Vietnam experience soon took place. I could see that outpost being hit squarely by hundreds of rounds of .50-caliber HEIT from all three PBRs. It seemed that every round fired was hitting that little mud-and-wood fort. The flagpole with the VC colors came crashing down. It was a great feeling I had in those few seconds.

The three boats all safely reached the Ham Luong. I led them to the *Harnett County*. We needed ammo replenishment and to take stock of our little foray. As we nestled aside the LST, Burney let the after gunner take control of the 7-13 boat. Burney first made sure the gunners dumped all the spent brass. He then went over to inspect the starboard side of his boat. He saw bullet holes in the stanchions for the awning and bullet scrapes on the gunwales. He was probably pissed out of his gourd. He did not show it. He simply asked me to come over and examine the battle damage to his command. He was the same old Burney, smoking a Salem and not talkative at all.

Burney simply said, "Mister Goldsmith, you were lucky. See those bullet marks? You were lucky."

Burney's little demonstration said a lot more to me than his words. He was telling me a lot more, something like, "You dumb, smart-ass, white boy officer. You nearly fucked up. See how close you got to getting your ass killed? Not to mention sailors who could have been killed."

I lamely replied, "We were all lucky."

A lieutenant junior grade on a River Section 531 boat came over as the 7-13 boat tied a line to a camel lashed to the side of the LST. The guy was about my age. I did not know him and never got to introduce myself to him. I do remember his words to me.

"Hey, don't you know that Com Rivdiv 53 (Lt. Comdr. Frank Steed in My Tho) has ordered all PBRs out of the Ben Tre?"

I had heard of that order but thought that it applied only to boats going up near the marketplace. I chose a smart-ass reply instead of some weaselly defense. I asked, "So, what's the Navy gonna do to me? Send me to Vietnam?"

Chapter 12

My belief that the U.S. Army could sweep the enemy out of
Ben Tre within a few hours was shattered when I was finally
relieved and returned to the barge. From the NOC guys I got
the word that the Army was having a tough fight at Ben Tre.
Their attack had stalled north of the town. Airpower was again
called in to blast out dug-in enemy within the town. It was
about 1930 on February 1. I also saw some radio traffic that
told me my job as senior patrol officer for the 534th was over.
Jerry Letcher had been promoted to full lieutenant (O-3). His
commissioning date had been six months prior to mine. I was
happy for Jerry. He was on the river at the time. I briefly
thought of calling him up on the radio to congratulate him but
decided to hit the rack and congratulate him in the morning. I
had been on patrol for over twenty hours. I had no clue what
the schedules for the next day were. That was no longer my
concern. Besides, even if I had remained the "senior patrol officer," it was Ron Wolin and Bill Earner who determined what
boats with what boat captains and which patrol officers went
where and when. In prolonged combat there was no set routine. The guys in command were sending out anybody and
everybody. Even YN3 Bruce Burns, our baby-face yeoman
(who had never been through boat training), traded in his
typewriter for a machine gun. John Smith took boats out
whenever he felt that his maintenance efforts were done for
the day. Some boats were refueled and recrewed within minutes after patrols if the boats still had full ammo loads and no
materiel casualties. I knew that if Wolin or Earner wanted me
they knew where to find me. I slept for ten hours. The longest
I would sleep for over a month.

When a tug on the arm awakened me the next morning I

knew that the battle had not been won. That day (February 3) had been my scheduled day off the river. I was not surprised that it was cut short. I took a cold shower, threw the smelly uniform I had dumped on the deck beside my rack the previous evening into a laundry bag, put on fresh clothes, and went back to war.

Most of that month was a blur to me at the time. Reviewing all the old combat action summaries many years later brought back some memories. When today's TV viewers watch the old footage of Vietnam's 1968 Tet Offensive on the History Channel, they see the ordeal of U.S. Marines at Hue and Khe Sanh, battles that lasted for weeks (Hue) and even months (Khe Sanh). The troops were fighting, dying, and just existing under squalid conditions that resembled trench warfare for American troops on the western front during World War I in the late summer of 1918 or the urban assault on German towns in early 1945. Not pleasant TV viewing. Americans at home, night after night, saw unrelenting destruction and carnage. Images that caused the commander in chief to call it quits and announce a bombing halt to North Vietnam that would last for years.

The Tet Offensive for me and all the other brown-water sailors in the Mekong Delta was a lot different. We shifted from place to place. We got some hours of uninterrupted, air-conditioned sleep. We could even get a hot meal occasionally. But most hours were spent in combat, waiting for combat, or racing to another combat situation on little boats. The Mobile Riverine Force, with its embarked brigade of 9th Division U.S. Army troopers, went from provincial capital to provincial capital to stifle the enemy. It was like the U.S. Marine "fire brigade" on the Pusan Peninsula during the late summer of 1950. PBRs were shuttled back and forth to save district towns. We succeeded in defeating the Viet Cong in the Delta while the news at home focused on a costly stalemate in I Corps against the North Vietnamese.

The 534th's experience was typical of that time. We fought at Ben Tre and all up and down the boundaries of Kien Hoa Province. We supported the Vinh Long district town of Cho Lach near the My Tho River. We came to the aid of the Vinh Long provincial capital on the Co Chien River. When no other friendly fire was available, we went up small channels in the middle of the night to fight off Viet Cong that were storming friendly outposts. Many of these little missions were never properly recorded. If no sailor was killed or wounded the engagement was marked down as just a combat "incident." No mention of sailors' names, bullets expended, friendlies saved, etc., unless the patrol officer took the trouble of making a full report at the end of the patrol. Many were just so exhausted that they never reported these "incidents."

I was pretty conscientious. I tried to make complete reports even if they showed only time, place, boats involved, and a few cryptic words when typed up in action summaries. My story of Tet for the 534th River Patrol Section is basically a personal story. Some of the personal experiences of the other 534th river rats would probably be more interesting. The only stories in this account are the ones I witnessed or for which I have written documentation. I guess I was more inclined than most to record my memories, and my involvement is probably not representative of the whole.

During February 1968, the 534th got involved in nearly fifty recorded firefights or incidents. I'm sure there were a lot more. Sometimes it just seemed a waste of effort to call in reports of enemy fire. There were just too many of them. Long bursts of enemy fire from the banks of the Ham Luong aimed at our boats as we went to support yet another outpost were no longer incidents. They were just ordinary occurrences and no big deal unless a sailor was wounded.

Late on the afternoon of February 4, six 534th boats were on station on the Ham Luong. I had the 7-13 and 7-14 boats near the Ben Tre River. Chief Raymond had two boats a mile to the south, and RD1 Wenzel had two boats two miles to the north. The battle still raged as the 9th Division grunts cleared the north side of the town block by block. Our boats had been busy evacuating wounded from the MACV compound the previous day. Four soldiers on stretchers on four occasions. Each time the boats had received enemy fire. But on February 4, MACV wounded were being taken out by Army dustoffs, and our boats were supporting local South Vietnamese in sweeps from their outposts along the Ham Luong. To me it finally appeared that the town of Ben Tre was truly going to be secured. The Ruff Puffs were engaged. Surely the Main Force Viet Cong were in retreat.

We got a recall message around 1700. The whole section was ordered to Vinh Long, a provincial capital thirty miles away by boat. As my two-boat patrol sped up the Ham Luong we received several bursts of automatic weapons fire from Tan Tan Island. We ignored it. A minute later we saw the 7-12 and 7-19 boats of Wenzel's patrol beached along the north bank in front of the large outpost across from the middle of Tan Tan Island. Sailors were firing an M-60 machine gun and launching grenades into the tree line three hundred fifty meters behind and on the left flank of the outpost. Other sailors were setting up the 60mm mortar on the engine covers on Engle's 7-12 boat.

I was on BM1 Burney's 7-13 boat. I had Burney close the boats on the bank.

RD1 Robert Wenzel, the patrol officer in charge of the boats on the bank, was busy talking on the radio. The after gunner on Engle's boat was firing the Honeywell in short bursts over the bermed walls of the mud fort. Two gunners were off the 7-19 boat. They were firing an M-60 machine gun and an M-79 grenade launcher from the raised observation deck of the outpost forty feet from the bank. Their fire was used as spotting rounds for the other gunners on Engle's and GM2 James Briggs's boats. Wenzel, still clutching the radio mike, told me he was in communication with an American adviser to Regional Force Popular Force (Ruff Puff) troops pinned down in front of the tree line, which formed a perfect L-shaped ambush site for the Viet Cong. The Ruff Puffs and the adviser were crawling on their bellies through grass toward the safety of the outpost. The PBR sailors' gunfire was over them at a height of only a few feet.

I asked Wenzel if he needed assistance.

"Mister Goldsmith, two more boats won't make much difference. I sure would like to have some Seawolves. I reckon none are available."

I made the radio request for gunship support and described the situation to the APL-55 NOC. The negative answer soon came back.

Wenzel was right. The Seawolves were busy that day in

Vinh Long and My Tho as they had been for four days. Saving the butts of Vietnamese Ruff Puffs was not a Seawolf priority when American brown-water sailors were fighting for their lives nearby.

Chief Raymond's two-boat patrol soon joined us. The chief and his sailors wanted to get involved more than I did. Fine with me. Sailors from Chief Raymond's boats took M-60 machine guns and grenade launchers into the outpost to help cover the Ruff Puffs. I decided to let Wenzel and Chief Raymond sort out the situation. They had had more combat experience. It was on to Vinh Long for me. I knew that the PBR base at Vinh Long had been overrun by the Viet Cong and that the 534th had been tasked to help retake the base—a mission much more important to me than saving a few Ruff Puffs crawling for their lives in a fallow rice paddy.

I expected to race the thirty-five miles from Ben Tre to Vinh Long by PBR. I was surprised when our boats got to the My Tho River and we discovered the APL-55 under way. One LCM-8 and two LCM-6s were pulling it at a speed of about six knots. The whole base was headed for Vinh Long. The two boats of my patrol tied up at the ammi pontoon astern of the barge. We got to enjoy a leisurely river ride for the next twenty-five miles and I had my first meal in the wardroom in a week.

I got to fire an 81mm mortar after dinner. Lieutenant Mel Shantz used the long transit time to prepare his support crews for combat. Lt. (j.g.) Billie Ray, Shantz's assistant, was topside drilling the cooks and technicians in their general quarters' assignments. Four pedestal-mounted 81mm mortars were the main battery of the APL-55. They were mounted at the corners of the second deck, thirty feet above the waterline. Each required a two-man crew. The weapon was basically the same one mounted on the sterns of Navy PCFs. Drop a round down the tube, swing the barrel around using a wheel, adjust the elevation, sight the target, and trigger-fire the round. Lt. (j.g.) Billie Ray told me that the APL-55's mortars had been in action before dawn the previous day while I slept. The APL-55 gunners and mortar fire from two 534th PBRs had routed two Viet Cong attacks on the Vinh Long district town of Cho Lach. The U.S. Army advisers there credited this Navy mortar fire with saving their compound and killing fifteen Viet Cong. With all the fighting going on at the time, that was the first time I had heard of the battle that raged a mile and a half away while I had been sleeping.

The round I fired was dead-on the sighted clump of raised earth on the north bank of the My Tho River at a four-hundred-meter range. The burst was much bigger than that of a 60mm mortar. I was impressed. I wished that PBRs had that kind of firepower.

By the time we got to anchorage in the middle of the Co Chien River, dusk had settled, and I got to witness another battle of World War II magnitude. In some ways it was Ben Tre all over again, except that the town of Vinh Long was on the main river, a river crowded with mobile riverine gunboats and support ships. Many of them were firing their weapons into the west bank, a bank chock-full of smoking and exploding structures. The APL-55 anchored three hundred meters from the abandoned PBR base. River Section 521 PBRs, gunships, artillery, and guns from the Co Chien PBR support LST were blasting away at undeterminable targets near the abandoned base. Green tracers were reaching up from the ground toward the gunships. The Mobile Riverine Force had a RAG (river assault group) on the scene. Forty or so landing craft were milling around on the Co Chien River as their commanders decided where to mount an amphibious assault. It was chaos, something I did not want to be involved in except as a spectator.

At any moment I expected Ron Wolin or Bill Earner to seek me out for some new mission. The 534th leadership had been busy on the radios for the last few hours planning, coordinating, reacting. The other available 534th river rats and I were merely pawns waiting to be moved.

I got the word that I would not be needed that night. I was to take boats out early the next morning to embark some South Vietnamese troops on a counteroffensive move. That was fine with me. I could relax in the wardroom for a couple of hours and get a full night's sleep before reentering the war.

My two hours in the wardroom that night seemed surreal. I played poker with Ron Wolin and a mixed bag of strangers—refugees from Vinh Long for the most part—while all hell was taking place a half mile or so away. Some of the poker players were Navy support officers from the abandoned PBR base. They pissed and moaned that the base had been holding its own, the PBRs all safe out on the river, but the senior U.S. Army guy in town had ordered the base evacuated three days before. Another player was a civilian in charge of the local CORDS program—a civil development program under the State Department. The guy let out that he was a former Green Beret major who had taken a leave of absence from the military to do "civil development work." That was his story. I figured he was probably doing a lot of good work with the local populace. He did seem concerned about the welfare of his resettlement camp, which had been abandoned, and the fate of his Vietnamese employees. I also figured him to be a spook (CIA agent).

As we played poker the APL's 81mm mortars fired above our heads. After folding a hand early I went topside to watch the show. Spooky was at work again around the perimeter of the airfield a mile and a half away and there was lots of ground tracer fire being exchanged within the town. In spite of having a good run of the cards, I decided to get a solid night's sleep. I went back to the wardroom and cashed in my chips.

My personal involvement in the war would come back as sure as the sun rose. I slept well. A steward's mate had to shake me awake at around 0500 the next morning.

I took the 7-12 (boat commander QM1 Fred Engle) and 7-19 (boat commander GM2 James Briggs) boats out just before dawn. As we got under way, Engle and his crew described what had happened at the outpost on the Ham Luong after I left the previous evening. The 534th PBRs had performed a miracle. They had saved every Ruff Puff (Regional Forces this time—guys with some proper military training) who had been pinned down at the ambush except for one KIA (killed in action) left behind. Only a few of the exhausted survivors were wounded. Nearly one hundred friendly survivors with three American enlisted advisers were transported by PBRs back to their base/villages near the Ham Luong district town of Tien Thuy, up the Soc Sai Canal three miles from the outpost. One of these American advisers told Engle that without the PBRs, he and all the troops pinned down at that tree line would have been killed.

Engle was not a demonstrative, exuberant boat captain in the mold of Tony Summerlin or James Shadoan. Those guys would have described the incident with much more colorful language. Engle was a white version of Irvine Burney. I made a mental note to have Bill Earner document the heroic achievement of the 534th sailors. I knew that RD1 Robert Wenzel, the 534th patrol officer who organized the rescue mission, couldn't care less about combat awards and recognition. All the combat was probably a major irritant to him; it was costing him money. But the big guy had pulled off a miracle. It had to be recognized.

We tied up at the designated landing site along the Vinh Long waterfront, where we were to pick up some ARVNs from the South Vietnamese 9th Division. The waterfront was covered in mist and smoke. Gunfire and bombs could be seen and heard less than a mile from the scene. The ARVNs were hanging around the quay wall, many more than I expected—about fifty of them. They might have looked spiffy in their new uniforms with their new M-16 rifles and M-79 grenade launchers if they'd had any military bearing. To me they looked like a disorganized mob of teenagers made to dress up for some sort of play war. The NCOs wore bright yellow or orange scarves around their necks and were shouting things to the grunts in the singsong Vietnamese language, but the troops were ignoring them. They wanted only to hunker down on their haunches and put their fingers in their ears to silence the loud explosions coming from nearby.

I got off the boat and sought out the American liaison officer. Wearing the bars of captain, U.S. Army, he was in a heated discussion with his counterpart, a little Viet wearing the pips of an ARVN major. I interrupted their conversation by touching the captain's arm.

"Captain, I'm Goldsmith from River Section 534. We are your transport. Get the troops organized in a single file and get them aboard the PBRs starting with this one first. My sailors will show them where to settle." I pointed to Engle's 7-12 boat.

It took over an hour for the Viet troops to get organized and properly positioned on the two PBRs. Even though the little guys on average weighed slightly over a hundred pounds, their equipment and numbers weighed down the two PBRs. It took minutes to build up to a maximum speed of less than fifteen knots. Our mission was to secure the My Thuan ferry landing on the My Tho River, an important road juncture and river town overrun by the Viet Cong.

It took another hour to reach the objective, which was slightly west of the Co Chien/My Tho River junction on the south bank of the My Tho. It took nearly an hour more for the South Vietnamese commander and his adviser to agree on a plan of action. The little town and the big boat landing were still standing. Not a soul was in sight, just some VC flags fluttering in the breeze from the balconies and roofs of the buildings lining the main street leading from the ferryboat landing. Through my binoculars I saw about twenty armed men four hundred meters away from the town going from the road across a rice paddy. They were headed for dense foliage at the mouth of the Co Chien River a half mile away. They were ripe for picking. The American adviser agreed. His counterpart did not. So instead of having one boatload of troopers land at the ferryboat landing to rush into the town and take these guys under fire while the other boatload went back to the Co Chien to intercept them, leaving a PBR freed up from troop-carrying to blast the enemy's escape route with 60mm mortar and 40mm grenade fire, nothing was done.

After the last of the enemy escaped into the foliage, the South Vietnamese commander told his adviser to tell me to have my boats blast the town. The adviser told me to fire a couple of belts of M-60 rounds and 40mm grenades into the buildings nearest the boat landing.

"Shoot at the tops of the buildings. Create some damage. This is all for show anyway. These guys are green recruits from the cities. They don't know shit about soldiering. Let them have a show before they get off the boats."

The two PBRs fired a couple hundred rounds of M-60 and twenty or so grenades into the top of the building closest to the ferryboat terminus and stopped after half a minute. Ten minutes later the South Vietnamese commander finally gave the order to land the troops. We did. And for another whole hour our PBRs milled around the ferry landing as the ARVNs secured the town—by looting it. When they returned for pickup at the ferryboat landing they were weighted down with radios, stereos, sewing machines, boxes of clothing, everything imaginable. Some little troopers were even carrying stuffed animal toys. They were a disgrace. Claiming that the boats could not take on the heavy load, I made the soldiers leave their loot behind. Somehow my arguments prevailed. The South Vietnamese looters took only stuff that could be concealed in the pockets of their uniforms.

A couple of hours later I was back on the APL-55. I got some chow along with the news that my patrol (the 7-12 and 7-19 boats) could relax for a few hours. Vinh Long was being secured. The Mobile Riverine Force's embarked 2d Brigade of the 9th Division had retaken the PBR base and virtually all the city. The U.S. Army and U.S. Navy had done their job. The APL-55 was going back to the My Tho/Ham Luong river junction. Ron Wolin told me I would be going out in a few hours to relieve boats that had been sent back to Ben Tre while my boats participated in the combat charade at My Thuan. The battle for Ben Tre was still undecided. Ron also told me that our CORDS/Green Beret/Army major/civilian poker player from last night's game was dead, killed in an ambush as he drove a truck to his refugee camp with cumshawed medical supplies and blankets taken from the APL-55. That news did little for my morale. I attempted to get some sleep in the bunk room and tried to make some sense out of this strange war. I decided I just wanted to survive.

At 1900 later that day my patrol sped down the Ham Luong to relieve Pete Richards's patrol at the mouth of the Ben Tre River. A mile before we reached the Ben Tre, we saw a large, suspicious sampan at a creek/river junction just north of the ferry landing. A man on the sampan was dumping heavy bundles into the river. The 7-12 boat raced to the bank. The man lifted the last bundle from his sampan onto the riverbank and started running just as we reached it. GM3 Wayne Murray jumped from his forward twin fifty mount with M-16 in hand. He was determined to kill or capture the guy. I ran to the bow but Murray was off and running. I ordered him back in my most commanding voice. I shot my M-16 over his head. I was primarily concerned with his welfare. The feisty gunner who grew up on the streets of New York City finally, and reluctantly, came back to the boat. He was pissed.

Murray had recognized before me that the bundles were bodies. When Murray finally came back to the boat, I examined those bodies on the riverbank. Twelve of them. All stinking, bloated, one bound by wire at the wrists. All blackened, one of them showing massive disfiguration of his head or what remained of it. I could not determine whether the cadavers were Vietnamese or American, white or black, until I recognized the octofoil insignia on their uniforms. These were 9th Division soldiers, probably nineteen- or twenty-year-old draftees just out of high school, every one the son of some mother praying for him. Maybe they had been captured and executed. Maybe they had been hit with "friendly" fire. Maybe the old guy dumping the bodies had tortured and executed them after they were wounded and captured. Maybe he was just some old guy cleaning up his property after a battle. I still have no clue as to what had happened to those soldiers.

I did what I regarded as necessary at the time: I left those remains on the riverbank to be washed out with the next high tide. I had no desire to preserve the scarred remains of American warriors fallen on a foreign shore. I would make a report. That was it. There was a war going on. I had to take care of the living. Much later, when night after night on TV I saw the trauma of uncertainty on the faces of mothers of Americans missing in action, I had some regrets. Perhaps I should have lashed all those cadavers together and asked for a Mike boat from the APL-55 to come down and haul them back to a mortuary. But, at the time, those bodies were just waste, no better than the bodies of Vietnamese we saw floating down the river. I also thought that they might be recovered in the morning. A couple of days later, when the survivors of Ben Tre really got into removing the detritus of war from their town, my perspective was reinforced. Hundreds, perhaps thousands, of bloated corpses clogged the river. If some of those stinking cadavers stayed near our boats at slack water when the boats had to cover some little area, we blasted them with gunfire to release the putrid gases so the waste would sink. Men, women, children, friend or foe. All were equal in death. Those still alive did not concern themselves with the dead. Unless, of course, the dead was one of our own—meaning, in our case, some other river rat. We would do and did do everything to recover the remains of our own. It's the same old story of war—comradeship, unit pride, and going to extraordinary lengths to recover your mates, but to hell with all the rest.

Less than an hour after leaving the bodies on the bank, the 7-12 and 7-19 boats got into another firefight at the mouth of the Ben Tre. Again we had to take a prisoner up the river to the police station. Again rocket fire and automatic weapons were used against us. Again we were lucky. The rockets were fired from behind us after we had dropped off the prisoner and built up speed. They missed by twenty yards. At first I thought the explosion was artillery fire because it was unusual for B-40 rockets to be so far off the mark, but the MACV compound claimed no artillery was being fired in the area. Once we were out in the Ham Luong, a couple of gunners claimed that they had seen rockets being fired from the rubble of the little fort that had briefly displayed that big VC flag four days earlier. By then that whole area of riverbank was just chaotic heaps of scorched earth. This time we had Seawolf gunships on call. They came within minutes to escort us back up the Ben Tre on a firing run. My plan was to go only a couple of hundred meters up the river and then use our M-60 guns at a safe angle and distance to spot where the gunships should put their rockets. No way was I going to let enemy rocketeers get a clean shot at us.

I was amazed at what happened when the Seawolves made their first firing run. The Cong gunners were really tough and crafty, concealing themselves in bomb craters and withstanding the rocket and machine gun fire of the helos until the gunships were passing them overhead. Then they rose and opened up. At least three streams of green tracers lashed out at the gunships. Belt-fed guns, not just ordinary AK-47s. The return fire was too much for the Seawolves. They banked and turned to the maximum limits. One gunship came out to the Ham Luong with its flex guns firing indiscriminately. The bullets hit within twenty feet of my boat. Several others and I immediately had our weapons aimed at the gunship in self-defense.

Another two seconds of indiscriminate fire would have seen a Seawolf getting shot down by PBR machine guns.

The Seawolf pilot made an apology.

"Pineapple Bowl Charlie, Seawolf 49. Sorry 'bout stuck guns. Hope nobody got hurt."

"Seawolf 49. Pineapple Bowl Charlie. Nobody hurt down here. Get those guns fixed. We just about shot you down."

"Roger that, Pineapple Bowl Charlie. Glad to hear no damage. Returning to base. Out."

The result was that the U.S. Navy was run out of the mouth of the Ben Tre once again. I did not blame the Navy pilots for not continuing the fight. No friendlies were in extremis. The pilots had no clear targets. One ship had gun problems. And they were probably a little gun-shy after nearly a week of round-the-clock emergency fire missions. And that one was certainly no emergency mission. After the Seawolves left the area my boats settled down on the Ham Luong to blast the VC firing positions from a distance. Slow harassing fire just to keep the gooks on their toes. They had no shots at us, but maybe we could hurt them with enfilade fire from our guns.

Less than five minutes after the Seawolves retired I heard an unfamiliar callsign on the MACV net. Some Army outfit wanting to get involved. I answered them on the radio. It was a pair of Army Cobra gunships from Can Tho. They were over the My Tho River flying east. I gave them my coordinates. Kien Hoa Province was off their charts. They wanted directions to the fight. I guided them just as dusk was settling.

"Gunslinger 5, this is Pineapple Bowl Charlie. Take the big fork in the river going south about twelve klicks before Dong Tam. We are thirty klicks down that fork. Two-boat units in the mouth of a smaller river to the east. You will see a lot of smoke. Stay over the main river until you see us. Over."

"Roger, Pineapple Bowl Charlie. Gunslinger 5 will be there shortly. Out."

A few minutes later two sleek Cobra gunships came speeding down the Ham Luong at only a hundred feet. They buzzed our boats at a speed that seemed twice as fast as that of the old Seawolf Hueys. This was the first time I had ever seen Cobras. The twenty-year-old warrant officer pilots (I am assuming their age because most really were that young, if not even a year younger) were hotdogging their ships around and seemed ready for a fight. I told them to expect one. Again our PBRs went up the Ben Tre, stopped, and spotted fire for helicopters. This time the first gunship was clear of his rocket firing pass over the enemy holes before the enemy could react. When the VC gunners did get up to fire they had no clear targets and fired blindly into the air. They became the targets. Unlike the Seawolves, which carried door gunners firing M-60s from the sides when passing parallel to enemy positions, the Cobras could direct their fire using swiveling, chin-mounted, rapid-fire 40mm grenade launchers or 20mm cannons while flying past the enemy. All it took was one more pass for the Army guys to suppress the enemy fire. Those young pilots whooped and hollered to us on the radio as they saw the effect of each other's fire. They really enjoyed their job. The difference between the Navy and Army gunships that evening was more than aircraft performance. The Navy pilots were more experienced—they realized how easily they could be killed. Navy pilots were primarily in their late twenties or early thirties, perhaps with wives and children. They rationed their heroic efforts to missions when they really counted. Those young Army pilots seemed to thrive on danger, perhaps because they had little to worry about except the task at hand. I hope those two Army aircrews survived Vietnam.

Chapter 13

The next day, February 6, 1968, marked the end of the battle for Ben Tre. The 9th Division completed the task of rooting out the die-hard snipers and sappers on the north bank. South Vietnamese Ruff Puffs had followed the 9th Infantry across the Ben Tre bridge by the hundreds, sifted through the rubble of the south bank, and eliminated any organized Viet Cong resistance there. Vietnamese civilians who had fled the fighting returned home, many finding only piles of smoldering rubble. They wanted to rebuild. But first they had to clear out the bodies.

A contingent of correspondents arrived by Army Caribou to the Ben Tre airfield on the morning of February 7. They were not the only visitors. Navy and Army brass from Saigon and Binh Thuy also arrived to tour the scene. Ben Tre was perhaps the most hotly contested fight in a provincial capital during that first week of Tet in the entire Mekong Delta. It was a clearcut American/South Vietnamese victory of arms if one considers the order of battle of the opposing forces and who was left standing. Lt. Col. John Dare, United States Army, Kien Hoa Province senior adviser, wanted to tell the story of the heroic defense of the town. Captain Paul Gray, United States Navy, probably just wanted to add to his personal glory. Peter Arnett, the young but seasoned New Zealand war correspondent for the Associated Press, had an agenda also. He wanted to get his byline on the front page of *The New York Times*. A difficult task considering the competition from all the press covering the continuing intense fighting and heavy casualties the United States Marines were experiencing at Hue and Khe Sanh.

Arnett needed a hook for his story. Simple pictures of huddled, frightened refugees amidst a backdrop of the ruins of what had been a beautiful river town would not be enough for a lead story. Major Chester Brown, United States Air Force, provided Arnett with his hook. Arnett had met Chet Brown several weeks earlier when Arnett had traveled to Ben Tre to do a story about rural development projects undertaken by the MACV advisers in the Delta. This day Arnett sought out Major Brown and asked for a tour. Chet Brown was glad to oblige. He took Arnett for a jeep ride of what was left of the town. Chet Brown probably described all the fighting that had gone on the first two days when it was touch and go, and how the PBR sailors and Navy Seawolf airedales were the only things preventing the MACV compound from being overrun. He probably described how he had to dodge sniper fire just to get to his little spotter plane on numerous occasions. He probably described how the 9th Division troopers landed in hot landing zones as dozens of F-100 jets were pounding hundreds of enemy nearby. He probably described how two entire Viet Cong battalions were routed by airpower and infantry. Arnett probably told Chet Brown that he was amazed at the level of destruction he was witnessing. That is when Chet Brown probably said, *"It was determined that it was necessary to destroy the town in order to save it."* Arnett's attention was naturally drawn to that declaration. He carefully penciled the exact words in his little reporter's notebook. Arnett had his hook.

A lot of river rats from the 531st and 534th went up the river that day. Some carried reporters. Some carried Navy brass from Binh Thuy. GMSN Marty Vice, forward gunner on Tony Summerlin's 7-15 boat, was at the wheel of the PBR as Tony talked to the reporters. Marty's toughest job that day was trying not to run over the corpses floating in the river. There were just too many of them for him to miss them all. Jack Harrell, as the senior American Navy man at Ben Tre, got to escort Capt. Paul Gray in a convoy of three 531st boats that went down the Ben Tre and up the Ambush Alley stretch of the Ham Luong. Captain Gray wanted to be exposed to enemy fire. I guess he felt he needed more glory in order to get his admiral's stars. He got part of his wish. A sniper cut loose with half a magazine from his AK-47 from the east bank of

Ambush Alley. The three PBRs silenced the enemy fire. Captain Gray got to fire one round from an M-79 grenade launcher.

Jack Harrell's toughest job that day was to politely refuse a request from one of Gray's assistants to write up the esteemed captain for a Bronze Star after the boats came back to the MACV compound. The sniper fire was a nonevent as far as Jack and the 531 river rats were concerned. Captain Gray, who supposedly had won a Navy Cross while flying A-1Es (skyraiders) during the Korean War, lost a lot more brown-water navy respect that day.

The next day Arnett's story covered most of the second page of *The New York Times*. The catchphrase—"the town was destroyed in order to save the town [sic]"—was picked up by television anchors and antiwar politicians all over the world. It helped make Peter Arnett famous and the town of Ben Tre infamous. Saigon command was furious. Six officers from General Westmoreland's staff were dispatched to Ben Tre to determine the identity of the unnamed American major who gave Arnett the famous quote. Three American majors were at the MACV compound when Arnett was there—two Army majors and Chet Brown of the Air Force. All were suspect. All were grilled. No one fessed up to the quote. Arnett was challenged by United States embassy personnel that if he would not name the source of the quote, then he (Arnett) must have made it up himself. To his credit Arnett never attributed the quote to Major Brown by name. Chet Brown went on to make lieutenant colonel in the Air Force before he retired. I believe he is still living. His experiences of combat flying in three wars—from B-17s over Nazi Europe to L-19s over the rice paddies of the Mekong Delta—would have to be a great read. I know that Chet Brown's war stories have to be a lot more interesting than mine.

After February 7, River Section 534 went back to the routine of two standard two-boat patrols along the twenty miles of the Ham Luong. We had twelve- to fourteen-hour patrols followed by eight to ten hours of rest instead of the nearly twenty hours on the river followed by four hours of rest that had become the norm during the previous week. The beer barge resumed business as usual. Wenzel's craps table thrived.

The nightly wardroom poker game returned. Major towns in the eastern Delta had been secured.

But it was a different kind of normal patrolling than we had done before Tet. Practically every day for the next three weeks our PBRs were called on to support a Ruff Puff sweep or to provide fire support to little South Vietnamese forts harassed by enemy fire at night. It was hard to tell who was being more aggressive, the South Vietnamese during the day or the Viet Cong at night. They were definitely trading blows. If it was not the Ruff Puffs it was the Mobile Riverine Force (CTF-117) that we supported. That great circus wagon of amphibious boats, slow armored gunboats, artillery barges, and thousands of sailors and 9th Division grunts came down the Ham Luong a couple of times. The PBRs' job was to chase down all sampans that were flushed out and attempting to evade the massive firepower and infantry assaults that took place along the Ham Luong's Mo Cay District or at the southern end of Tan Tan Island. Our support mission caused us to get involved in numerous little fights. Enemy movement at night on the river increased. We racked up a lot of confirmed kills and captured sampans. This was definitely not a period of routine sampan searches.

Of all the many scrapes that the 534th experienced during that period, I remember most of all three incidents that occurred while supporting the Ruff Puffs in the Ham Luong and Truc Giang districts. The first occurred at 0500 in the morning of February 12, 1968. I took the 7-16 and 7-17 boats up the Soc Sai Canal (a twenty-meter-wide channel off the eastern bank of the Ham Luong halfway between the Ben Tre River and the My Tho River) to investigate what was taking place at the riverfront market a half mile from the district town compound. That was done at the request of the district advisers in the Ham Luong compound, who had lost touch with the little outpost behind the marketplace. The adviser offered Ruff Puff guides from a large outpost on the main river. I agreed, but only after I confirmed that a Seawolf fire team was on call.

I had been up that little tributary only a couple of times and sure did not remember any outpost at the boat landing—just a couple of one-story, wood-and-stucco stores. We picked up a couple of Ruff Puffs from the outpost where Wenzel had saved the Regional Force company. The two little guys seemed game. They had a PRC-25 radio and M-2 (automatic) carbines. One even spoke a little English. Somehow he communicated to me that he believed that eight Popular Force irregulars had been driven from their outpost fifty meters inland and were hiding by the boat landing. So that was our mission. We were to tie up at the little boat landing and evacuate eight friendlies evading a superior force of Viet Cong—at night with absolutely no room to maneuver. I decided to call on the Seawolves. Before we entered the little river, I got the boats together and explained the mission to all the sailors. The 7-16 boat (TM1 Malcolm Fullam, boat captain) and the two South Viets would approach the boat landing with me while QM1 Radford's 7-17 boat covered us. We would call out to the friendlies and give them thirty seconds to come forward. If we received fire, the only weapons to be fired were M-79s, M-16s, and the M-60s. We would clear the area as soon as possible and leave the eight friendlies on the beach if we did not see them coming to us. I had seen what those fifties could do to the district town, and we had a hundred or so friendlies only a half mile away and directly in line with the marketplace. I also knew that if we stayed and slugged it out with even only a squad of Viet Cong in that narrow channel, we were extremely vulnerable. I radioed my intentions to the Seawolf fire team that arrived just as we entered the little tributary. I told them if we got into a fight to not use rockets and to only fire their machine guns where our M-79 rounds were impacting, unless they received heavy ground fire. We were ready. I even let the little Viet trooper who spoke some English practice speaking into the battery-powered megaphone we carried.

We cruised silently up to the rickety, barely distinguishable, bamboo boat landing. There were no lights, no sounds. I could barely hear the gunships overhead. I handed the power megaphone to the little Viet and we both stood up on the starboard engine cover. It was show time for the Vietnamese to shout to his comrades to come forth and be recognized.

The South Vietnamese soldier spoke only a few words before three or four automatic weapons opened up from the marketplace ten yards away. No tracers, just some flashes of light and loud cracks. Very loud cracks. The bullets were directed at the source of the amplified sound of the Viet soldier's voice—right in front of me. The Vietnamese man knocked me over as he jumped sideways to get out of the line of fire. By the time I got to my feet Fullam had slammed the starboard throttle full ahead, the port throttle in full reverse, and had the wheel turned all the way to the stops to port. The gunners on boat 7-17 were firing their small arms into the marketplace. I fired three M-79 rounds as we cleared the area and the Seawolves blasted the area with their machine guns. It was all over within seconds. The boats raced out of the small river.

I radioed what had happened to the advisers in the nearby district compound, figuring it was a failed mission. The remains of the men from the abandoned guard post would be discovered in the morning, perhaps after booby traps or sniper fire maimed a lot of friendlies. Another little victory for the stealthy Viet Cong. I was wrong. The next day I got some great news. The fire from the PBRs and gunships had driven off the squad of enemy. The eight friendlies from the outpost had been hiding in the bushes on the riverbank. They all survived and gave credit to the PBRs and Seawolves for saving their lives.

A week later (February 19), once again I had the 7-16 and 7-17 boats on a routine patrol. This time it was a day-patrol. At 1045 we were in the crossing area of Tan Tan Island looking for trouble when trouble once again came to us over the radio from the Ham Luong district advisers. The Ruff Puffs from an eight-man lookout tower on the east side of Ham Luong needed PBRs to insert them back into their village two hundred meters south of their little watchtower. The Viet Cong had occupied their village and had come to the watchtower and demanded them to surrender or their families would be killed. The Ruff Puffs' reply was to go on their radio and ask for urgent assistance. They specifically asked for PBRs. As luck would have it our boats were only a half mile away. I guess the Ruff Puffs had seen us nearby. We got to the outpost within two minutes. The eight Ruff Puffs, all clothed in black pajamas, barefoot, and carrying heavy World War II–era M-1 semiautomatic rifles or M-2 carbines, were waiting for us on the bank. Two of them had pineapple grenades nestled in grenade launcher baskets protruding from the muzzles of their rifles. I had seen such rigs in World War II film footage of big, burly GIs attempting to take out sniper positions with rifle grenades during the Battle of the Bulge. That day the extra-long rifles seemed out of place. I was amazed that the little one-hundred-pound fighters were actually going to storm Viet Cong with those heavy, awkward weapons. But they were the only weapons the little guys had to rescue their families.

The Ruff Puffs had something else going for them that day besides grit. They had the firepower of two American PBRs, which must have given them some confidence. The fact that their families were in the hands of the enemy made them determined.

We took the Ruff Puffs aboard the 7-16 boat. They crouched down on the bow under the forward fifties. The boats went downriver hugging the bank. We did not have far to go. When I saw the landing site approaching I saw a lot of things that I had not noticed over the previous months. This stretch of the riverbank was laced with small hidden streams that snaked into the nipa palm underbrush. I glimpsed villages up every stream. The landing site was a cleared little cove surrounded by tall coconut palms. Thatched huts and beached sampans indicated a typical large Vietnamese fishing village. No one was in sight.

As soon as the bow touched the bank, half of the South Vietnamese home guard soldiers were off the boat. Three leaped to the bank and started running forward with their heavy weapons pointed forward. Before the others cleared the boat all hell broke loose. Grenade explosions ripped the tops of the palm trees. Bullets whizzed over the boats. The PBR gunners opened up. Fullam pulled the throttles into reverse. The other four Ruff Puffs jumped off the boat as it was backing off. They ran straight forward firing their weapons as our bullets passed over their heads and enemy grenades exploded in the trees. I thought they were racing to their deaths. When the 7-16 boat was twenty yards off the bank the after gunner let loose a belt of M-79 grenades from the Honeywell over the heads of the Ruff Puffs, who continued to run forward apparently unscathed by the enemy fire.

It was over an hour before we learned the fate of those Ruff

Puffs who stormed that bank under enemy fire in the finest tradition of professional assault troops, like the U.S. Marines at Tarawa. They had killed seven Viet Cong, suffered only one wounded, and had, most important, saved their families from death. I was dumbfounded. I had expected every last one of those guys to killed. That mission was certainly one of the most satisfying jobs I ever accomplished in my lifetime.

What was the difference between the heroics of those part-time soldiers and the disgraceful behavior of the regular South Vietnamese 9th ARVN Division troopers at the My Thuan ferry landing? It simply boiled down to the fact that the Ruff Puffs were motivated because the lives of their families depended on them. They did the impossible on pure emotion.

On February 27, I had a patrol on the Ham Luong, a half mile upriver from the watchtower manned by the intrepid Ruff Puffs. Our job was to capture Viet Cong suspects trying to evade a Regional Force sweep down to the river from positions near the Ben Tre airfield. A typical operation of the time. See some young males attempting to get out on the main river by sampan from a safe distance of half a mile or so. Let the guys get well into the river, radio the advisers to call off friendly artillery fire, and race like hell to cut the suspects off. See weapons blast the sampan out of the water. Usually we just got some very meek draft-age guys with no *can couics* who were happy to be turned over to American sailors rather than subjected to the combat nerves of South Vietnamese Regional Force troops operating miles from their homes under constant threat from booby traps, snipers, and ambushes. That day we did not flush out any suspicious characters. We did get to pick up a Viet Cong suspect captured by the Ruff Puffs when they reached the Ham Luong and called my patrol over to pick up him up. I was on QM1 Howard Stevens's 7-21 boat. We made for the bank, where an American sergeant adviser had called us over. There was one suspect in custody. A seventeen- or eighteen-year-old, naked except for black shorts. Tall for a Vietnamese. Had the build of a champion swimmer—narrow waist with a wide, muscular chest, and not an ounce of fat. He had thick, black shaggy hair and a clenched jaw. His hands were bound behind his back with a nylon manacle.

I jumped off the bow of the boat near where the prisoner was being held by a young American Army sergeant adviser. The sergeant introduced himself and gave me some advice.

"Lieutenant, be careful with this sumbitch. We had to pull him out of a hole. Hasn't said jack shit or opened his mouth."

The forward gunner helped me get the surly young prisoner up on the bow of the boat. I had my left hand on the boy's shoulder and gently pushed him forward along the port gunwale for the trip back to the stern. In my right hand I carried an M-16. Just as he cleared the coxswain's flat with some pressure on his left shoulder, I indicated to him to drop down on the port engine cover. He spun around ninety degrees, opened his mouth wide, and kicked himself off the gunwale, disappearing into the muddy ten-foot depths. I fired a full magazine into the water where he had jumped. The boat commander reversed engines and the boat circled the spot. We dropped a couple of concussion grenades into the water. The grenades brought up some stunned fish but no Viet Cong prisoner.

I had briefly met one hard-core Viet Cong up close and personal. A teenage boy who had a full life ahead of him if he had chosen to go to the POW stockades. He had been captured without a weapon. He could have lied about his association with the enemy. He might even have been eligible for easy time in a Chieu Hoi resettlement camp. After a few months he could have made the choice to switch sides or be sent to a major POW camp, where he would still be fed, clothed, and treated well. Much better than what we knew was in store for river rats if they were captured. We had received recent intelligence reports about a PBR gunner from the Mỹ Tho boats who had been blown off his boat by rocket blasts and captured. He was dragged from village to village. At each village he lost another extremity. He was just a torso at the end of his exhibition. That is why I still carried an M-26 grenade in the right pocket of my fatigues while on patrol.

Maybe the Viet Cong was worried about a similar fate being dealt him. I doubt it. I believe the guy was determined to display the ultimate defiance to the American barbarians. His gesture depressed me.

One of our most notable little victories on the river during that period occurred at 1815 on February 19, the day the Ruff Puffs stormed into their own village. Ron Wolin had just relieved me on patrol. It had been a long day for me and I had purposely taken the boats closer to the APL-55 by the 1800 time we were to be relieved. There was nothing to pass on to Ron, and his two-boat patrol simply cruised at slow speed in the dark shadows a hundred meters off the west bank as the boats made their way down the Ham Luong. After a few miles or so, the boats would reach Tan Tan Island. It was not appropriate to be that close to that spider-hole-infested riverbank. Evidently some Viet Cong on the east bank had seen my patrol departing at high speed to the north but did not detect the 7-20 and 7-21 boats of Ron's patrol as they cruised in the shadows of the trees on the western bank thirty minutes later. Three twin-engine sampans started a mad dash across the river from the east bank only a few hundred yards downstream from the PBRs coming down the river. The Viet Cong hot rod sampans were headed for the Cai Cam.

Ron's patrol with QM1 Milliken and QM1 Stevens as boat commanders intercepted the sampans just as they started to enter a creek south of the Cai Cam. The boats opened up with all weapons, and the Viet Cong abandoned the sampans and scrambled to the bank. One sampan disintegrated in a large secondary explosion. After pouring thousands of bullets into the area of nipa palms where the sampans had sought refuge, the boats closed in. Near the burning sampan were ten other sampans besides the two that had not exploded. They were camouflaged with brush. Some were filled with rice and supplies. Most had two engines. A couple were over twenty-five feet long. The PBR sailors began to retrieve the sampans one by one using grapple-hooked lines. Eight sampans were pulled off the bank before the boats were taken under fire from concealed positions ten meters into the nipa. The PBRs silenced the enemy fire and destroyed the remaining four sampans with their fifties. There were no friendly casualties or known enemy casualties.

Once safely out into the wide Ham Luong, the sailors examined their booty. The big prize was a twenty-eight-foot sampan with twin five-horsepower engines at the stern. The sampan was full of black and khaki Viet Cong uniforms, entrenching tools, and documents. Included in the uniforms was some sort of dress Viet Cong black pajama-style uniform complete with bright brass buttons. Looked like the equivalent of Navy Service Dress blues. The documents included Viet Cong certificates of training completion, the Viet Cong equivalent of Navy "A" School certifications. One was to a nineteen-year-old female.

The sampans captured or destroyed that evening could transport a whole company of Viet Cong across the river. It was a big loss for the Viet Cong in the area. Ron Wolin was so proud of the twenty-eight-footer that he had Lt. John Smith patch up the bullet holes, paint the sampan brown-water green, erect a canvas awning amidships, and fabricate mounts for M-60 machine guns. It became known as the 534th's command sampan. It was used against the enemy at night in clandestine insertions and during the day as a utility craft for Ron and the constant stream of visitors. It even made the front page of the *Jackstaff* and got some great recognition for 534 sailors.

The last two weeks of February had the river rats finally going back on liberty to Ben Tre and My Tho. Mostly to My Tho because the two-mile trip up the narrow Ben Tre had too many bad memories. The guys went on liberty for different reasons than before. No longer were they interested only in getting drunk or visiting some whorehouse. They had a curiosity about what had happened to friends and familiar landmarks. The sailors came back with all sorts of tales of the action at My Tho. The Victory Hotel, our former billet, had been subject to heavy fire. SEALs and PBR sailors had to defend their living quarters at night and fight their way down to the boats during the day. Some favorite restaurants had been reduced to ashes. Bodies of dead Viet Cong were left on the streets, sprinkled with lime dust to reduce the stench, and pounded into the pavement by every South Vietnamese military vehicle passing through. This macabre scene lasted for days. I decided to pass up post-Tet My Tho. I visited the MACV compound at Ben Tre and the Ham Luong district advisory compound instead. I wanted to meet the guys we had supported and go over the recent battles with them. At both compounds PBR sailors were treated as heroes. I naturally welcomed the attitudes of the advisers.

I did not like walking the half mile from the boat landing to the Ham Luong district compound. The narrow path between the boat landing/marketplace had to be swept for mines and booby traps each morning. The Army advisers seemed nonchalant even as they pointed out a recently marked trip wire to a buried grenade that was awaiting destruction. I remarked to a young sergeant that I was sure glad I had not gone infantry. The sergeant laughed and said that being on a little plastic boat on the river for twelve hours each day was his idea of being a sitting duck in a shooting gallery, and that he would take the job of an infantryman over my job any day. We both laughed.

For me, night patrols during that period were devoted to attempting new (to me at least) methods of catching Charlie napping. I realized that the enemy was a creature of habit. He would use the same old crossing areas. There were three areas along Tan Tan Island and a couple near the choke points of Ambush Alley that seemed to be favorites. I would have one boat with engines off lashed to the other boat running with unsynchronized engines. The boat with engines off would then be cast adrift near a crossing area. A sea anchor (a big, weighted canvas bag) would be silently cast over the side of the drifting boat while the other boat cleared the area. The theory was that the sea anchor would keep the boat from drifting with the river current.

One morning at around 0300 I was on a drifting PBR less than a hundred meters from the abandoned fish stakes where I had captured the rice-laden sampan months earlier. Using the "534th command sampan," 534th sailors had recently caught enemy sampans in that fishing hole. I tried my luck again in the familiar area.

I was lucky that morning, but in a way I never expected.

I was curled up on the deck in the coxswain's flat, near the radios and beside the alert boat captain or whoever was on watch at the controls of the drifting PBR. Suddenly bright flashes of light entered my closed eyelids. A split second later there were two tremendous claps of thunder. Then the concussion hit.

The whole boat was lifted off the water. I was bounced around inside the coxswain's flat. The guy at the controls of the boat lit off the engines and got the boat out into the middle of the river. Everyone on the boat was shaken. Nobody knew what had happened. Enemy mines? Friendly artillery? A few days later I discovered the truth. I described the incident, which did not even rate an official report (no casualties, no enemy contact, etc.) to Jack Harrell when I went back to the Ben Tre MACV compound.

Jack let me in on one of the latest American "secret weapons."

"Jawja boy, you were the near victim of friendly bombs from the United States Air Force. They got this thing they call 'sky spots.' An F-4 with a couple of five-hundred pounders will be guided by a new ground radar system to a point in the sky and will release the bombs from over five thousand feet to hit within ten yards of the intended target. That night you and the Air Force had the same target. You were lucky the system worked. Another fifty meters east, those two bombs would have blown your boat to bits." Jack was grinning as he slapped me on the shoulder. He was obviously proud of F-4s, pilots, and American technology. Once a fighter jockey, always an airedale! Jack Harrell was more amused than I was about what had nearly happened to me.

I got a lot more satisfaction out of what I regarded as "mini B-52 strikes." A deal of my very own design.

The idea came to me when I fiddled with a new toy we had received a couple of weeks before—Starlight night observation devices (NODs). The little night scopes were intended to be mounted on M-16 or M-14 rifles so grunts could get off shots against enemies sneaking up on them out in the field at night.

When we first got them, the river rats thought the things were worthless. We would use them as handheld monoculars to view battle scenes at night when gunships, flares, artillery explosions, and burning huts made the devices useless. Once exposed to bright light, the greenish image in the scope simply blanked out. Our Raytheon Pathfinder radars could detect sampans on the river better than the Starlight because they covered 360 degrees. The scopes were best for spotting people on land not lit up by flares and tracers. The problem was that most of the riverbank was thick foliage. Still, I spent some time scoping out familiar crossing areas on Tan Tan Island, attempting to see some Viet Cong sneaking a sampan out into the river. Maybe thirty minutes a night for several nights.

One early morning I was looking at the area where Ron Wolin had captured all those sampans. I saw little orbs of light perhaps twenty meters from the bank. They seemed to be strung out in a loose line formation. Without the Starlight scope there was only blackness to be seen. Using a red-lensed flashlight I checked the chart taped to the armor inside the coxswain's flat. Sure enough there was a ten-foot-wide stream in the area where I saw the lights. By then I realized that the lights were probably little candles or lit cigarettes on sampans. I got the after gunner to prepare a forty-eight-round belt for the Honeywell. I took one last look in the night scope and cranked out all forty-eight rounds into the area. To anybody on sampans in that area, the rapid rain of exploding grenades in the branches over their heads must have seemed like a miniature B-52 strike. I did this little stunt several times over the next few weeks before the Viet Cong figured what was happening and did not burn candles in their hiding holes.

Ever the big mouth, I would get on our standard PBR patrol FM radio frequency (which I assumed the enemy monitored) and announce, "Good morning Viet Cong on Tan Tan Island. That wake-up call is courtesy of Pineapple Bowl Charlie!" Later I would regret making those little announcements.

Chapter 14

The first five days of March saw only four combat actions by RivSect 534 sailors. One involved heavy fire from the bank of the Cai Mon River as PBRs 7-20 and 7-21 exited the river with a wounded Ruff Puff. One sailor was slightly wounded. The other three combat actions were suppression of sniper fire from the banks of the Ham Luong. At 1300 on March 5, PBRs 7-16 (TM1 Fullam) and 7-17 (QM1 Evans) with BMC Raymond as patrol officer took a cruise down the Ham Luong past the Mo Cay Canal. Through cuts between the mid-channel islands they spotted an armada of fifty or sixty sampans strung out for a half mile on the eastern bank of Ambush Alley. Chief Raymond did the smart thing. He positioned the boats close to a channel cut and called for artillery support. While waiting for Major Brown and his little L-19 spotter plane to arrive, the 7-16 boat fired its 60mm mortar into the concentration of sampans from a safe distance of three hundred yards. Chet Brown arrived on the scene within minutes and directed the mortar fire until the last of the rounds was shot. Then the heavy guns from the Ben Tre soccer field blasted the area. Results were unknown. If Ron Wolin or Robert Wenzel had been the patrol officer, the results could have been a lot different. They would probably have taken the two PBRs down Ambush Alley on firing runs and the PBRs would probably have racked up a lot of confirmed sampan kills, but they would also have suffered heavy friendly casualties under the sustained fire of what could have been hundreds of regular Viet Cong fighters in the narrow confines of Ambush Alley, a stretch of water that had earned its name.

The evening of March 6, just after dark, GM2 Briggs's 7-19 boat ran down an enemy sampan attempting to reach Tan

Tan Island. Ten occupants jumped from the sampan as the PBR bullets began to hit it. Five Viet Cong were confirmed killed, another five possibly killed. Six uniforms and a quantity of Russian-manufactured small-arms ammunition were captured. We had no friendly casualties.

The next day I had a day-patrol on the upper Ham Luong, and RD1 Robert Wenzel had two boats on the lower patrol area. I had not been involved in combat for a week, and only one sailor had been wounded during that time. Our luck was holding, and the level of enemy activity seemed to have decreased. I looked forward to a pleasant day of cruising up and down the river looking for VC suspects on sampans.

Less than an hour into the patrol, Wenzel radioed to me that he was taking a VC suspect to the Ben Tre police station. For some reason I took my two boats downriver at high speed to get to the Ben Tre River. I just had a feeling. Perhaps it was the fact that Wenzel never radioed his intentions. Perhaps it was because I felt that the Ben Tre was still a mighty dangerous place. When my patrol approached the junction of the Ham Luong and Ben Tre, the radio blared out screams of distress. I recognized the booming voice of BM1 Tony Summerlin.

"Foxtrot 1 hit by a rocket! We got wounded and are heading back to the Ham Luong! Somebody call a dustoff!"

Looking up the Ben Tre River, I saw two PBRs racing toward me. They were firing their guns into the south bank. Déjà vu all over again. I remembered the boat carrying the prostrate Frank Walker down that same stretch of water. I called for the dustoff and gave the coordinates of a half acre of island just south of the Ben Tre River. Not a great helicopter landing site, but a close one that could be secured. I radioed Summerlin to follow my boat, the 7-21, to the little island. My two boats got between the island and the east bank of the Ham Luong a hundred meters away. I did not want any Viet Cong to feel bold enough to creep out to the bank and shoot down a hovering medevac helicopter. Summerlin's 7-15 PBR landed on the island less than a minute later. I had QM1 Stevens back up the 7-21 boat to the 7-15 boat so I could assess the situation of the wounded.

What I saw was both poignant and dramatic. Wenzel was

flat on the port engine cover, screaming and cursing, while
Tony Summerlin pressed a large, bloody battle dressing on his
right thigh. The engine covers and stern were covered with
fresh blood. I went to the back of the boat, where three sailors
were kneeling over the body of the after gunner, EN3 David
Webb. I pushed aside GMSN Martin Vice, who was attempting to administer mouth-to-mouth resuscitation to Webb;
Vice's efforts were causing blood to squirt from the ears of the
wounded man.

When I saw Webb I was horrified but pragmatic. I jumped
up and got on the radio to confirm that the evacuation site was
secure and tossed out a red smoke grenade. Then I went back
to help Tony Summerlin with Wenzel's wounds. Webb was a
lost cause. A B-40 rocket had hit the breech of his .50-caliber
after gun. He was barely alive, a smoking, bloody, rag doll.
One eye had been blown out of his head and his hands were
just bloody, blackened stumps. His flak jacket was shredded.
So was his chest. His groin had been split up the middle. The
three other sailors were doing their best to bring the boy back
to life. I just wanted to make sure Wenzel survived. I ripped
open another large battle dressing and took off my belt. I gave
Summerlin the battle dressing and prepared to wrap my belt
around the dressing as a tourniquet. When Summerlin momentarily released his hand pressure on the older bandage,
Wenzel's blood squirted three feet into the air, spraying Summerlin and me. We somehow got the other bandage over the
massive inner thigh wound and secured both bandages with
my belt just as the medevac helicopter arrived.

The Army pilots and medics were a professional team. The
skids of the chopper had barely touched the muddy bank
when two men with a stretcher ran over to the boat. They
agreed with me that Wenzel was the priority. Summerlin and I
helped the medics carry Wenzel to the open side door of the
helicopter. Meanwhile the other gunners on the boat continued to try to will life back into their buddy Webb. After Wenzel was strapped down in the helicopter, the crew came back
for Webb.

Within fifteen minutes both wounded sailors were operated
on at the Dong Tam Field Hospital. Webb lived for nearly an
hour. Wenzel was given plasma and the leg artery was patched

up. He went to a better-equipped hospital in Saigon before being medevacked out of country. He spent months in the Pensacola Naval Hospital before being medically discharged as totally disabled.

Only after the helicopter had taken off did I realize that Summerlin and SN E. L. Strait, the M-60 gunner, had shrapnel wounds. Those guys barely realized that they had been wounded themselves. Strait had been concerned only about his friend Dave Webb. Summerlin wanted to make sure Wenzel stayed alive in order to settle up some gambling debt. Evidently Wenzel owed Tony a lot of money. I understood the different perspectives. Summerlin and Wenzel were regarded as big and mean, old-salt, drinking and gambling buddies by the young gunners. Those two guys ruled a roost largely populated by young gunners who had little combat experience. But to those three gunners attempting to revive Webb, he was one of them; his mortality was their mortality. Webb was the first 534th sailor killed in action.

The next day Pete Richards and I inventoried Webb's personal effects. Pete cleaned out Webb's locker while I cleaned out Wenzel's. We were both touched. Pete was surprised to learn that Webb was married and twenty-four years old. We both thought the guy was nineteen or so, a typical, good-natured, innocent young kid right out of high school. Webb in fact was a three-year Air Force veteran who had married a Japanese girl while stationed in Japan. He had shipped her home to his parents in Florida and then enlisted in the brown-water navy in order to save up money to start a new family. All his money had been sent home to his bride. Wenzel's locker contained all sorts of gambling equipment, several hundred dollars in cash, three checkbooks with balances totaling over twelve thousand dollars (the equivalent of over fifty thousand in today's money), and some pictures of his young Vietnamese mistress. I let Bill Earner decide what to ship home to Wenzel's parents in Alabama.

It was during this period that a new but experienced poker player joined the wardroom. Gerald Dooher, Lieutenant USNR, MC (Medical Corps). "Doc" Dooher to the rest of us. Doc was a radiologist from Denver. He took over the recently supplied and refurbished medical facilities on the APL-55. He

had two operating theaters, a recovery room, a bunch of supplies, and three medical corpsmen to assist him. He was fresh
meat from the States, just out of his residency, when he was
shipped to the Mekong Delta to be the jack of all medical
trades on the APL-55 to pay back Uncle Sam for footing the
bills for his training. He soon became very bored so Lt. Mel
Shantz turned over operation of the beer barge to Doc. Doc
rigged up some piped-in music and made plans for spending
the beer profits in fruitful ways. But most of all he cleaned out
the wallets of other officer poker players in the nightly games
in the wardroom. Doc's very irreverent sense of humor was a
refreshing addition to the wardroom. When all the other officers seemed to dwell on the war, he would tell us ribald stories
drawn from his medical experiences. Jerry Dooher never ran
out of funny stories.

The war continued. We got to see Father McCoy again at
the memorial mass for Webb. At an awards ceremony on the
upper deck of the APL-55 a few days later, Ron Wolin got his
Silver Star and first Purple Heart. I and a bunch of others got
lesser awards for our actions during first few days of Tet. We
were all proud.

There were more incursions by river assault groups
(RAGs) from CTF-117 along the Ham Luong. A RAG went
up the Ben Tre River to assault Viet Cong positions on the Ba
Lai River. Pete Richards got his chance to run the Chet Say as
the Mobile Riverine Force and grunts from the 9th Division
entered the enemy Ba Lai redoubt. Pete remembers being on
QM1 Milliken's boat and taking off his helmet to rub his hot
head while transiting the Chet Say while all hell was going
down on the nearby Ba Lai River. His hair came out in
clumps, a sure sign of major stress. While looking at a handful of hair in his hand he heard the sound of approaching jet
fighters. He looked up to see two afterburning F-4s scream
overhead, then pull up into an almost vertical climb as the familiar voice of Maj. Chet Brown, flying his little L-19 at an
altitude of fifty feet, announced over the radio, "The United
States Air Force proudly salutes the river rats of the United
States Navy!"

Pete Richards completed the transit of the Chet Say with

only a few hundred rounds of enemy small arms and one rocket being fired on his two-boat patrol.

I continued to avoid enemy fire during the month. I did, however, have some memorable experiences. One night I took it upon myself to clear a boat engine's water pump that was clogged by debris. The pump would just spin with a high-pitched sound and spurt out a little water, a fairly routine occurrence, especially during the rainy season when the river was full of flotsam. Usually the problem was a branch or twig snagged around the impellers. The procedure was to secure the engine, lift the engine cover, unfasten the top housing of the pump cover, reach into the pump housing, and pull out whatever was clogging the pump. That particular night it consisted of one big, nicked-up, angry water viper. I grabbed the snake in the middle as soon as I reached my right hand into the pump. Somehow I flung the twisting snake over the side of the boat before it could strike me. That was the last time I cleared a pump at night. My experience was not unique. A lot of other river rats had to pull live vipers out of pump housings during the Vietnam War.

I witnessed a big combined arms attack by Navy Mobile Riverine boats, U.S. Army grunts, and old South Vietnamese AD prop-driven fighter-bombers up the Mo Cay Canal. A lot of medevac helicopters landed to take off wounded sailors and soldiers. Seventeen friendly KIA. That's when GM1 Ned Caldwell related his bad experiences up that canal with the SEAL platoon to me, an action that was never reported in the River Section 534 logs because getting conned by SEALs into taking on a "dumb" mission that turned into a fiasco had embarrassed the sailors.

In the middle of one late-March day, I was on patrol in the upper Ham Luong. Absolutely nothing going on. The sailors were eating their C rations and the boats were drifting when we saw a fifty-ton Navy YFR steaming around the bend in the wide river. It was belching smoke from its deck and sailors aboard the little supply ship were frantically dumping smoldering cases of ammunition over the side as our boats raced to it. We pulled alongside the low stern of the little ship. A couple of sailors and I went aboard and helped the ship's crew dump pallets of smoking M-79 ammunition into the river. It turned out that the supply ship had taken a 75mm recoilless round into its deckload of ammunition. Fortunately those cases of ammo just burned instead of exploding. There was no after-action report, just some thanks from the civilian (a retired Navy chief quartermaster) boat commander and another little memory for me.

At 0645 on March 20, 1968, BM1 "Boats" Shadoan and the 7-17 boat were headed full speed back to the APL-55 for breakfast after being relieved from a night patrol. In the early morning mist Shadoan saw a large sampan crossing from the north bank. Shadoan steered for the sampan, hoping that it would turn back so he would not have to bother searching it. Instead, someone on the sampan fired a rifle at the 7-17 boat. A dumb-ass Viet Cong. In the uneven fight that followed, the 7-17 boat killed five Viet Cong and captured ten others, four females and six males. Six of the ten were wounded. In the captured sampan were uniforms, grenades, and one M-2 carbine. The 7-17's breakfast was delayed for an hour as the crew transported the captured Viet Cong, naked on the PBR's bow, back to Ben Tre.

I had a night-patrol with the 7-13 and 7-14 (Burney and Caldwell) boats on March 28. The boats we relieved (7-20 and 7-21) had received a hundred fifty or so rounds of automatic weapons fire from Tan Tan Island a couple of hours before we relieved them. I decided to concentrate our night's effort around that old familiar crossing corridor just south of the Cai Cam, near where the relieved boats had received the enemy fire. I hoped to be able to do my little trick with the Starlight scope and a belt of grenades from the Honeywell. There was no joy that night. Just long hours of drifting, conducting muffled radio transmissions when I repositioned the boats, and searching in vain for little lights deep in the foliage of Tan Tan Island.

Shortly before dawn I took the two boats downriver to help QM1 Carl Evans's two-boat patrol with the extraction of a SEAL platoon just south of the Mo Cay Canal. Radio traffic indicated that the SEAL Team 2 unit from My Tho had made enemy contact and needed PBRs to go up a tributary and help them. When my boats arrived on the scene, Evans's two boats were out on the main channel with the SEALs, loaded down with captured supplies. A Viet Cong defector had led the SEALs to an arms cache. The result was a fierce little battle in which the SEALs had prevailed and uncovered a bonanza. The booty was transferred to the LCVP that a couple of hours earlier had transported the SEALs to Evans's PBRs before inserting near the suspected enemy arms depot. My boats stayed around as dawn broke and the SEALs continued to go back ashore for gear that had been left ashore near the extraction site. At about 0730 the LCVP was heavy with SEALs and booty. The captured materiel included machine guns, recoilless rifles, automatic weapons, mines, and cases of Chinese-manufactured small-arms ammunition. It was the largest haul of enemy supplies that I would ever see. A major accomplishment for the SEALs.

Lieutenant John Smith arrived late that morning to relieve my patrol. Very late. The exchange took place past 0830—two hours later than normal. The first extended hour had been interesting, what with all the materiel being brought back to the LCVP. The second extended hour was just a hungry pain in the tired ass.

There had been some sort of mechanical casualty to one of the boats. I was not in a good mood. I made some sort of sarcastic comment to Smitty as Engle's 7-12 boat came alongside the 7-13 boat I was on, something like, "If we had a decent maintenance crew, boats could get relieved on time." John Smith was, of course, the 534th maintenance officer. He was not amused by my crack. He had probably busted his butt for a couple of hours repairing a stuck throttle, water gate assembly, or whatever had prevented one of his boats from getting under way earlier. Smitty looked me in the eye, spat, and saltily replied, "Some stupid smart aleck of a pissant junior officer like you, Goldie, probably fucked up the controls yesterday and did not have the balls to report it. Somebody has to make things right."

I was properly chastised by a dedicated twenty-year regular, a mustang (commissioned from the enlisted ranks) Navy lieutenant whose billet did not call for him to go on combat patrols. Smitty was an all-Navy professional doing much more than was required. I reminded myself of the story Smitty had related at a wardroom dinner table a couple of weeks before, just after he returned from a week's emergency leave to attend the funeral of his father. An Air Force MP at Tan Son Nhut Airport had told him he could not board a commercial airliner in his green utility uniform. (Smitty, like me and a lot of others, had lost his Class A uniforms on the YRBM-16.) Smitty told us that he had grabbed the throat of the MP and told him, "All the fucking MPs in Saigon can't keep me off that plane taking me to bury my father." My dressing-down by Smitty paled in comparison to what that young MP must have experienced.

That day would be Smitty's last patrol and his last day in Vietnam.

Seven hours later I was getting ready to go back out on a night-patrol. I went up to the NOC to get the intel brief and learned that Smitty's patrol and the two-boat patrol of Jerry Letcher were just getting ready to run the Cai Cam River. Engle's 7-12 boat was also carrying our new river division chief, Lt. Cmdr. Harlan Cust, on only his third combat patrol. There was no Seawolf cover and the boats would be transiting from the south, evidently something cooked up by Wolin and Cust on the spur of the moment. A very dangerous run. I decided to delay early chow to listen to the radios in the comm center. A cryptic "checkpoint tango" from Smitty indicated that the first boat was under the bamboo footbridge. Another five minutes and the boats would be out safely on the Ham Luong if they traveled at twenty knots.

Four and a half minutes later Engle's voice came screaming from the radio speakers along with the background sounds of rapid machine gun fire.

"Pineapple Bowl. This is Pineapple Bowl Sierra. Taking fire from east bank. Pineapple Bowl Sierra shot. We need a dustoff!" No over or out.

The comm center technicians tried to get confirmation, clarification, coordinates. That was their job. I grabbed a mike and switched to the emergency channel monitored by the dustoff evacuation helicopters at Dong Tam. I radioed that at least one American wounded required immediate evacuation and gave them the coordinates of a small, uninhabited mid-river island four hundred meters north of the Cai Cam. The voice at the other end acknowledged my words and said that the helo would be there as soon as possible. Then I recognized the voice of Jerry Letcher on the RivSect 534 net. He said that all boats were now out of the Cai Cam. I grabbed another mike and told Jerry that a dustoff was on the way to such and such coordinates. Then I ran down to get my two boats under way as soon as possible.

I got to see the evacuation helicopter lifting off. Two boats were still up on the bank and two boats were out into the river. My boat beached alongside Engle's 7-12 boat. Jerry Letcher was tending to Lieutenant Commander Cust, who was dazed but not injured. He had had the traumatic experience of being knocked down by John Smith's body as a high-velocity round had hit Smitty under the rib cage and knocked him off his feet. It was the first time I had seen the young river division commander. He was sweating and shaking. Jerry was wiping his sweaty brow and lifting a cup of water to his lips. I asked Engle what had happened.

"There were two short bursts from an AK-47. Maybe four or five shots. The shooter must have popped up from a spider hole. Near where I took that rocket back in December. Nobody saw a thing."

I picked up John Smith's flak jacket. No big splatters of blood. Just a little hole in the front just right of the zipper, and a little spot of blood in the back surrounding the rifle round that had penetrated the back of the flak jacket only halfway. I pulled the bullet out with my fingers, an AK-47 round. It appeared to be unscratched, a good indication that it had not hit a bone. Perhaps Smitty was lucky with no vital organs damaged and his spine unscathed. I certainly was looking forward to giving him that souvenir from the back of his flak jacket when he returned to duty.

Chapter 15

April 1968 was certainly a memorable month for me. A month of violence, bad memories, good memories, triumphs, and tragedies. Martin Luther King got killed. Tense and tender moments among the troops. I almost participated in a murder. I almost got killed another couple of times. Old friends were rejoined. Party times. The River Section 534 lost the first MK II PBR in combat.The month a record number of Purple Hearts were established for RivSect 534. One of the Purple Hearts was mine.

The month started routinely. More sniper attacks, more sampans sunk with unknown casualties. More Ruff Puff sweeps to cover.

On April 2, I took two boats into the east bank of the Ham Luong just a mile north of the ferryboat landing to see what the Ruff Puffs might flush out onto the river. It was about 1000 in the morning. This time the Ruff Puffs had artillery support. The river rats on my patrol stayed well clear of the bank as air bursts hit the tops of the coconut palms ten meters inland. Through my binoculars I spotted two figures coming to the water's edge and huddling down in the bushes. I radioed the Kien Hoa MACV tactical operations center that two suspects could be apprehended by the unit if the artillery fire was lifted. The MACV TOC came back with the word that the artillery fire had stopped. My two boats raced into the bank. The two men in black shorts and black shirts attempted to make themselves invisible as we closed on them. A couple of rifle bursts over their heads got their attention. A gunner got off the boat and, with his shotgun, persuaded the men to climb aboard. One was a teenager. The other was older, perhaps the father. I searched the pockets of the scrawny younger one. In one pocket of his shorts I retrieved a five-round stripper-clip of ammunition for a communist SKS rifle. I shoved it into his face, thinking: Caught in the act you little sucker! Evidently the older man had the same idea. He spit into the face of the young man and attempted to strike him. The gunner with the shotgun pushed the old man down on the deck. That's when an artillery burst hit the treetops less than thirty meters away. A chunk of steel flew by my face and hit the port engine muffler at the boat's stern. The boat captain rammed the throttles in full reverse before the next round hit the treetops. I reached down and attempted to pick up the thumb-size piece of shrapnel. The red-hot, razor-edged chunk of metal blistered *and* cut my fingers. I was pissed. I wanted to strike out at whoever had fired that artillery round that could have easily taken out an eye or killed me. Instead I struck the young Viet Cong in the face with my fist. The only time I ever laid a hand on a prisoner. I got on the radio and told the MACV TOC that a PBR was almost hit by artillery. A few minutes later we secured the prisoners with nylon manacles and the Ruff Puffs came to the bank. I could also see a couple of American soldiers on the bank, waving at my boat. I wanted to give them a piece of my mind. The PBR closed the riverbank and I walked to the bow. Before I could say a word, a young, sweating American sergeant assisted me from the boat with a few words. "Lieutenant, *xin loi* [Vietnamese for 'sorry'] 'bout those rounds. We got a new radioman back at our battery." I forgot my anger and shook the hand of the grinning soldier. The sergeant said that the two prisoners were part of a small group of Viet Cong part-timers manning a propaganda booth outside a nearby village.

"There must be a few more of them hiding nearby. You can take these two birds back to the police station. My troops will search for their buddies and weapons after we destroy their little booth."

Less than two minutes later both young American advisers were killed by grenade booby traps as they attempted to pull down the bamboo booth and its VC flag. I saw the smoke and heard the muffled blasts. Their bodies were carried back to the Ben Tre airfield by the Ruff Puffs. Another incident that never made the monthly summary but is permanently engraved in my memory.

For me, April 6, 1968, was basically a quiet day on patrol in Area 2. A couple of sweeps down Ambush Alley with everyone at general quarters followed by a couple of hours of searching sampans, water taxis, and junks headed to Ben Tre from the south. The boats on patrol in Area 1 got into a fight and killed one Viet Cong who was evading a Ruff Puff sweep. My boats did not even test-fire their weapons. It was just another hot, sticky, long day on the river until late in the afternoon.

The memorable happening was not due to any action on the river. The boat captain (a seasoned veteran whose name will not be mentioned here) was listening to his little AM transistor radio in the coxswain's flat as we buttoned up and made ready for another run past the Mo Cay Canal before running Ambush Alley. I was pulling a drink of ice water from the five-gallon insulated jug beside the small-arms locker and had just picked up my flak jacket as some sort of newsbreaking announcement came over the little radio. I did not hear the radio report but I sure remember the next words from that boat commander.

"Hip, hip, hooray! That black nigger Martin Luther Coon has been killed!"

I was dumbfounded. GMSN Willie Brown, a slight, nineteen-year-old African American, was the forward gunner. He reacted immediately to that obscene exclamation as he would to enemy fire from the bank. Willie jacked rounds into his fifties and swung the mount around as fast as he could. Fortunately the stops built into the gun mount held. I rushed forward to keep Willie from grabbing the M-16 he kept at his feet. By the time I reached him he was a sobbing little boy and not the fraternal killer he well could have been.

I spent the next half hour alternating between crying with Willie Brown and getting that boat commander to make apologies to him. The boat captain was distraught himself after he realized what his words had done. He was the type of guy who would have sacrificed his life for Willie Brown if need be. PBR crews were that bound together. Now, the boat captain did not know how to approach his young gunner. I suggested to him that he could begin by cutting down the Confederate battle flag flying under the national ensign from the jackstaff over the awning. He did that and then went over and hugged Willie Brown. While the two of them, one a quiet young black seaman from inner-city Baltimore, the other a tough, profane, white, first class petty officer from hardscrabble rural Mississippi, cried and consoled themselves, I took the boats back to base. I was still shaking when I made the landing.

Bill Earner received my report and immediately transferred Willie Brown to Briggs's 7-19 boat. He also gave the boat captain a personal counseling session. That day was the last day any flag or emblem besides the American flag ever flew from the jackstaff of a River Section 534 PBR. Only Old Glory, with no other pennant beneath it. Several state flags, one from New York, joined the Confederate battle flag and a Jolly Roger skull-and-crossbones emblem as missing in action. No one ever bitched. The word had gone out. Everyone knew it was the proper action at the time.

That night on the beer barge there were some restrained sailors. Most were listening to the radio news piped in from the comm center. There was no rock 'n' roll music over the speakers that night. All the news concerned the assassination of Martin Luther King. Several others and I paid little attention to the radio speakers. We ordered round after round of beer for our little tables. The junior officers from PBR classes 35 and 36 back in the "summer of love" were having a joyful reunion.

River Section 535 had come to share our home. The ten-boat section with all its personnel had made the eighty-mile transit (only thirty-five by air) from its former base at Binh Thuy on the Bassac River. The ever-boisterous John Smock led the 535th guys in describing their adventures. Pete Richards and I matched his stories one for one with our exploits of the 534th. The 534th saved Ben Tre. The 535th saved Chou Doc. After a while we shared stories we could *all* relate to. For my part, I told how the 535th's Lt. (j.g.) Richard (Rich) Sloane, my roommate at Vallejo, had saved my life in San Francisco's Haight Ashbury district the weekend before we shipped out. A good story.

"While Rich and I were seeing what the Haight Ashbury scene was about, I had replied to the solicitation for some spare change from a scruffy, barefoot, thirteen-year-old girl with something like, 'Little girl, here's a dime to call your momma to get you out of here!' The little hippie was not amused with my words. She immediately spit in my face, clawed at my eyes, and cursed me like a sailor, yelling for assistance at the same time. A whole bunch of scurvy street people came to help her. That's when Rich, the streetwise New Yorker from Queens, upended the little girl with a swift kick and we beat feet back to our rental car."

After I finished my little story, Rich Sloane sucked up the dregs of a beer and said, "Goldie speaks the truth, but he sure don't know when to keep his mouth shut. He's one Georgia boy who would not last long in the big city, but I still like him."

John Smock then went on to relate the farewell salute and benediction given to Capt. Paul Gray at Binh Thuy the previous day by Father McCoy. It seemed that the game warden commander had suddenly been relieved of his command with no ceremony other than the padre's middle finger salute to his departing helicopter. Father McCoy was conducting a memorial mass when the helicopter rose from the nearby landing pad. Without breaking a beat the padre had gone from making the sign of the cross to waving the familiar vulgar hand sign to the helicopter as it flew overhead. It took a lot of restraint for the sailors commemorating a departed river rat not to start cheering. (Captain Gray had not been the beloved, courageous commander that Don Sheppard [the Bassac Interdictor] fictionalized in his book, *Riverine: The Story of a Brown-Water Sailor in the Delta*, 1967.)

Much later we would discover the truth about the "silver eagle's" summary departure from Vietnam. On March 28, 1968, Gray had grandstanded a little too much. He wanted to show a visiting dignitary what a PBR firefight looked like from a safe altitude in a helicopter. He had ordered a PBR from Binh Thuy to run a bunker-lined complex off the Ti Ti Canal, a dangerous, heavily contested waterway. A fierce one-sided firefight did take place. Unfortunately, a U.S. Army Green Beret captain hitchhiker on the first boat got killed and a river rat gunner received a life-threatening, permanently disabling head wound. The visiting dignitary aboard that admin helicopter was Rear Adm. J. V. Smith, newly appointed Commander of Amphibious Forces, Pacific (COMPHIBPAC), the command that owned all the brown-water assets and was responsible for training all brown-water sailors. Admiral Smith was the son of Maj. Gen. Holland M. "Howlin' Mad" Smith, USMC, the legendary, tough Marine commander of the grunt Marines at Iwo Jima. John Victor, a pretty tough guy himself, was definitely not amused by the result of Captain Gray's orchestrated PBR action. Gray was relieved of command and shipped out of Vietnam as soon as possible. Poor guy never got his admiral's stars and his name is conspicuously absent from most histories of Vietnam's brown-water navy. His relief, Capt. (later Rear Admiral) Arthur Price, went on to be a well-respected brown-water hero, usually described as the epitome of what a river rat commander should be and, in his case, definitely was. Art Price was several cuts above his predecessor in everything except bullshit.

Early on the evening of April 14, I had a two-boat night in Area 2. Just as dusk settled, I took PBRs 7-15 and 7-18 down to the Mo Cay Canal area for our second sweep to the end of our patrol area before running Ambush Alley on the return trip. A good time and place for the enemy to cross a sampan or two. Sure enough, we apprehended a little eighteen-footer landing on a mid-channel island. It had come out into the main river after curfew and I took no chances. Both boats went to general quarters. There were two people aboard the little sampan, an old man and an old woman. They saw us coming and took no evasive action. The sampan had only one 2.5-horsepower engine and there were no weapons or supplies aboard, just a little AWOL bag with an Air France logo on the plastic sides. I figured that the bag contained clothing. I had seen the old man before. He was wrinkled and sported a Ho Chi Minh mustache and goatee. He seemed very friendly and started talking immediately as Tony Summerlin put the bow of the 7-15 boat up against the stern of the little sampan. With gestures and some French words the old man indicated that the engine had stopped and that he just wanted to get back to the west bank of the river. Another chance for PBR river rats to aid some poor peasants in need. Something we did often.

But I had to go through the formality of searching that little flight bag. When I asked/indicated to the old man to hand over the bag, the old lady covered it with her body and started babbling in unintelligible Vietnamese. Tony Summerlin ordered the M-60 gunner to go aboard the sampan and retrieve the bag. The gunner had to pull the old lady off the bag, which he handed to me as he was assisted back aboard the PBR. The bag was heavy. I set it down, sat myself down on the port engine cover, and unzipped the zipper. The bag was stuffed with cash. Fifty or so bundles of Vietnamese bank notes in large denominations—1,000 dong, 5,000 dong, and even 10,000 dong. I had never before seen a 10,000-dong note. The Vietnamese dong, commonly referred to as the piaster (the old French word for the Viet unit of currency), was probably officially worth around 110 dong to the dollar, maybe 220 dong to the dollar on the black market. Whatever, our find was big-time money. Also included in the bag were some little slips of paper. I recognized them as Viet Cong tax receipts.

"Holy shit! We just captured the Viet Cong's payroll!" I was excited.

I dumped the entire bag of bill bundles on the deck behind the coxswain's flat for the other sailors to see. The sailors gawked and shot forth a lot of expletives, usually preceded by the word "fucking."

That's when the sailors starting talking and dreaming. I'm sure a lot of them had heard or read about sailors sharing captured war booty. The exuberant young sailors passed around the bundles of notes before I re-collected them. The guys on the 7-18 cover boat fifty meters away wanted to know what was happening. I radioed back that we had captured two VC and a lot of documents. I ordered Tony Summerlin to get the two old folks aboard the PBR, secure them with nylon manacles, and lash a line to the sampan. No more runs up Ambush Alley for us that night. We went back to the Ben Tre/Ham Luong river junction. By that time the sun was down and I did not want to risk taking a towed sampan up the Ben Tre River to hand over the suspects.

My college accounting major came into play. I wanted an accurate accounting of the cash. It took me nearly an hour to count and recount the bills in the illumination of a red-lensed flashlight. My count was 790,000 dong—more than a year's pay for an average sailor, after taxes, at the official exchange rate. I then spent a half hour shackling up a coded message to the Kien Hoa MACV compound. The message was for Jack Harrell to meet my boat at the ferry landing at 0700 to pick up important suspects. After the message was acknowledged, I relaxed on the deck with the stuffed Air France flight bag as a pillow. I believed that we could dog the rest of the night. We had already accomplished a better achievement than most night-patrols.

Unfortunately, the night did not turn out to be as restful as I had desired. Sailors kept coming up to me with one proposition after another. They began with, "Mr. Goldsmith, you can take one third, and the crew will share equally in the remainder."

I got involved in the little game (at least I thought it was a game, much like the RivSect 522 sailors and I had enjoyed when Bill Larsen was on his "ambush" position months earlier). I deflected the first proposition with a mildly believable supposition.

"Hell, the old guy might be some friendly village chief who collected money to go to Saigon and buy materials for some orphanage. He might even be President Diem's uncle. Let MACV intel sort him out in the morning. They are expecting him to be turned over in the morning."

The sailors conferred among themselves for a few minutes. They wanted to know about the message I had sent out to the MACV TOC. I truthfully replied with the gist of the short message. The sailors conferred again before approaching me. This time they said that they had a perfect solution.

A young gunner, who probably went on to become a successful lawyer, made their case. "Mister Goldsmith, these suspects probably came out of the Mo Cay right after our first sweep after curfew. They have no identification. Anybody coming out of that canal after curfew has to be Viet Cong. They are terrorists. They've got Cong documents. You told us that. We should eliminate them and the sampan. An hour later it would have been dark, and we would have wasted them as a matter of course. You can tell Ben Tre that they jumped over the side. You don't even have to see what happens, and you get 50 percent of the money."

Tony Summerlin, who seemed to enjoy what was taking

place from his boat commander's perch in the coxswain's flat, finally got involved. He asked some hard questions, as if the deal had been accepted. "Who's gonna be the guy who kills these two dinks? He deserves more than an equal share. And how we gonna make sure the bodies don't get washed up on the bank and get identified as obviously murdered? How do we know that the dinks are not some big-time secret South Vietnamese agents? Somebody gonna have to slit their throats and open up their guts to make sure they sink, and I sure don't want any VC blood stinking up the deck of my boat."

That caused the crew to reflect a little, giving me enough time to move the bound couple forward beside the coxswain's flat where I could stay within touching distance. I spent the rest of the night clutching the Air France bag in my lap either in the boat commander's seat or the seat beside it. There were no catnaps for me that night.

In the morning the couple was turned over to Jack Harrell. I never found out what happened to them or what became of their money. Just to confuse some of the young sailors whose bitches about me being soft on Viet Cong had started to circulate back to my ears, I planted a rumor that the old man was a friendly village chief who had collected the money from his hamlets to go to Saigon to purchase a tractor to replace water buffaloes killed by PBR sailors the previous month. That rumor was credible; a young gunner's mate, already reduced from GMSN (gunner's mate seaman) to SA (seaman apprentice) for insubordination, had killed a couple of water buffaloes in March because he had the power of two .50-caliber Browning machine guns, he was in a bad mood, and the animals were close to the riverbank. That young bad-apple of a sailor received his due. He was brought up on charges, shipped out of Vietnam, and discharged from the Navy under less-than-honorable conditions—the only River Section 534th sailor to receive such punishment. I hoped that my little disinformation about the Viet Cong suspects coupled with the sailors' knowledge of the shitcanned gunner would make 534th crewmen a little more respectful of VC suspects with or without property.

For me, the next two weeks consisted of hot, boring days and nights on the river interspersed with good times on the beer barge and at the wardroom poker table; others were involved in some hairy combat. A couple of the actions called for Seawolf support, and one called for fixed-wing aircraft support. John Smock's war diary indicates that the 535th section was more involved in combat during that period than the 534th. The 534th's monthly summaries show only the boats involved. Burney's boat, Shadoan's boat, Engle's boat, Caldwell's boat. Nobody was killed or wounded. I had gone for weeks without being shot at or called upon to rescue Ruff Puffs. All the action the past few days seemed to involve the Ruff Puffs, who were doing daily battle with Viet Cong on the My Tho River side of Kien Hoa near the Chet Say Canal. I could see that from all the radio traffic I monitored when times were slow.

I must have been getting bored when I took a newly assigned patrol officer, Lt. (j.g.) Ken Kaiser, down Ambush Alley on his third orientation patrol. Ken was fresh from the States. Jerry Letcher and Chief Raymond had taken the new guy out on one night- and one day-patrol in Area 1. I was to take him for a day-patrol in Area 2. After that Ken would be fully qualified to take out a two-boat patrol for River Section 534. I figured that a couple of daylight runs down Ambush Alley would be the best way for Ken to see what he was going to experience in the months ahead. I had long since given up doing consecutive daylight runs down Ambush Alley. On the first run we might or might not draw enemy fire. On the second run we would probably receive fire from concealed bunkers. Our boats could control that stretch of river by staying in the main channel to the west, shielded from direct fire by the low, uninhabited islands. From a safe distance, we could spot sampans in Ambush Alley by radar or visually. That old chief from the 531st had given me good advice back in October. I had passed it on to the new guys. Still, I wanted Ken Kaiser to get used to enemy fire. The time had come.

The run down Ambush Alley started from the north. Usually our PBRs made the Ambush Alley run from the east after first scouting out the area with a south trip down the Ham Luong past the Mo Cay in the main channel. I decided to be different that day. Just another attempt to break up any discernible pattern observed by the Viet Cong from their holes and bunkers. A mile downriver we took some fire. I was on the lead boat, QM1 Engle's 7-19 boat. A couple of AKs were fired in three-round bursts that came very close to my boat. The boats quickly outran the enemy fire. We fired only a few hundred rounds in return. That had just been harassment fire, no rockets, no recoilless rifles, no belt-fed machine guns, no hundred meters of dug-in enemy gunners. I turned the boats around. Since I had a good fix on the enemy's firing position, I told the gunners to fire at my rounds as I put down my M-79 grenade launcher and picked up an M-16 loaded with twenty rounds of tracers. I radioed GM2 Briggs's boat (carrying Ken Kaiser) to direct its fire to where Engle's gunners were firing. The result was the usual overwhelming fire from six machine guns and two rapid-fire grenade launchers directed against a small patch of riverbank by speeding, bouncing boats. Bullets going short and skipping off the water were adjusted to hit the bank, and grenades were hitting all around. With all the bullet splashes, I could not determine if we were receiving return fire. Within seconds the boats had cleared the area. I hoped that our concentrated fire had put the fear of God into those two or three snipers but I felt that our fire had not harmed them. They were probably well protected. Still, a big .50-caliber HEIT bullet might come close to their heads. Shrapnel from a 40mm grenade burst might penetrate their firing slit, close enough that they might start firing blindly and waste precious VC ammo the next time they shot at a PBR.

After the boats were four hundred meters upriver from the enemy's firing position, they slowed down to look for battle damage and check or replenish the ammo trays. That's when Briggs radioed that he had some men slightly wounded. I immediately led the boats to a wide area of the Ham Luong. I was concerned about what "slightly" wounded really meant; guys could be seriously wounded and not recognize the extent of their wounds because of shock.

When I got aboard the 7-12 boat, I found out that the wounds were indeed superficial. Two rounds of enemy small-caliber fire had impacted on the ceramic armor, one on the side of the coxswain's flat and one on the splinter shield of the starboard M-60 position. The armor had caused the AK-47 rounds to disintegrate and spray small bits of copper and lead all around. Three guys had been hit. GM2 Briggs had small splinters in his right arm. The M-60 gunner had some in his right leg. Ken Kaiser, the most seriously wounded, had a bleeding butt. I took it upon myself to examine and treat his wounds while Briggs and the M-60 gunner treated themselves. Ken was a hefty guy. His ample right buttock had been penetrated by a half-dozen little splinters. I used my pen knife to scrape out the slivers of metal. A little alcohol swab and a few bandages fixed him up.

"Okay, Ken, pull up your drawers. You just earned a Purple Heart on your third patrol. Two more Purple Hearts and you can go home."

Briggs looked back at me. "Mister Goldsmith, I figure I can go home now. I just got wounded for the second time."

PBR enlisted were entitled to two war wounds before being considered eligible for rotating home before the end of their one-year tour. Officers had to get three Purple Hearts before they could go home early. I thought that policy was correct. The enlisted river rats had to endure a lot more time on the river than officers. Oftentimes PBR sailors' little nicks due to fragments of fiberglass or tiny aluminum shards never got documented. Naturally, most of the unrecorded wounds were suffered on boats entirely manned by enlisted, without an officer around. It was a mark of honor for some river rats to pass off superficial wounds as nonevents. Some staff puke from Saigon or Binh Thuy might claim a Purple Heart if he bruised himself while the gunners on his boat suppressed an enemy sniper, but not a true river rat. That day I told Ken Kaiser that he had earned a Purple Heart. Briggs, who probably had spent some serious time in a hospital for his first wound while with River Section 542 in the Rung Sat out of Nha Be, wanted his little nick also recorded as a wound. Well, what was good for a green-pea officer was good enough for him. I would have been the last person on earth to argue the point. Splinters in the butt, a bullet crease of the leg, burns on the hands from changing a hot machine gun barrel were all war wounds in my book if the guys were actively engaged with the enemy when injured. Individuals still had the option of completing their tours no matter how many little stars were pinned to their Purple Hearts. Nobody wanted some whiner around if he claimed his tour was over because he had a couple of Band-Aid wounds. We river rats often told the new guys that "Purple Hearts will be passed out with the C rations. Get one fast and easy. The second one might be a bitch."

"Briggs, you got another Purple Heart. You also got to sit down with Wolin and Earner tonight to explain to them why you get to get out early. I think you might be the first case like this that they've heard."

"Mister Goldsmith, just put my wound in the record. I'm not gonna skate out. You know that, don't you?"

"Briggs, the decision is up to you. I know that I want you here with me until I rotate home in September."

"Mister Goldsmith, I guess you will have to do without me after I rotate home in July."

He was smiling. Briggs was not a whiner. That was it. He would continue to take his chances on the river. Briggs was a career Navy man. A second Purple Heart on his record would add to his retirement points. He just wanted to make sure his little wound was recorded.

Later that evening in the wardroom, Ron Wolin told me that I would be joining him in running the Chet Say Canal the next day. That info and the nonchalant manner in which Ron informed me jangled every nerve in my body.

"Ron, don't you know the Cong have been real active in that area for the last few days? Hell, the Ruff Puffs patrolling near that canal from the My Tho side were beaten back just today. Charlie was mortaring that little Viet fort at the My Tho/Chet Say junction just a few hours ago."

"Wynn, that's why we are going up there. I've set up Seawolf cover. You and I have made that trip before. We will do it again tomorrow."

I did not play poker well that evening. After I folded my last hand, I went up to Doc Dooher's medical spaces to join the colorful crew of after-hours drinkers and philosophers. Jerry Dooher left the poker table with me. He probably sensed that something was wrong when I said I wanted to get "a sleeping aid up in medical." Doc's medical spaces had plenty of beer. He also had a good supply of gin and grain alcohol. Only a select group of people knew about his little blind pig operation. I often enjoyed the music and conversation; that night I hoped the alcohol would settle my nerves and help me sleep. All I could think of was what was going to happen the next day up the Chet Say Canal. When Doc Dooher asked me what was on my mind and I replied that I was concerned with running the Chet Say Canal, the drinkers gave me a toast. A comm center petty officer promised to make a tape recording of the radio transmissions of the run to send to my next of kin. We all laughed.

I got little sleep that night. No bad dreams. Just a foreboding, and a feeling of helplessness as I tried to sleep. I imagined the scene: I'm on a stationary PBR twenty yards from a wall of green that's spitting bullets and rockets directly at me.

When I tried to eat breakfast around 0530 the next morning in the wardroom I gagged on the rolls and coffee, but the bad feeling in my stomach came from fear, not alcohol. Rich Sloane, who was getting ready to take out a RivSect 535 daypatrol, already knew about my run up the Chet Say and gave me some encouragement.

"Goldie, as soon as I finish my coffee I'm gonna give you some extra protection."

Rich came back a few minutes later with two pieces of gear very new to me. The first was a twenty-pound vest of inch-thick ceramic armor. The second was an eight-pound panty made from the same Kevlar material as a flak jacket.

"Goldie, I got this gear from a Seawolf pilot down in Binh Thuy. The ceramic armor can stop a fifty-caliber bullet. The groin protector will protect your balls from missile fragments. I think the Women's Clubs of America paid for the design. Just don't try to go swimming wearing this shit. And good luck."

I lugged the heavy gear down to the waiting boat—Engle's 7-19. Briggs's 7-12 boat was also ready as the second (cover) boat. It had a new toy aboard, one of Ron Wolin's latest innovations, a 20mm cannon mounted forward in place of the starboard Browning. It was one of several such heavy guns Ron Wolin had recently obtained from who knew where. Ron was a believer in firepower. The bigger the gun the better. The sight of the new 20mm in the forward machine gun mount caused another wrenching in my stomach because the weapon had never been tested in combat on a PBR. The 20mm cannon fired a much bigger round than the .50-caliber Browning, but the Browning was an old, reliable weapon whose idiosyncrasies were well known on the boats. Five hundred bullets could be placed in a continuous belt in the ready locker for each barrel of the Brownings. The 20mm cannon could accommodate only two hundred rounds in the ready tray. What was wrong with that picture? To me it was a no-brainer; the boat needed more ready bullets, not fewer. The 20mm cannon would be great if we were expecting fire from enemy armor or armored attack aircraft. But a 20mm cannon was only marginally more effective against bunkers than the .50-caliber Browning. The rate of fire was approximately the same. The 20mm cannon's ready ammo would be expended long before that in the ready tray of a fifty.

When the sailors saw the heavy personal protection I carried aboard they started to share my concerns. One young sailor asked the question that most of them wanted to ask. "Mister Goldsmith, what the hell are we going up against? Do we have to go down the Ba Lai?"

"We will have a routine patrol on the Ham Luong until around 1445. The CO will take over Shadoan's and Stevens's boats and lead us up the Ben Tre to run the Chet Say to the My Tho. We will have Seawolf gunship cover. There has been a lot of gook activity up the Chet Say the past few days. I expect we will receive a lot of automatic weapons fire. The 7-12 boat will be tail end charlie. Briggs, your boat might get hit by a rocket from the get-go just east of the Ba Lai. We gotta practice some towing drills today just in case tail end charlie gets disabled."

"Why does my boat have to be tail end charlie, Mister Goldsmith? Why not Engle's 7-19 boat, with you bringing up the rear?"

Briggs's questions were both heartfelt and disturbing. Ron Wolin had told me to be on the third boat. He had also told me to stagger the guns—the third boat's guns all to starboard and the last boat's guns all to port. I wanted to be on a boat with all guns to starboard. I sure did not want to be on the last boat.

"I've got my orders to be on the third boat. You and Engle can flip a coin as to whose boat is last in the column. 'Course I will have to explain why I switched boats. In spite of the

CO's suggestion (I sometimes took orders as suggestions) to have the guns staggered, I want all guns on your boat to be directed as you want. The threat is mostly from that right bank. If there is a major ambush and the last boat is disabled, any boat going back to assist will be a sitting duck when it turns around. Hell, if I had my druthers, I would be on the first boat. But maybe the Cong will take the first boat under fire first. Briggs, you, me, Ron Wolin, and everyone else gets the luck of the draw."

I hoped my words would not spook the sailors but would make them aware that I expected a fight and wanted them ready for that fight. We searched few sampans that day. Two hours of the next six we did things we had practiced up the creeks of Suisun Slough in the San Francisco Bay area. One boat would be beached on a little, uninhabited upper Ham Luong island. I would have a smoke grenade tossed ashore from the beached boat. That was the signal for the other boat to come in to the rescue. The boat on the beach was supposed to be totally without power. Two sailors on the beached boat were supposed to be down with serious wounds. The other two were fighting for their lives. The object of the training was to get a powerless PBR pulled off the bank by the stern and then towed by the bow by the other PBR while gunners were still firing. Then it was a drill of first aid for sucking chest wounds, bleeding leg arteries, or whatever. I would toss concussion grenades a few yards near the boats as the two rescue sailors were rigging tow lines. The sailors performed the drills much better than I expected. I was impressed at how quickly they could rig up the tow lines.

The 7-12 and 7-19 boats were loitering in the Ham Luong when Ron Wolin and the 7-16 and 7-17 boats came speeding downriver and entered the Ben Tre. My two boats followed. As we passed the bridge I donned my special gunship personal armor. With flak jacket, flak groin protector, a heavy ceramic vest over the flak jacket, and a steel helmet, I looked like an early version of the Teenage Ninja Turtles. I had other gear—my pistol belt with all its attachments, my holstered .45, two seven-round .45 ammo clips, a first-aid pouch, a canteen full of water, and a pouched inflatable life vest. My jungle fatigue side pockets were stuffed with M-16 magazines and bandages. I also still had the M-26 fragmentation grenade in a pocket.

The extra personal protection was a big encumbrance. Wearing the heavy ceramic vest would be a definite hazard if I was blown into the water; I would sink like a rock. Wearing it on a boat was probably a court-martial offense, but disregarding Ron Wolin's order to stagger the guns by boat was also a court-martial offense. What the hell. Disregard one order, might as well disregard another order. As my Irish bride has often said, "In for a lamb, might as well be in for a sheep." Those words probably first meant that an Irish peasant caught stealing a lamb to feed his family during the famine would be hung just the same as a sheep rustler caught stealing a whole flock. My feelings at the time were similar; whatever orders or regulations I violated to give me an edge were secondary to what was to come. My boats were going to get hit hard to starboard. *Maybe* they would survive if they had their guns trained. *Maybe* I would survive with all the nonregulation armor protection. *Maybe* I would be killed. *Maybe* I would be court-martialed.

As we neared the Ba Lai, we conducted radio checks with the Seawolves. Seawolf 44 was out of Dong Tam, a familiar callsign that brought some comfort. But something not at all comforting to me was the fact that Ron Wolin had the boats going so slow. Hell, we were just cruising up the Chet Say at a slow pace of fifteen knots. Viet Cong rocketeers would have the chance to get off some great first shots. Ron Wolin, my buddy, was going to get me killed. I expected the 7-19 boat to be hit within the first minute. I was at the starboard gunwale, just forward of the engine cover. The safety of my M-16 was off, and I had twenty rounds of tracer ammunition in the magazine. Another twenty-round magazine of tracer ammo was in my right blouse pocket. The tracers were to pinpoint the Viet Cong firing positions so the gunships would immediately be able to concentrate their fire suppression. I kept looking back at Briggs's boat. When was the shit gonna hit the fan? We had gone almost a mile down the canal. It was three minutes of nerve-racking anxiety.

When the first rockets were fired, it came as a relief. I saw the blasts at the water's edge and the explosions at the back of the 7-12 boat. I ran to the coxswain's flat and ordered Engle to turn around while I grabbed the radio mike and screamed over the sound of the firing machine guns.

"Seawolf 44, Pineapple Bowl Charlie. Will stop my unit at rocket site and mark it with tracers!"

There was no time for acknowledgment. I did not even know if my transmission was blocked by Briggs's frantic call for help. Engle had turned the 7-19 boat around in a few seconds and brought the boat's speed to over twenty knots. We passed the limping 7-12 boat as it tried for the north bank of the canal. The boat was sinking but all guns were firing. The bullets from their guns must have come very close to our boat as we sped by. When we approached the firing position of the rockets, I ordered Engle to make a crash turn. The boat had not settled down from this maneuver, the gunners had momentarily stopped firing, and I had only a second or two for reflective thoughts. I thought of my father, who had died of a sudden heart attack two years earlier. I regretted that I had never really told him how much I loved him. Today, I thought, I will probably join him in eternity. I raised my M-16 rifle and cut loose on full automatic at the green-and-brown riverbank twenty yards away.

I had done a good job of spotting the rocket position, and Engle had done a great job of stopping the PBR in front of it to shield the wounded 7-12 boat. The Viet Cong rocket crew at that position did another good job. Before my M-16's magazine was empty, one of those little men put a B-40 round into the starboard engine less than four feet from where I had been standing. If that rocketeer had done a great job he would have hit the starboard fuel tank below my feet and just forward of the engine that his rocket destroyed. Then I and at least three American sailors would have joined my father that day.

Over ten minutes later I regained consciousness. My head was resting on the deck just inside the coxswain's flat. I struggled to my feet and looked around. The 7-12 boat was two hundred meters upstream from the raging battle to salvage Briggs's 7-19 boat. The gunners on the 7-12 boat were not firing their weapons.

Engle looked at me. "I thought you was dead, Mister Goldsmith. We took a rocket in the starboard engine. The port engine is overheating. We can barely maneuver."

"Anybody else wounded?"

"Marko sez his back hurts. He could have broken his back. Check yourself, Mister Goldsmith. I really thought you got killed."

GM3 David Marko was the forward fifty gunner. A stout little guy. I asked him if he could fire his twin fifties. He gave me a thumbs-up in spite of being in some pain. I looked for my M-16. It was missing in action, blown over the side along with most of the ten cans of M-60 ammo that had been opened and positioned between the engine covers. I grabbed an M-79 thrown on deck from the small-arms locker and told Engle to get closer to the other boats. We could not help them where we were and I sure wanted to be closer to other PBRs. Even PBRs taking heavy enemy fire. I needed them and they needed me. Then I noticed a cut on my left arm near the elbow. I was bleeding but felt no pain. I realized that I had been lucky again. I was feeling good. This was not to be the day I rejoined my daddy. I would live to get married and have children. This day was not my time. I experienced an inner calm that was beyond all previous experience.

The 7-19 boat could make only about twelve knots on one engine. Steering was difficult. Engle got the boat within about thirty yards of the other three boats. "Boats" Shadoan's 7-17 PBR was broadside alongside the partially sunken stern of Briggs's boat. It was blasting away with all guns against an eighty-meter front on the south bank. QM1 Howard Stevens's 7-16 boat was twenty meters downstream covering the other boats with a steady barrage of fire. VC rockets and automatic weapons continued to rain down around the three boats. Two rockets hit the water near BM1 Shadoan's 7-17 boat. I was firing M-79 rounds as fast as I could. The gunners on the 7-12 boat were taking their lead from the sailors firing on Shadoan's and Stevens's boats. The sailors were attempting to conserve ammunition. A second or two would pass without the gunners firing. Then they would recognize more enemy fire and put some pressure on their triggers. Twice I caught sight of a blast on Shadoan's boat. Each time I cringed, then I realized that these were the back blasts of M-72 LAW rockets fired by sailors.

Seawolf gunships were rocketing and machine-gunning the south bank at unbelievably low altitudes—as low as twenty feet. I put an M-79 round between the windscreen and tail rotor of one of them. I had fired the round before the chopper came into view. Then I realized that five gunships were now supporting us. A heavy fire team of three gunships had recently arrived to support the original two. The first team had shot all their rockets and were low on 7.62mm machine gun ammunition. They had stayed until relieved by the three new ships. Then they returned to Dong Tam to rearm and came back within fifteen minutes. Fifteen minutes of all-out war. It was one hell of a firefight: life or death for every sailor on four plastic boats, everyone trying to stay alive by suppressing the fire of the enemy at close quarters but ever mindful of their depleting ammunition, doing their best to save a mortally wounded PBR and shipmates who no longer had a boat to call their own.

The 7-12 boat had been hit at the waterline by two rockets, both near the stern on the starboard side. Three sailors had been wounded. They were all firing their guns when Ron Wolin came to the rescue with the 7-16 and 7-17 boats. The 7-12's engines and pumps were undamaged but the boat had taken on a lot of water. A MK I PBR could have taken those hits and kept on trucking because the older boats had hundreds of pounds of Styrofoam between the inner hull and the outer hull. Ron Wolin had decided to salvage the guns and classified documents on board before attempting a tow. The transfer was done over a twenty-minute period during which the River Section 534 boats and sailors were in the fight of their lives. Without the Seawolves' firepower, Ron would never have attempted a salvage operation. Thermite grenades and explosives would have destroyed PBR 7-12, its weapons, and our documents.

After all the weapons, including that heavy 20mm cannon, were removed from the 7-12 boat, a tow was attempted by James Shadoan's 7-17 boat. Only GMG2 Briggs and GMSN Willie Brown were left aboard the 7-19 boat, Briggs in the coxswain's flat and little Willie Brown manning an M-60 machine gun up on the bow. As soon as the 7-12 boat was pulled thirty feet out into the canal it rapidly began to sink by the stern. The tow line was stretching and about to part until it was cut by a sailor manning the tow on Shadoan's boat. Shadoan put his pumps in reverse and Willie Brown was able to jump to the stern of Shadoan's boat with his M-60. With his command swiftly sinking beneath him, Briggs jumped out of the coxswain's flat, cut down the ensign, stuffed it into his shirt, and jumped over the side. He was recovered by QM1 Howard Stevens's boat in a matter of seconds while Viet Cong bullets kicked up water all around him. The return fire of a dozen machine guns put a stop to the enemy fire. By the time Briggs was aboard the 7-17 boat, all PBR gunfire stopped. The three-ship Seawolf fire team was hosing down the south bank with everything it had and their fire silenced the enemy. By then our PBRs had fired over twelve thousand rounds of machine gun bullets and the Seawolves had fired over a hundred thousand rounds. The gunships had also expended over a hundred 2.75-inch rockets. I figured that the enemy troops along that eighty meters of canal bank had run out of ammo. We had also lost the first MK II PBR in combat.

Now it was decision time for the survivors. Ron Wolin ordered me to lead the boats east to the My Tho. To me that was a bad idea. Another two miles of the Chet Say lay ahead. I believed that the Viet Cong ambush party we had encountered had shot its wad but that others still waited ahead. I made my case as calmly as I could.

"Pineapple Zulu, this is Pineapple Bowl Charlie. We have one Whiskey India Alpha [one wounded], one engine destroyed, and the other engine overheating. We might need a tow. Recommend Romeo Tango Bravo [return to base] by going back the way we came. Still believe major enemy force located to the east. Over."

Somehow my words persuaded Ron Wolin to take the boats back the way we came. There was no enemy fire as we progressed through the hundred-yard ambush site. Engle's 7-19 boat was tail end charlie. All boats were restricted to the twelve-knot speed of tail end charlie. Every time Ron Wolin called for more speed from the 7-19 boat, I reminded him that it had only one overheating engine. Just past the Ba Lai we were joined by seven other River Section 534 and 535 boats that had been scrambled to come to our aid. Seawolf 44 with his two ships had rearmed and joined the heavy fire team in giving us air cover. With five gunships flying air cover, I never felt so secure in my life. I was faintly amused when some dumb-ass Viet Cong opened up on a boat in the middle of the formation with a machine gun. That whole south bank of the Ben Tre River was blown apart in short order by dozens of Seawolf rockets and thousands of bullets from ten PBRs. When the boats reached the Ben Tre marketplace, the flag off the sunken 7-12 boat was first waved at the hundreds of Viet civilians by Briggs on the 7-16 boat. Every 534th sailor wanted to touch and wave that flag. The flag was passed down the line until it reached me on the limping 7-19 boat. I could almost hear the national anthem as I waved that proud flag in the face of all those curious Vietnamese. I had shed all the armor protection and was dancing, prancing, and taunting the dumbfounded local populace by sticking our national emblem in their faces. I was alive. I had taken the best shots the enemy had. Let those VC sympathizers deal with it. My feelings at the time.

An hour later in the wardroom, while I was drinking coffee from a shaking cup, Ron Wolin and I were comparing notes for the firefight's action report. A couple of Seawolf pilots from the recent battle joined us. They had landed unannounced on the helo deck. They were typical gung ho naval aviators, all smiles and swagger. They said that they really enjoyed the action up the Chet Say and were eager to support us on some more runs. Those guys were on a high. Ron and I profusely thanked them but gave them no encouragement that we would be running that canal in the near future. I was more impressed by young ENFN (engineman fireman) W. F. Brewer on Briggs's boat, who had requested permission to come up to the wardroom to speak to me. A new guy, he had only three patrols under his belt. The second one had been the day before, when those two or so AK-47 rounds had wounded three sailors. He was wounded twice by fragments of B-40s within seconds of each other. He had been blown off his feet twice, only to get back up and reman his gun. I had never talked to him. Did not know his name. He told me that he believed I had saved his life. I thanked the bandaged-up sailor for his kind words and expressed my admiration for his courage. He had been firing the after fifty on the 7-19 boat when the two rockets hit within a few feet of him. I was glad that he left the wardroom before he let out to Ron Wolin that I had disobeyed orders about staggering the boat's guns.

I later learned from Briggs and the forward gunner on his boat, GMSN Wayne Forbes, that several Viet Cong were observed sneaking up on the 7-12 boat while it was stranded on the north bank of the Chet Say. Briggs and Forbes took them under fire with pistols and rifles. Forbes claimed to have killed one of them. The official report indicated no known enemy casualties, one PBR sunk, and seven sailors wounded. I received my one and only Purple Heart. Ron Wolin got the second star on his, and GM2 Briggs got his third wound award and a sure-fire early ticket back to the States. Briggs again declined the option. He left Vietnam on time with three Purple Hearts, just as Ron Wolin did in August. Both were real stand-up guys. The only man seriously wounded enough to be medevacked out of country was GM3 Marko. He never returned to duty. Evidently his spine had been compressed when he was thrown back against the steel bulkhead of his gun tub.

The maintenance guys did a great job on the 7-19 boat. They replaced two engines, patched and painted the hull, and had Engle's boat returned to duty within two days. CWO2 Rich Chesbro (John Smith's replacement), CWO3 Ralph Fries (River Section 535 maintenance officer), and CWO3 John Dorso (YRBM-18 maintenance officer) and their crews worked almost nonstop in the hot sun on the maintenance barge. The rebuilding of the 7-19 boat in a short couple of days was typical of the miracles that brown-water maintenance personnel did. Maintenance sailors were sometimes given the task of mating halves of heavily damaged boats together into one complete boat. Several times they were presented with boats salvaged from river bottoms. Instead of two boats being surveyed from Navy lists, only the boat with the bow section would be scratched. Sometimes a sunken and salvaged boat would get new electronics and have the engines repaired and the hull patched, and it would be back in combat within a week.

Chapter 16

Two days after the ambush up the Chet Say, the YRBM-18 (I still want to call it Apple-Five-Fiver) received its first SEAL assault platoon. Until that time the SEALs who *supported* PBRs on the Ham Luong were based at My Tho. By early 1968 the BUD/S (Basic Underwater Demolition SEAL) program was churning out SEAL platoons to the extent that every two river sections would have one two-officer, twelve-enlisted assault platoon assigned to support PBRs. These platoons were supposed to gather intel and react to PBR intel by going on raids near the riverbanks in order to make PBR operations more effective.

We got Mike Platoon from SEAL Team 1 and a small contingent of BSU-1 (boat support unit-one) sailors with two slow armored SEAL support boats. The platoon had come from Nha Be, where it had run operations in the Rung Sat for several weeks after deploying from Coronado with a stop in the Philippines.

This Mike Platoon SEAL outfit is often described in all the published stories of SEAL Vietnam exploits as "unlucky." Unlucky they were. A first-class fuckup also commanded them.

Dave Rickman was a young lieutenant (j.g.) fresh from BUD/S training. He was a former Notre Dame collegiate swimmer and a high school buddy of Pete Richards's. He was a boisterous know-it-all, "don't tell me anything" asshole as far as I was concerned. I discovered that soon after Pete introduced us.

Pete and Dave were both from upper-middle-class, Catholic, Main Line Philadelphia families. They had those things in common besides the fact that they were old chums. The big difference between them was that Dave was a talker and Pete was a listener. Pete was really sensitive to other people, perhaps a little too much into other people's feelings as far as I was concerned. Pete would invite sailors up to officers' country to share coffee and conversation in the wardroom lounge whenever Wolin and Earner were not present. Not really appropriate at the time in my book. I really liked Pete and I knew that anytime I wanted a sympathetic ear, I could count on him. Pete was not a poker player. He spent his free time writing letters to his wife, Betsy. Letters filled with human-interest stories about his experiences on the boats. He had two young daughters at home. One barely two (Chrissy) and the other just a baby (Patty Ann). Two years later I would get a chance to baby-sit those little girls. Pete's year in Vietnam must have been harder on him than my year was to me. It would be years before I became the daddy of two girls. Today I cannot imagine not seeing them for a whole year, especially when they were at that age.

Dave Rickman was something else.

Dave Rickman was my type of guy in my previous life as a college party animal. He was single and did not give a shit about authority. Cocky, insolent, boisterous, and irreverent, he would have been the life of a wild frat party. But he seemed to care less about his men or his mission. He was superjock sent to Vietnam to kill gooks, he thought, an attitude that was inappropriate for the time and place. That became evident real soon.

The first order of business for Rickman on his new assignment was to make an insertion. No time to get intel. No time to get the feel of the new op area. Tides, moonlight, lay of the land, and so on meant nothing to him. He just wanted to kill some gooks, to get to the nearest free-fire zone as soon as possible. Time of insertion was whenever he wanted. He had the power.

His first insertion was on Tan Tan Island. The SEALs went inland for hundreds of meters. They saw and encountered nothing. Dave Rickman wasted his resources on a dry hole. Upon getting back to the YRBM around 0400, he went directly up to the junior officer bunk room and crashed into his rack, leaving his muddy uniform, his muddy boots, his muddy web gear with attached grenades, and a mud-coated automatic

rifle in a pile beside the bunkroom door for PBR patrol officers going out on day-patrol to stumble over in the morning.

Dave Rickman was a little miffed the next morning when
he enjoyed a leisurely breakfast in the wardroom and discovered that PBR patrol officers coming in from night-patrol
were not interested in his heroic tales of "greasing" a couple
of gooks back in the Rung Sat the previous month. They were
more interested in when he would clean up his shit on the
deck of their stateroom. Rickman was not shamed or apolo-
getic. He really believed that it was up to the steward's mates
to clean up his mess.

Rickman rested on his laurels for a couple of days. Meaning he did nothing but sleep, drink beer, and bullshit in the
wardroom. I was really beginning to dislike him in spite of the
fact that he was a childhood friend of Pete Richards's, probably my closest friend at the time.

I probably allowed my feelings about Dave Rickman to
taint my memories about SEALs. Only when I really went to
work on this book did I realize that Rickman was an exception. At the time, and for many years later, I took stories of
SEAL exploits in Vietnam with a grain of double-laced vinegar salt. I might concede now that most of them were ad-
mirable brown-water sailors. I would be proud to share a beer
with them today.

PBR sailors like me went out on twelve- to fourteen-hour
patrols day in and day out. We got no "proficiency" or "jump
qualified" pay; we got no "per diem" pay. Our tours were the
full three-sixty-five days unless we were killed or medevacked
out of country. Our only relief was the one week (usually only
five nights out of Vietnam) R & R we could enjoy after at least
five months "in country." SEALs could count the two or three
weeks they had spent in Subic Bay getting acclimated to the
tropics against their half-year tours, which qualified them for
daily twenty-five bucks per diem pay for being away from
their permanent assignments. For Mike Platoon that meant
two four-hour insertions a week, usually by PBR, for a dry
hole on Tan Tan Island, with Dave Rickman continuing to
dump his muddy gear on the stateroom floor. This SEAL platoon was given the luxury of going out only two or three times
a week for a few hours and getting more pay than the PBR

sailors. As far as I was concerned at the time, all SEALs were blowhards. I had never seen one earn his salt in combat.

And I saw only Dave Rickman at the wardroom table.

His second in command, a young ensign who was into yoga and transcendental meditation, freaked me out with his yoga exercises and reading habits the one afternoon we shared the wardroom lounge. ENS Jamie Briarton was a pacifist philosopher thrust into the macho world of guerrilla warfare. While I looked for an action thriller or war book to catch my fancy, the ensign just acknowledged my presence with some polite words and went on with his deep thoughts or breathing exercises. I wanted to know more about him. I wish I could have known him longer. I really enjoyed the guy's company that afternoon and the few times we shared a meal at the wardroom table. He did not say boo about himself or the SEALs. As tired as I was of Rickman's bluster, that was a wonderful relief.

I did wonder, What the hell is going on? A SEAL platoon skippered by a dumb-ass, loudmouth jock with a seemingly wimpy, reflective, second in command? Both of them on their first tours? My doubts about SEALs mounted.

Rickman was advised by Ron Wolin to go visit Jack Harrell to get the lay of the land. Dave did spend some time with Jack, who told him about his *hoi chan* (Viet Cong defectors) and how the SEAL platoon could work with them. Dave Rickman must have also known about the PRUs (provincial reconnaissance units). They were the cornerstone of America's war against the VC infrastructure in Operation Phoenix—a CIA-funded operation to use any dirty trick, any former VC terrorist, and large amounts of blood money to eliminate suspected Viet Cong cadres by using the communists' own methods: assassinate, kidnap, turn were the modus operandi employed. Rickman must have known that Jack's bunch were the same as PRUs. Only the color of the money that paid them was different. Jack's guys got paid from regular MACV accounts; the PRUs got paid from Agency accounts. Jack wanted the SEALs to work with his mercenaries in ops close to Ben Tre and other supposedly "friendly" areas in the "sneaky pete" operations that SEALs were supposed to have mastered. Rickman once again demonstrated his arrogance: he was not going to work with Jack or a bunch of mercenary gooks; his job was to get a high body count. From all the PBR and SEAL action reports, Rickman was convinced that Banana Island—Tan Tan Island (referred to by SEALs mostly by its shape, though it was the location of some long-neglected banana groves)—was a fertile hunting ground.

Some SEALs had an ingrained bias against NILOs (naval intelligence liaison officers). If the intel was not from a vetted SEAL, that intel was shit. That certainly was Rickman's attitude. He knew how to kill the enemy. He had "greased" a couple himself in the Rung Sat the previous month. He would continue on his own terms. Why go out with unknown locals into some area where a few bad guys were surrounded by good guys? Tan Tan Island was to continue to be his target. It was a free-fire zone. Gunships and artillery had a free rein to waste anybody on the island. Why shouldn't his SEALs?

In the early morning hours of April 28, I had a two-boat patrol in Area 2. The SEALs were to make another insertion on Tan Tan Island, so I had my boats positioned near the northern boundary of Area 2 in case the SEALs and the other two-boat RivSect 534 patrol assisting the insertion needed help. Over a mile but just a couple of minutes away, we heard some rapid gunfire. We heard the screams over the radio. We had no clue what had happened. There was no call to us for assistance. My patrol went back to Ambush Alley and the mouth of the Ben Tre River.

The next morning I learned that a SEAL had been killed on the armored LCPL (landing craft, personnel, light) fifty meters from the insertion point. He had been killed by dozens of rounds from his own 5.56mm Stoner machine gun. Another SEAL had been seriously wounded. The story was that somehow the gun went berserk and that BM1 Walter Pope had stuffed the exploding muzzle to his chest to protect his shipmates. I did not believe that line for a second. Rickman and his entire platoon were fuckups as far as I was concerned.

A week later another SEAL from that platoon died. That death was just as bizarre. The man had drowned after Rickman had attempted to insert his team by dropping them off the stern of a moving 534th PBR. It was to be a totally clandestine insertion so the silent warriors were to swim ashore with no noisy boats making a landing. Unfortunately the SEALs were dropped off exactly where Dave Rickman desired—three hundred yards from shore. Rickman personally pushed off the first two men before jumping off the stern himself. Insertion from a moving PBR might have worked if the SEALs had had only twenty or so yards to go before reaching the riverbank at high tide. But three hundred yards was much too far to swim carrying sixty-plus pounds of gear. Even the strongest swimmers had to fight for their lives. And the ones who got close to the shore did not have the strength to get up the shallow bank of slippery, sucking mud. At that time of day, even fifty yards from the bank, a SEAL dropping off the stern of a PBR would have found himself up to his thighs in mud. It was low tide—something that Rickman never really understood. After swimming a hundred yards or so, some of the SEALs discarded their equipment; they recognized that others were going under and their inflatable vests could not keep them afloat. They had to pop emergency flares to get the River Section 534 PBRs to return and pick them up. The 534th sailors came back quickly and retrieved every SEAL they could find. But one man was missing. The body of SFP-2 (shipfitter, pipe, second class) David Devine was recovered the next day by a 534th PBR. That "insertion" had been a first class disaster.

Mike Platoon had some sort of stand-down for a week or so, when I hoped they would get their stuff together.

Meanwhile, our PBRs continued to support Ruff Puff sweeps in the environs of Ben Tre in their attempts to eliminate the last of the small, hard-core guerrilla squads. These squads continued to harass friendly forces attempting to rebuild the outposts that had been destroyed around the Ben Tre River during Tet. Prisoners were taken. Thousands of bullets were fired. Sampans were destroyed at night with unknown enemy casualties. Sailors were wounded, none serious enough for medevac. Every day there were little incidents. I remember only the ones that involved me. The "op sums" just provide dates, coordinates, and hull numbers of the boats involved.

One afternoon I was with two PBRs returning from dropping off a VC suspect at the police station. Ruff Puffs inserted by Vietnamese LCVPs were sweeping the south bank of the Ben Tre. We could see and hear sporadic firing. My boats were at good speed with all guns aimed at that bank. We did not relax until we reached the Ham Luong. I was taking off my helmet and flak jacket when I saw a flash on the stern of an LCVP tied up at the ferry landing. The flash was followed by a big bang. A 75mm recoilless rifle fired from over three hundred meters away had hit the king post on the stern of the Vietnamese landing craft. A South Vietnamese sailor was literally blown in two before my eyes. My boats had crossed the line of fire at a much closer range just moments before. The enemy gunners who had fired the round must have had my boats in their sights; we were lucky. The fact that we presented moving targets with eight machine guns at the ready probably contributed to the enemy recoilless team's decision to take out a stationary target farther away. I had my boat fire a belt of grenades into the Viet Cong firing area and radioed the coordinates to the MACV advisory compound.

Later that day I was presented with the steel, waterproof, mustard-colored canister used to transport that 75mm round. It was the only thing left by the Viet Cong at their firing position. The Ruff Puffs had gotten there within half an hour. An American Army sergeant adviser gave me the ammo canister as a souvenir. Later someone deciphered the dates and markings on that steel tube for me. That shell had been manufactured in China less than four months earlier. The Cong were getting their stuff into combat as fast as we were, if not faster. Somehow I was not surprised. Cambodia's off-limits border was less than forty miles away. Our supply lines were a lot farther.

Two days after witnessing the Vietnamese sailor being blown apart, I had another day-patrol in Area 1. A SEAL from Mike Platoon wanted to go along for the ride. The SEALs were going back on operations the next night. The SEAL appeared to be a squared-away sailor. I gave CS-1 (commissary mate first class) Donnie Patrick a good tour. He seemed really interested in the various known enemy areas and wanted to get a feel for where the villages were located. I kidded him that he was probably the leanest and youngest first class cook in the whole Navy. Until I met Donnie, the only first class cooks I had ever known were portly guys in their forties. Patrick was lean and younger looking than his thirty years. He just laughed and said that he knew more about demolitions and guns than he did about cooking. He had been a SEAL for two years and was a leading petty officer for Mike Platoon. His volunteering for a thirteen-hour recon on a PBR definitely cast him in a better light than his platoon leader.

The next evening the SEALs went on an insertion in the Cho Lach District of Vinh Long Province on the upper Ham Luong (Patrol Area 1). Even though I had a patrol in Area 2, I had my two boats within a mile of the insertion site around 0100 because Mike Platoon would probably need some more help. As usual there were no radio transmissions. This time the SEALs were going ashore on an SSB (SEAL Support Boat) manned by BSU-1 (Boat Support Unit 1) guys—a lieutenant junior grade boat officer and three gunners. The two River Section 534 boats on patrol in Area 1 were covering the insertion.

I saw a big flash followed by a big boom over the water. The radio channel was immediately flooded with screams for assistance from the BSU-1 boat and the accompanying PBRs. I got my two boats going. By the time my boats arrived, the BSU-1 boat and the two other River Section 534 boats were under way at top speed back to the YRBM-18. My boats followed them. When I got to the base a medevac helo was already on deck. The first of three. Doc Dooher's people and other sailors were carting wounded men up ladders to the helo deck. As the PBR sailors from my boat went to help carry the wounded, I made my way to the BSU-1 boat.

Its deck resembled a slaughterhouse. Blood and guts covered the thirty-foot steel boat. The lieutenant junior grade boat commander and his three gunners were starting to clean up the mess. Two were picking up a headless, legless torso and putting it into a body bag. Another was swabbing away the blood. They were all sobbing.

I picked up what was left of a leg by its jungle boot and placed it into the body bag.

"Do you know who it is?" My question was directed at the lieutenant junior grade.

"It's Patrick. He got blown up as soon as we landed. He

was the first one off. All the others were on the bow, just ready to get off. Every damn one of them went down."

"What happened?"

"Patrick was carrying a lot of C-4. He stepped on a mine or was hit by a rocket. Who the hell knows what happened? I didn't see a thing until bodies were being thrown all around me after the explosion."

Whatever happened that early morning—and my guess is that Patrick threw himself on an armed grenade one of the other SEALs had dropped—resulted in one SEAL KIA and seven others medevacked out of country. Dave Rickman and Jamie Briarton were surveyed from the Navy with 100 percent disabilities. Five enlisted wounded SEALs may have shared the same fate. I know only that they were medevacked out of country. One SEAL on the boat was completely untouched, like the four members of the BSU-1 boat. They had been shielded from the blast by being low and surrounded by armor. Another SEAL from Mike Platoon had escaped the carnage by being away in My Tho; he was unable to join the insertion because his PBR ride back to the YRBM-18 had broken down. Those two were the only men left standing of Mike Platoon, a SEAL platoon that never killed, captured, or wounded any enemy during its three-week deployment on the YRBM-18.

My two-boat patrol soon went back to the disaster site. We made noisy mock insertions in attempts to draw enemy fire. No fire came. We then blanketed the site and a whole hundred square meters beyond it with hundreds of M-18 Honeywell-launched M-79 grenades. Probably a waste of ammo, but everything seemed a waste to me at the time. I cranked out two belts myself. I just hoped that some curious Viet Cong were around that site. I wanted to make them uncomfortable.

Chapter 17

The morning after the Mike Platoon fiasco I was really pissed. Not so much by what had happened to the SEALs, but by what had just happened to me. Bill Earner had given me the bad news. My requested five-day R & R (rest and relaxation) to Australia was postponed. I had been counting on getting there after eight months "in country"—the time that I was told and believed was necessary to qualify for an Australia R & R. I had been dreaming about Australia for weeks—a dream of doing nothing but having fun and relaxing on some warm beach (I was so taken with my vision that I had completely forgotten that a beach in Australia in June would be like a Charleston beach in January). In Australia there would be no guns, no tension, just great food, drink, female companions who could speak the language, and the ability to do nothing or anything twenty-four hours a day for a whole five days. Everything would be "dinky."

My Uncle Wynne in Dallas, who had fought in the southwest Pacific in World War II and was only miles from his older brother Bill when he had been killed on Biak Island, advised me to check out Australia. It had made his hell in the Pacific almost pleasurable. Uncle Wynne told me that the hearty, hardworking, fun-loving, independent breed of people in Australia actually enjoyed Americans, especially guys coming in from combat duty. Australia would be my kind of R & R. Now, I was told, Australia R & R required *nine* months in country. A big bummer. Australia was too popular. Too many guys like me, lured by visions of long-legged, sexually liberated, blond surfer girls or old war stories from fathers and uncles had made the country too popular for the troops.

The married guys like Pete Richards and John Smock who had gone to Hawaii seemed refreshed by their R & Rs and getting reacquainted with their wives. Their trips had been confirmed weeks in advance. Hawaii after five or six months was a dead cert for R & R. Australia was different. This damn war had too many single guys like me lusting for Australia. Instead, I was told, I could go anywhere authorized for R & R within the next two weeks. Hawaii, Taiwan, Hong Kong, Manila, and Bangkok were readily available. Decision time again. I chose to wait another month for Australia. Too many stories about good times with the Aussie ladies prevented me from going to those other sites. I could wait another month.

I did take advantage of every opportunity I had to get off the river. Bill Earner and Ron Wolin encouraged me to take some time off. We had Ken Kaiser and another commissioned patrol officer, Lt. (j.g.) Frank Alla, to take up the slack. Let the new guys carry the load. I agreed wholeheartedly.

Courtesy of a Navy RD-4 flight out of Vinh Long, I went on a one-day excursion to a beach on Phu Quoc Island with a couple of other guys stationed aboard the barge. That trip was something right out of *M*A*S*H*. The Navy crew of the twin-engine plane was stationed in Saigon. Whenever they had the next day free from scheduled flights, they would put out word of their availability. In exchange for gas for the converted civilian airliner, several cases of beer, steaks, and maybe a war souvenir or two, they would fly brown-water sailors lucky enough to be near an airfield with free aviation gas over to that little island in the Gulf of Thailand. They probably did it at least once a week. No manifest, no flight plan. Getting enough gas could be a problem. Beer and steaks were no problem. Mel Shantz and his Supply Corps assistant, Lt. (j.g.) Fred McGowan, made sure of that. Viet Cong flags were no problem. Our little Vietnamese seamstress in My Tho had survived Tet and her business was booming.

The crew knew which airfields had gas. Fortunately, the Vinh Long airfield had a supply of high-octane aviation fuel and was only a short boat ride away. Mel Shantz and his minions made sure that the Air Cofat* crews were assured of this info. Any U.S. military aircraft landing there got gas, no questions asked, no requisitions to sign if that bird was on a combat mission. The Army guys gassing up the plane probably got a couple of cases of frozen steaks and lobster tails as a tip for that noncombat mission. One hand washed the other.

The flight was unusual for me and the ten or so other combat guys paying the freight, but not for the aircrew. It was just another romp for them and their female companions, the girlfriends of the flight crew. They were secretaries from the U.S. embassy, female journalists, and so on. Whatever their trade, they were all good-lookers. Three of them—one for each flight crew member—were casually dressed in sarongs and seated up front. A couple of the young lovelies spent some time up in the cockpit. The paying passengers seemed out of place among the familiar folks. There was no in-flight movie or snacks. I did not mind.

I enjoyed my few hours relaxing at the warm surf line on the Gulf of Thailand in my skivvies (my swimsuit had been lost on the YRBM-16, and the only swimming I had done during the past months had been in full uniform after falling off sampans) while I watched the flight crew and their female companions frolicking in their swimsuits and going out of my sight beyond the dunes. Phu Quoc Island did have a nice beach. I just lay down at the shoreline to get washed by the warm salt water while dreaming of Australia.

I also got a chance to play messenger boy, ferrying some documents to Saigon in order to visit an old college buddy stationed at COMNAVFORV. That time I got the admin flight from Air Cofat's old UH-34 to Vinh Long and continued on a C-130 transport on space-available to Saigon. Air transport was the only way to make the trip to Saigon. There were still ten blown bridges along Route 4 from My Tho to Saigon, a reminder of Tet.

That trip was more interesting than the flight on the RD-4. The C-130 Hercules that day was indeed the "trash hauler"

---

*Cofat was the name of a French cigarette that was still attached to an old French tobacco company building taken over by U.S. Naval Support Forces in Saigon. The pilots flying the administrative aircraft out of Saigon called their operation Air Cofat.

that it is labeled today. Two goats roamed around freely in the cargo bay. I kept waiting for one of them to pull out the ring pin of a grenade on the vest of some of the dozens of sleeping Vietnamese Rangers who shared the cargo hold with me, a bunch of civilians, and all sorts of weapons casually strewn about the cargo deck. The only briefing to the passengers had been a short request from the pilot to have weapons unloaded until landing.

Perry Patterson was a Navy lieutenant junior grade like me. Perry had sent me a short message after seeing my name as being one of the wounded on the April 24 action report. We had lost track of each other over the last three years. I relished the opportunity to get back in touch with him. Those short helo and trash-hauler flights got me back to Saigon to see Perry.

Perry was not quite the same old caustic, sarcastic, hard-drinking college buddy I had known. No longer an extremist supporter of Senator Barry Goldwater's conservative foreign policies, he had toned down the "nuke 'em all" histrionics he had mouthed at college bull sessions. He was married and his wife was expecting a baby. He had opted for Navy OCS to get out of the draft as he waited out law school admissions. He was commissioned, trained in communications, and sent to Saigon within a period of ten months. He no longer seemed so sure that nuclear war to save the world from communism was really such a good idea. Maybe fighting the commies in the backwaters of the world was not a great idea either. Reading all the daily reports from Navy and Marine units must have contributed to his change of attitude. Perry might have enjoyed the easy life in Saigon. I doubt it. Just reading all those casualty reports would have to be a big downer for anybody.

Perry's tour was a little different from mine. He basically had an eight-hour-a-day desk job running a watch section at NAVFORV's communications center. Perry probably had a great bird's-eye view of what was really happening. He saw all the radio traffic—from the top secret, admiral's eyes only to the mundane combat action reports from PBR river sections, Marine battalions, and other units.

He also had a membership in the exclusive Cercle Sportif, the Saigon club reserved mostly for government and business elites. Perry had inherited his membership from the guy he relieved, who had inherited his membership from yet another guy. By 1968 only the best and brightest of Americans were admitted as new members. This meant they had to be at least a full bird colonel (O-6) on COMUSFORV's staff or at least a senior diplomat. The rear area junior staff guys took care of themselves. They carefully passed down their memberships to another generation of rear echelon, lower-ranking warriors such as Perry as a matter of pride from the days when being an Army captain (O-3) or a Navy lieutenant (O-3) in Saigon had carried some respect.

Perry and I enjoyed gin and tonics and a great French lunch served poolside by Vietnamese waiters who spoke only French and were immaculately attired in stiffly starched black-and-white uniforms. I keep watching for Ambassador Bunker or General Westmoreland to show up in their tennis whites. I saw a lot of fit and tanned middle-age Caucasian males play tennis on the nearby clay courts, but I never recognized any big name. They were probably merely Air Force or Army colonels or one-star generals. Perry and I exchanged wild memories of college pranks and major wartime screwups by our leaders. It was an enjoyable, memorable day, an experience far removed from the river when each day or night I fully expected combat.

The merry month of May continued to be happy times for me and for most of River Section 534. Only several sniper incidents. No wounded sailors. Just hours searching sampans in the hot sun and tedious hours at night drifting along Tan Tan Island or trolling for Cong in Ambush Alley. Meanwhile, our shipmates from River Section 535 were getting a rough introduction to their new patrol area, from one mile east of the My Tho/Ham Luong river junction, where the YRBM-18 was more or less permanently anchored, to ten miles to the east, just past the Co Chien/My Tho river junction where the My Tho simply became the Mekong River all the way into Cambodia and beyond. That stretch of river water had many little islands, a big choke-neck turn, and a lot of canals to the north usually controlled by the Viet Cong. One area on the north bank of the river in the Cai Be District of Dinh Tuong Province was still considered a Viet Cong secret area. The distinctive bulbous bend in the Rach Bai Rai River before it ran into the My Tho River was well known by Mekong Delta brown-water sailors as "Snoopy's Nose." The Mobile Riverine Force had visited Snoopy's Nose several times and it had been rewarded with bloody-nose, costly victories. No matter how many NVA and Viet Cong were killed in that area during the previous year, the enemy kept coming back the thirty miles from sanctuaries in Cambodia through the Plain of Reeds, into the eastern Delta, right through Snoopy's Nose.

During Tet, the Viet Cong had taken over a lot of the little islands on the My Tho River near Snoopy's Nose. It was the 535th River Section's mission to pacify them. The Vinh Long Province/Cho Lach District senior American adviser, a Green Beret Army captain named John Sabattinni, on his third Vietnam tour, had a lot of plans for his newly arrived brown-water support. Sabattinni had molded a great group of Ruff Puffs in Cho Lach. His counterpart, a feisty *dai qui* (Vietnamese Army captain) named Le Thom, was just as aggressive as Sabattinni. They just needed some firepower and mobility.

River Section 535 was up to the task. Jack Doyle, Sabattinni, and Thom soon became partners shortly after Jack Doyle met the adviser and his Vietnamese counterpart in the district town of Cho Lach.

The 535th had experience in special operations. They had seen a lot of combat before and during Tet around Can Tho on the Bassac, inserting and covering local South Vietnamese troops. They had experienced a lot of wounded around the Ti Ti Canal in support of Captain Paul Gray's quest for his stars. But it was at the zero hour of the NVA/VC Tet Offensive on January 31, 1968, that the 535th had really been tested.

Three days before Tet, Lt. Jack Doyle, the OinC, had led four River Section 535 PBRs and an LCM-6 support boat to Chou Doc on a special mission code-named Bold Dragon 1. Rich Sloane was Jack Doyle's second in command for this operation. Chou Doc was almost directly on the Cambodia border. The little brown-water task force's mission was to assist two Special Forces camps manned by ex-VC and NVA deserters, Nung (ethnic Chinese), Cambodian mercenaries, and a handful of regular ARVNs at Chou Doc in case the enemy violated the Tet truce with a major ground attack. Chou Doc was only a klick from the Vinh Te Canal that marked the border and was a ripe target. Jack Doyle's 535 sailors made contacts with all the friendlies in the area and scouted out the canals. Two days later a SEAL platoon from Binh Thuy arrived by helo to assist the 535th.

Early on the morning of January 31, a reinforced NVA battalion had attacked and overwhelmed the little border town. One Special Forces camp was so much in danger of being overrun that 535 PBR sailors had to go ashore and fight as infantry. To prevent the guns at Camp Ann from being captured, some PBR sailors manned the walls with machine guns while others destroyed the tubes of 105mm guns with the thermite grenades normally reserved for destroying beached PBRs to keep them from being captured. That was done while ammo stores and a fuel dump were exploding all around them. Hours earlier, two RivSect 535 boats had saved the asses of the SEAL team they had inserted, which had been attacked by a company of NVA crossing the border. The SEALs had been outnumbered and outgunned. "Demo Dick" Marcinko, later known as the "Rogue Warrior," the young SEAL officer whose life was saved by Jack Doyle's River Section 535 PBRs, was later inserted with his dozen enlisted into Chou Doc proper to assist a Special Forces team and their PRUs in rescuing American civilians, who were trapped in enemy-controlled buildings. Meanwhile, RivSect 535 boats blasted away at enemy strong points so the Special Forces–led irregulars and SEALs could rescue the American civilians. One 535 PBR took a recoilless round hit and the Mike 6 support boat was also hit by a rocket. Thirty rounds of machine gun fire hit another 535 PBR. The River Section 535 sailors fought on the ground with shotguns and grenades while attempting to secure landing zones for medevac helicopters for the wounded Special Forces troops who did the most of the fighting.

The 535 PBR sailors, the Special Forces with their mixed bag of Cambodian and Nung mercenaries, the SEAL team, Navy Seawolf gunships, and Army Cobra gunships defeated a numerically much stronger NVA and Viet Cong force at Chou Doc. That two-day battle earned a Presidential Unit Citation for River Section 535, as the 534's actions at Ben Tre had done for River Section 534. One 535th sailor had been killed in action and two others were wounded seriously enough to be medevacked out of country. One SEAL was killed by sniper fire as the NVA evacuated Chou Doc, which was being pounded by gunships and Navy PBRs.

The SEALs at Chou Doc benefited from a big public relations campaign. Demo Dick Marcinko left Vietnam shortly afterward and went on a SEAL recruiting and propaganda tour back in the States before returning to Vietnam for another six-month tour. Marcinko was a bold warrior. That is a fact. But from reading his first book, *Rogue Warrior*, published years later, I guess Marcinko really believed what that public relations tour had fabricated—that his SEALs had saved Chou Doc, and that Lt. Jack Doyle and the 535th sailors were just along for the ride.

Marcinko at least admitted in his book that there was an intrepid PBR "chief petty officer" [sic] named "Jack" on the boats transporting his team to victory. Enough said about the "Rogue Warrior's" memory and truthfulness.

I heard firsthand accounts about the Tet attack at Chou Doc over beers on the beer barge and at the wardroom table. I also got to know the other 535th officers besides John Smock and my buddy Rich Sloane. Jack Doyle, the hero of Chou Doc, was a regular at the nightly poker games. Jack was from the Boston area and came complete with Irish wit and distinctive accent. Jack enjoyed a jar or two on the beer barge. And he could really spin a story. The operations officer/XO was Lt. Bill Dennis. Bill was from Alabama. A quiet guy. A friendly guy. Bill and I enjoyed the way each other spoke. We had the same slow, accented southern speech pattern. After Frank Walker had been medevacked, I was the only southern guy in the wardroom. Bill Dennis and Ron Wolin had been in the same PBR class back in California and got along as the best friends they were at the time. Lieutenant (j.g.) Mike Glynn seemed stressed out. I'm sure he was at the time. The 535th was getting shot at and engaging the enemy around the "choke point" of the My Tho River day in and night out. Mike had only weeks to go on his tour. He had a wife and baby waiting for him. He was nervous, skinny, and wasted. Every time I saw him going or coming in from patrol he was clutching a 12-gauge pump shotgun. I guess that Ithaca Featherweight shotgun was his security blanket. The second time I saw him getting off a PBR with yet another load of VC suspects while carrying the shotgun, I gave him a new nickname—"Shotgun Glynn." That moniker stuck.

Nicknames were fairly common. "Handgrenade" had stuck with Bob Hunt. Tony Summerlin was often called "Zeke," a nickname going back years. The commissioned patrol officers called me "Jawja Boy," "Georgie," or "Goldie." None of the names were offensive to me—unlike the "Chickenshit Goldsmith" sobriquet that some of the enlisted had earlier applied to me.

Some nicknames that were applied to guys probably would not be accepted in today's "politically correct" environment. For example, Frank Alla was tagged "Mini Guinea" by John Smock. Alla was a short Italian-American from the Boston area who wore a highly brushed and waxed handlebar mustache. He looked like a diminutive Groucho Marx. Frank's stature, his mustache, and his preening of it had been a natural setup for the nickname.

Frank Alla did not seem to mind being called "Mini Guinea." Frank was just glad that John Smock had taken him under his wing while at Binh Thuy and helped get him out of his boring staff job as an admin officer for River Squadron 5. In addition to his normal admin duties, Frank had gone out with John on numerous combat patrols. He got enough combat experience to convince his boss to send him to the 534th—the 534th because his boss was familiar with the casualty reports and a bit irritated with Frank's never-ending ideas for improving the ways the admin unit could support the guys in the combat boats, like allowing them to carry painkilling drugs for emergencies the way the SEALs did. His boss saw the stats for the 534th. Frank Walker wounded and medevacked, John Smith wounded and medevacked, and then Ron Wolin and Wynn Goldsmith were wounded and possibly medevacked. Frank Alla got his wish for a combat assignment the day I was wounded. At the time he thought that he was my replacement. So did his boss. Or maybe his boss just wanted to rid himself of a junior officer full of irritating enthusiasm for new ideas and an itch for a combat assignment.

I was delighted that his boss was a dumb-ass who had

never followed up on the status of the wounded before cutting Frank's orders. Frank was my type of guy. A little wild and crazy but not stupid. A guy who felt he could contribute. Frank, who had not endured the rigors of PBR school, contributed mightily. Frank appreciated the enemy's capabilities, but he also understood what PBRs could do well. Get the enemy on our terms, give them no quarter, and avoid doing stupid things. Things that some of the old-hand boat commanders—bored after a few weeks of sampan searches that followed several months of constant combat action—began to try. One boat had recently run the high-tide bank of Tan Tan Island at max speed. The crew enjoyed the exhilaration of being on a seven-and-a-half-ton boat pushing off only a few inches of water alongside a riverbank at thirty-five miles an hour. The palm fronds reaching out over the bank were just under their heads. Then the few inches of hull in the midsection actually touching water hit a submerged log an inch below the surface. The seven-and-a-half-ton PBR went airborne for sixty feet before landing in the tops of the nipa palms, high and dry.

Two months earlier the men of that stunned boat crew would all have been killed by Viet Cong manning spider holes along the bank. But two months earlier, no 534th PBR captain would have dared run that bank. Instead they got to wait for hours as an LCM-8 boat dispatched from the YRBM-18 pulled the boat and its chagrined crew back onto the water. Fortunately no enemy snipers or rocket crews were anywhere near them.

But the crew did have some 'splaining to do to Ron Wolin and Bill Earner.

Chapter 18

The 535th was getting enemy fire night and day. Some missions were great successes. On one of its first night-patrols in the new op area, a two-boat patrol with a SEAL platoon from My Tho caught a small flotilla of VC sampans near the choke point. The 535th patrol officer called in the other 535th two-boat patrol for support. The SEALs were merely passengers as three 535 PBRs ran down and destroyed seven sampans with machine guns and grenades. The next day eighteen enemy bodies complete with web gear, grenades, and Viet Cong documents were recovered. No PBR sailors had been wounded and no SEALs had even fired a weapon. A little incident mentioned in two lines in a RivSect 535 combat action report that was expanded to a half page in a SEAL's memoirs many years later.

While the 535th was seeing so much action up on the My Tho, Ron Wolin and Jack Harrell decided to put some pressure on the Kien Hoa Viet Cong along the Ham Luong River. We, the commissioned and noncommissioned patrol officers, started to take our PBRs out after dark with Jack's band of former VC—for us something new and very different.

Until that time, the Kit Carson Scouts—that band of Viet Cong deserters mixed with an assortment of Cambodian and Nung mercenaries who lived with Jack in his Ben Tre villa—had been regarded by me as just a bunch of hired guns to bodyguard Jack and collect intel in a town beset with spies and double agents.

I believed until writing this book that those guys were part of the highly classified Phoenix Program. Something I learned about only after I left Vietnam.

The Phoenix Program was a CIA-funded and -orchestrated

effort to eliminate the Viet Cong infrastructure. Using old-fashioned police and FBI techniques of building files on associates of captured or turned Viet Cong, the intel people selected targets for kidnap or murder. Reports of being a bad guy by three different vetted good guys got somebody on a list of people to be captured or killed. I found this out when I took a two-boat patrol to a prearranged meeting with a PRU squad at the Ben Tre ferry landing around midnight. At the time I believed that I was the first 534th patrol officer to insert PRUs. Over thirty years later I found out that they were just Kit Carson Scouts. Whatever the color of the money that paid for them, they were hired bounty hunters.

I thought I would pick up the equivalent of a South Vietnamese SEAL squad—guys loaded down with bear-hunting gear about to go out on some hit-or-miss insertion like most of the SEAL operations at night. Instead I was greeted by Jack Harrell, all six-foot-three-inches of him, wearing black pajamas and a conical straw hat, cradling an AK-47, and wearing Ho Chi Minh sandals. Behind him were a half-dozen smaller Asian men similarly attired and carrying AK-47s. None had radios, demolitions, grenades, machine guns, or other gear. They looked exactly like a Viet Cong light infantry nighttime raiding party. That was the point.

As we got under way, Jack explained the night's mission.

"Wynn, we are going up the Soc Sai half a klick past the district town boat landing. Hopefully we will be in and out within half an hour."

"Jack, why the hell are you all dressed like Cong? What's this little half-hour job about?"

"Wynn, we are after only one guy. We think we have a good fix on him. He is a hamlet leader and supposedly a stalwart good guy. We know he is an important VC cadre. His family and all the other villagers in that hamlet are gonna believe he got kidnapped by Cong. If this op works, the Cong in Ham Luong District are gonna get a lot less support from the natives."

Jack was his smiling self. He then introduced me to the guy who was going to locate and identify the Viet Cong agent, a Vietnamese man who spoke very good English. I got to know him (his name sounded like Bow Wee) on the fifteen-minute boat ride. When his English failed, Bow Wee spoke French. His French was a lot better than mine. Using three languages, we communicated very well. I learned that he had been born and reared in Hanoi, had gone to university, been conscripted into the North Vietnamese Army, was commissioned as a first lieutenant (*thrung qui*) and assigned to infiltrate the South to fight against the imperialists. He had switched sides after a year or so of leading Viet Cong and NVA infiltrators around Saigon. Now he was fighting for "democracy" against his former comrades.

I did not ask the circumstances or the price of his conversion. I did not want to piss off the guy. I trusted Jack Harrell that his talkative traitor/spy/patriot was a good guy. I did ask Bow Wee what would happen if the target happened not to want to be taken from his home in the middle of the night by strangers.

"If he resists, we kill him. Then we chop off his head and take it back with us to prove we got right man."

The insertion turned out to be a dry hole. The target was not home. Just some more hours of stress for PBR boat crews manning guns up a twenty-yard-wide creek, waiting to save some good guys before they gave the signal to pick them up from the bank. A typical, unreported incident for the 534th during May 1968. Once again, if nobody got wounded or there were no confirmed enemy KIA, it was a nonevent in the monthly summaries.

A couple of nights later I was on the river when the other 534th patrol out that night had inserted and extracted Jack's band of mercenaries with a captive. Jack Harrell was not on that op. I guess Bow Wee was completely in charge. Something must have gotten out of hand during an impromptu interrogation of the prisoner on the back of the boat QM1 Carl Evans was riding as patrol officer. Evans called me by radio.

"Pineapple Bowl Charlie, this is Pineapple Bowl Echo."

"Echo, this is Charlie. Roger. Over."

"Charlie, this is Echo. The dinks are cutting the tongue out of a prisoner. How can I stop them? Over."

How the hell could I or anybody not on the scene stop a mutilation on his boat? was my first thought. My second thought was to evoke the name of Jack Harrell.

"Echo, this is Charlie. Tell the guy in charge that Howling Pistol Bravo will send his head back to Hanoi in a handbasket if he does not stop torturing that prisoner! Over."

Evans acknowledged and signed off. We heard no more radio transmissions.

I guess everything turned out as well as expected. A bleeding but live prisoner was deposited by Evans's boat back at the Ben Tre ferryboat landing. I never asked about or was told his fate.

Besides the beginning of PRU-type insertions along the Ham Luong during the first days of May, I remember all the war stories that the 535th officers related at the wardroom table. They had many.

First story. Lieutenant Jack Doyle, that loquacious, intrepid CO, related what happened to him on the afternoon of May 4, 1968.

It was about 1400 in the afternoon. Jack was leading a two-boat patrol around the islands of the choke point on the My Tho River. Hours of boredom and tension had passed since first getting under way. Captain John Sabattinni and Dai Qui Thom came out to the 535th in the river aboard a sampan. Their sampan and another carried a dozen or so armed Ruff Puffs from Cho Lach. Just like Jack's PBRs, they were looking for Viet Cong. They also had an objective, an island less than one hundred meters away. Some informant had told the Vietnamese district commander that a meeting of VC leaders was to take place on it. Jack Doyle, John Sabattinni, and the Vietnamese district commander drifted on the river and made small talk while watching the island for a few minutes.

They saw a sampan race across a creek on the targeted island and head for a small (four-hootch) hamlet on the opposite bank. The man on the sampan was obviously in a hurry. Doyle, Sabattinni, and Dai Qui Thom went into action. The sampan carrying Sabattinni and Thom followed Jack's PBR up the creek. The two craft beached and the three warriors got off to investigate, followed by other sailors and Ruff Puffs. Jack Doyle was the first onshore from a PBR. He was wearing sunglasses, a floppy hat, no helmet, no flak jacket. Fortunately he had an M-16 rifle. After Jack took two steps toward a hootch, a Viet Cong rifleman popped up from a spider hole fifteen feet in front of him and fired a shot at Jack point-blank with his Chicom SKS 7.62mm rifle. Jack fell backward into the mud, firing his M-16 on full automatic, and before the young VC could chamber another round Jack had killed him. But a hornets' nest had been stirred. Dozens of Viet Cong soon came scrambling out and opened up on the ten or so Ruff Puffs and PBR sailors ashore. The friendlies were about to be overwhelmed. The 535th PBR sailors on Jack's boats did what had to be done. One sailor came ashore cradling an M-60 machine gun. He rushed past Jack and fired a two-hundred-round belt of ammunition nonstop. Other sailors came ashore and fought like Marines until the enemy fire was suppressed so that the friendlies on the bank could get back aboard their boats. By that time, Seawolf gunships from Dong Tam had arrived. The Seawolves were soon joined by Army Cobra gunships. That little four-acre island was virtually destroyed. A meeting of fifty Viet Cong cadres was seriously disrupted and the Cong were probably all killed. Every hootch, every tree was consumed by fire by the time of the last gunship pass.

Jack Doyle was rightfully proud of his sailors. He broke out a bottle of gin for them when they returned to the barge that day. Jack also became a savior/hero in the eyes of Dai Qui Thom. The feisty Vietnamese commander was full of ideas for other operations. Jack was probably proudest of the Chinese SKS rifle he recovered from the young VC he killed.

Second story. On May 18, 1968, I came back from another routine day-patrol on the Ham Luong. Soon after my boats landed on the YRBM-18, I got the news that a 535th boat had been seriously shot up and four sailors medevacked. At the wardroom table that evening I received a detailed account of how John Smock had entered a canal on the western border of the Cai Be District of Dinh Tuong Province, just east of Snoopy's Nose. A canal stretched for miles up into the Plain of Reeds. A canal that was just over a mile from where the YRBM-18 was anchored. A canal that John had been up twice, the last time less than a week before, when his patrol had captured five VC suspects. This time the patrol was more or less ordered up that canal. The canal was the target of a propaganda raid championed by Dai Qui Thom. John's boats were to distribute anti-VC leaflets up the canal. I can only imagine what John must have thought of that little mission after the 535th boats had already established a pattern of going up the enemy-controlled canal.

The Viet Cong were waiting for River Section 535's 7-30 and 7-31 boats that morning. The first shot fired was an enemy rocket that hit the cowling of the 7-31 boat carrying John Smock. The rocket blasted through the coxswain's flat, seriously wounding John, the boat coxswain, the forward gunner, and a Vietnamese maritime policeman. The boat commander, manning the M-60 at the time, was less seriously wounded. Somehow he and the wounded coxswain (Engineman Third Class Summerhill) regained control of the boat as other rockets and heavy small arms including .51-caliber machine guns took both boats under fire. The two boats were able to bring enough suppressive firepower to bear to allow them to get out of the canal. Eight of the ten people aboard the two boats were wounded. John Smock and three others had to be medevacked by dustoff at the nearby Cai Be district town. Another buddy of mine shipped off to the medics.

By then Ron Wolin had offered the services of the 534th to Capt. John Sabattinni for operations on the Ham Luong; Ron was the type of guy who wanted to go where the action was. I took 534th patrol boats into Cho Lach from the Ham Luong three or four times. The first time I took a patrol into Cho Lach from the Ham Luong, the narrow stream from the Ham Luong to the district town looked like a perfect setting for Viet Cong ambushers: dense foliage on both banks part of the way; productive rice paddies part of the way; occasionally a clear area for a village. The absence of VC flags and *Sat My* signs was noted. There were no peasants running away from our boats; they just smiled and waved at us. Looking back over all the years since that three-mile trip from the Ham Luong to the Vinh Long district town, I still have an idyllic vision of what a peaceful district the Vietnam Mekong Delta was and what the rest of the country had possibly been years earlier. I saw no war scars. No blown-up bridges, no scorched villages, no Agent Orange defoliation, no palm trees with the tops blown off by artillery fire. Just a fruitful, lush, tropical countryside and productive rice paddies.

But, I was taking no chances. When I went to Cho Lach that first time I had my boats at general quarters. When I got off at the marketplace and met John Sabattinni for the first time, I had an M-16 in hand. The town was pristine. Not a sign of being in a war zone. Sabattinni was bareheaded and wearing a dark-green T-shirt. Nobody around the marketplace—dominated by a Catholic church—was armed. Sabattinni was a compact, well-tanned, blond guy with a closely cropped flattop haircut. He looked like a smaller Tab Hunter, a B-grade actor featured in a lot of war movies during the late 1950s.

Sabattinni was a warrior, but he was also a great schmoozer and a natural born salesman. His home was your home. Come enjoy his home. His pleasantries usually ended with a, "By the way, you have something that my people desperately need. The civilians need medicine, my troops need pop flares and mortar ammo. You Navy guys are great. Would some of your people like to have a great, six-course Vietnamese meal? I can arrange it. We are going to do great things together. How 'bout we start planning something for tomorrow?"

I had a two-boat patrol that supported Sabattinni's Ruff Puffs during the last week of May. The operation was a half mile inland from the Ham Luong. My boats' mission was to take care of any Viet Cong evaders coming down to the Ham Luong. The 535th had a two-boat patrol up the Cho Lach Canal supporting the same operation. My patrol area was a two-mile stretch of main river where our boats had never had enemy contact. I thought my boats were being underutilized as I followed the progress of the Ruff Puffs by plotting information from Sabattinni's radio transmissions on my chart.

Sabattinni's troops made contact with a dozen Viet Cong. He radioed that the Cong were about to escape and asked for Seawolf gunships to prevent the enemy's escape. So that was the Navy's mission. We were the guys who could call in on-the-spot air support for the Ruff Puffs, who rarely enjoyed that luxury.

Seawolves were assigned on a priority basis. A PBR unit in heavy contact, a SEAL team unit under fire, American soldiers operating with Navy units in desperate straits, were all priorities for Seawolf scrambles. Ruff Puff support was never even mentioned. Scrambles were different from planned PBR support ops. They were supposed to be the reserve for life-threatening emergencies involving brown-water sailors.

The 535th patrol officer, Lt. Bill Dennis, made the call for Seawolf support as a "Scramble 3"—American fighting men in need of air support but not really in immediate danger. I thought there would be a long interrogation from the Seawolves about exactly what Americans were in danger. A "Scramble 3" was a low priority. Bill described the situation correctly. His boats were farther away from Sabattinni's troops than my two boats. The HAL-3 Dong Tam Seawolf detachment radio guy radioed back within seconds that the birds were on their way. Seawolf ready crews would go to a cockfight in Thailand just to get airborne. They were armed and waiting in the wings every hour. Those guys did not give a damn about the color of the butts or the military status of the friendlies on the ground once an American unit leader asked them for help. They just wanted to do their thing.

They did their thing. Within a few minutes a two-ship fire team was on station above the Ruff Puffs, who were running and firing their weapons on a dirt track leading into the nipa less than a quarter mile from the Ham Luong. The 534th sailors could hear the firing. We could see the Seawolves.

I remember Sabbath's radio transmissions to the Seawolves.

"Seawolf 42, this is Rollup Niner. The Cong are on that track two hundred meters to the north headed for the woods. Take them under fire now. Over."

"Rollup Niner, this is Seawolf 42. We see a column of what appears to be civilians herding water buffalo. Where are the VC in relation to these folks? Over."

"Seawolf 42, this is Rollup Niner. Those people with the water buffalo are all Cong. Take them under fire. Over."

"Rollup Niner, this is Seawolf 42. Understand you want me to take the people herding the water buffalo under fire. Over."

"Seawolf 42, Rollup Niner. Grease them! Kill them all! Over."

"Roger that, Rollup Niner."

By then the last transmission from the Seawolves was blurred by all the rockets and machine guns being fired from the two helicopters. A dozen Viet Cong and a half-dozen water buffalo were killed within seconds. I could see only the gunships unleashing their loads at a half-mile distance.

Chapter 19

On June 12, 1968, John Smock returned to duty via an Air Cofat utility helo to the YRBM-18. It was good to see him again after three weeks. John was a little slower because his leg wounds still were causing him pain, but he was looking tan and fit. He had spent the last week at the China Beach convalescent Naval hospital on the coast near Cam Ranh Bay. He had had two hours of surgery at the Dong Tam Field Hospital and another two hours of clean-up surgery at a major hospital in Saigon followed by ten days' hospital rest before being shipped to China Beach.

Other than having a right upper thigh that resembled a small pepperoni pizza and which required constant dressing changes, John was his usual self. He showed what a trooper he was when he requested patrol duty as soon as possible. Jack Doyle took John Smock at his word. He needed patrol officers like John. John Smock went back on the river the next day, bandages and all.

A couple of days after John Smock's return, I went to a memorable party. Jack Harrell was getting short—his in-country tour was near its end. Jack and his MACV buddies decided to throw a couple of going-away parties. He needed at least two bashes because Jack had a lot of friends and not everyone could attend on just one date. Ron Wolin, Frank Alla, and myself attended the first. We were picked up at the Ben Tre ferry landing by one of Jack's Kit Carson scouts in the purloined jeep. I had come off a night-patrol and had five hours' sleep. I was looking forward to some big time off the river. I was ready to party. I would not have to go out on patrol until the next evening.

We were dressed for the occasion. We had on our cleanest

greens and were wearing our black berets. Ron and I had only our .45 sidearms. Frank Alla had an M-3 grease gun—a World War Two–era .45-caliber full automatic—besides his pistol. As it turned out, Frank was more appropriately dressed than Ron or me.

After a short jeep ride we were at the gate of Jack's "villa," a two-story masonry structure with a back courtyard and balcony facing the Ben Tre River. I guess in friendlier times the place could properly have been described as a villa. When I entered it for the first time I thought I was entering a bunker. Steel bars covered the windows (to defeat RPGs) and there were sandbags at the windowsills. M-60 machine guns were armed and resting on the sandbags. The furnishings were weird. Wooden crates of Chinese and American munitions served as tables. Mortars and RPG launchers provided the proper decorative touch. Every type of infantry weapon seemed deposited at random on the floor, which was also covered with a lot of the ordinary litter of a bachelor pad at college—empty beer bottles, food-covered plates, and so on. The only artwork on the walls were cello-taped Playboy centerfolds. The only thing missing was rock music from the stereo. Jack recognized that the sound of his party had to be subdued.

When we arrived around 1700 a lot of folks were crowding the house, most of them American advisers of all ranks. The party was a feast of food and drink. I stuck with *Ba Mui Ba* beer and did not indulge in the wine and hard liquor. I did pig out on the culinary delights—prawns, pork, noodles, and rice drenched in *nuoc mam* sauce served by a couple of Vietnamese ladies. I was having a really good time. Around 0100, after a dozen or so beers, I crashed in a corner on the second floor. I went to sleep believing that I would be awakened around 0700 to get on a PBR that would take me back to the YRBM-18 for more rest before I had to go back on patrol late in the afternoon.

About a half hour after I had gone to sleep, the local Viet Cong in Ben Tre ruined everything. A squad of enemy party poopers took the place under fire. I was blasted awake first by the M-60 machine guns at the windows. I pulled out my pistol and huddled down as far away from a window as I could. Ron Wolin soon came over to me.

"Wynn, get your ass in gear. We are getting out of here!"

Ron got on a PRC-25 radio and ordered the nearest 534th patrol to the ferryboat landing. He then had Jack Harrell get a couple of his mercenaries to get the jeep ready for our run to safety. I jumped on the back of the jeep with my cocked .45 at the ready. Frank Alla was beside me with his finger on the trigger of the M-3 grease gun. The jeep went out of the gate at full speed and headed for the ferryboat landing as gunfire continued around Jack's villa.

I still do not know what caused me to be left on the river after Ron and Frank were ferried back to the YRBM-18 by a waiting 534th PBR. Was it because I got drunk early and needed to be punished, or was it because Ron thought I was irresponsible and had gone to bed earlier than Frank and himself? Whatever, Ron Wolin wanted a commissioned officer on our boats near Ben Tre until the morning relief boats arrived, and I was elected. Ron told me to stick around with the boats on patrol while he went back to the barge. At the time I took his orders as a compliment for my dedication to duty.

Stick around I did, dreading any weapons fire as the last fire from around Jack's place ended. Thank God, the PBR boats were relieved without having to fire their weapons. My headache was not further irritated. By 0930 I finally got to sleep on the YRBM-18, awakening around 1430 to prepare for the scheduled evening patrol. I had had six hours of sleep over the previous two days, but I had no complaints. Being in charge of several thirty-one-foot, plastic boats in the middle of a muddy river in a combat zone while in a sleep-deprived, hangover condition was no sweat. I was surrounded by competent, bushy-tailed sailors.

I guess that night-patrol was the usual one—a few hours of searching watercraft before curfew, a few hours of running down Ambush Alley at general quarters with every sailor alert and at his gun, sandwiched between hours of drifting near the banks of the Ham Luong north of Ben Tre. By that time the Viet Cong had sent their main force battalions back to secret areas to regroup, retrain, and lick their wounds. There were no fights around outposts. There were no flares in the air or streams of tracers from Spooky gunships. A peaceful time in the eastern Delta.

Around 0300, while I was on a drifting PBR at the north end of Tan Tan Island, I heard a frantic call on the Kien Hoa MACV frequency.

"Willow Rule, this is Able Alpha Six! Require immediate dustoff for one Uniform Sierra Whiskey India Alpha. Coordinates Xray Zulu three niner five, five zero three. Lima Zulu is secure. Over."

"Roger that, Able Alpha Six, this is Willow Rule. Dustoff on the way. Out."

By that time the jargon was second nature to me. I had to put a red-lensed flashlight on the chart to determine where a wounded American would be waiting for a medevac helicopter in a secure landing zone. It was five miles away and only half a mile from the provisional Mo Cay district town. A place that was supposed to be secure. The incident was not my concern. An American Army adviser wounded far away was going to be medevacked. I stretched out behind the coxswain's flat for an hour or so before the boats were to sneak down to another known crossing area.

The next day I got the really bad news from the comm center guys (my after-hours drinking buddies in Doc Dooher's blind pig). Those guys had all the skinny that Ron Wolin and Bill Earner thought too sensitive for the troops. The medevac chopper from Dong Tam had arrived within minutes to pick up the American wounded. As soon as it settled into the little field, it was destroyed by rockets and small arms. Two Army pilots and two Army medics were killed.

No Mo Cay district adviser had made that call. It was just another example of Viet Cong tradecraft. I was impressed. The words I had heard on the radio calling the mission really sounded like American Army talk. The tone and accent of that transmission calling for the medevac had seemed genuine. The fact that the Ben Tre radio watch did not request passwords from the day's list to authenticate the guy making the distress transmission did not surprise me; those guys at the Ben Tre (Kien Hoa) TOC had always been sloppy. What pissed me off the most was that the voice I had heard calling for the chopper had to be that of a turncoat American. That there were some Americans who would purposely set up a medevac helicopter for destruction bothered the hell out of me.

Occasionally I would listen to the AM radio propaganda broadcasts the enemy sent from sanctuaries in Cambodia. Some of it was inflammatory, and possibly dangerous, such as the words from well-known black militants like Stokely Carmichael urging the brothers to frag white officers. Most of the stuff from Radio Hanoi was laughable. The American body counts it claimed were distorted much more than our body counts of Viet Cong and NVA. Radio Hanoi had reported that 250 American sailors died in the destruction of the YRBM-16. It had also reported that two American warships had been destroyed at Ben Tre during Tet, along with similar disinformation.

But that voice on the radio, calling for the medevac, was something else. It reminded me of what a young SEAL sniper told me when my boats had covered a SEAL dry-hole extraction months before from Tan Tan Island. I believe it was in early January. A My Tho–based SEAL squad of seven or so was coming out from Tan Tan around 0800. It was still the monsoon season, and a heavy shower had just passed. The river was encased in heavy fog.

The SEALs had to be extracted by 534th PBRs. The SEAL support boat did not have an operational radar. My two boats were just backup. Chief Raymond's boats had picked the SEALs up on schedule and on time. At the SEAL support boat, I was curious about the long, bolt-action rifle with telescopic sights that the SEAL was carefully putting back into a hard aluminum case lined with rubber foam. I had asked the guy why he had such a weapon. He had replied that it was a tool to kill "that longhaired blond hippie working with the gooks. I got a glimpse of the son of a bitch. He moved around a tree, and I never got a clear shot."

A few days after the helicopter had been lured into the death trap, another unsettling incident occurred out on the Ham Luong. During a routine night-patrol someone speaking in American-accented English called out my callsign over our FM radio channel. The unidentified caller said, "Pineapple Bowl Charlie, you will never leave Vietnam alive. Liberation forces will destroy you and your boats." I did not believe the call was a prank pulled off by a disgruntled GI. It was just one more disturbing thing about the war.

A few days after that incident, the 535th brought in about thirty suspects they had rounded up on a little island near the choke point. As I understood it, the purpose of the island sweep was to please "Empress Josephine," the nickname of Dai Qui Thom's feisty little wife. It seemed that Josephine was not too happy with the fact that there was a whorehouse in Cho Lach that openly serviced the Ruff Puffs. Josephine ordered her husband to move the whores out of town. Dai Qui Thom had gone to John Sabattinni for advice. John had called Jack Doyle. That is how the 535th got involved in Operation Lay House.

The prisoners were being held under guard out on the hot decks of an ammi maintenance pontoon. A couple of them had been shot up but their shoulder and arm wounds were patched up by Doc Dooher's medics. Since they had been firing weapons when captured, they were segregated from the rest. Every one of the enemy suspects suffered in the heat; the steel decks fried their bare feet. Then Lt. Bill Dennis came to the rescue of the suffering Vietnamese. He got sailors to rig up a canvas awning to shelter them from the hot sun and personally went around giving drinks of ice water to each of them, including the two young men who had been shot up before being captured. It was a tender scene of American compassion for our enemies. I had to take some pictures. The next day we learned that the two young Viet Cong had suffered a particularly slow execution. They had been tied to the bottoms of fish stakes at low tide by Dai Qui Thom's troops, and for many hours had felt the rising water get higher and higher until they eventually drowned.

Less than a week after I had witnessed Bill Dennis tenderly caring for those captured Viet Cong, he was killed.

The day was June 22, 1968. I was returning from a day-patrol in Area 1 on the Ham Luong. It was around 1700 when my boats approached the YRBM-18. I could tell that something was wrong. Instead of eight to ten PBRs nestled alongside the stern pontoons there were only a couple. On the upper deck of the barge I saw guys looking toward the northwest with binoculars. I jumped off my boat and climbed the ladders to the top of the barge to see what all the excitement was about. Even without binoculars I could see a column of smoke on the north bank of the My Tho River.

That was all that remained of River Section 535's 7-50 boat. Bill Dennis had taken a two-boat patrol up some little canal (the same canal where John Smock had been wounded the previous month) to chase down a Vietnamese woman in her evading sampan. The two PBRs were led into a trap. The first B-40 rocket had hit the port fuel tank underneath the coxswain's flat. The boat was lifted several feet out of the water and a fireball erupted in its center. BM1 William Delph, the boat commander, died at the controls. His last act was to slam the throttles to the stops and turn the wheel all the way to port. The forward gunner jumped out of his gun mount and into the water before the fire could reach him. Bill Dennis and the two other sailor gunners on the stern were wounded. They went into the water. Witnesses from the cover boat recall GM3 Patrick Ford, the after gunner, assisting Bill Dennis and the other after gunner, EN3 Cline, into the water as machine gun and rocket fire continued to hammer down on them. Only the unwounded forward gunner was rescued by the cover boat as it fought its way out of the canal.

By the time I came on the scene it was two hours after the ambush. For the previous hour and a half there had been a big search-and-rescue effort. Every available 534 and 535 boat had gone into high gear and boats from PBR Section 524 out of Vinh Long had joined in. A hundred or so of Dai Qui Thom's Ruff Puffs were inserted on both banks of the canal and swept the area around the burning boat. John Smock led a salvage team to the burning boat while others searched the banks for survivors or bodies. Ten or so CO_2 fire extinguishers were used up before the fire was contained enough so sailors could poke around in the ashes for remains and salvageable equipment. There was little of anything. Maybe the fifties could be saved. They were removed. The remains of BM1 William Delph were put in a .50-caliber ammo can and placed on the 534th boat of BM1 James Shadoan. Then the 535th sailors burned what was left of the boat. It was a very emotional experience for "Boats" Shadoan; he and Delph had been best buddies ever since PBR school. The body of Bill

Dennis was discovered and recovered. It was not evident whether he had died of wounds or drowned. The remains of GM3 Ford and EN3 Cline were discovered over the next two days. Ford's body had been in the hands of the Viet Cong, who had stripped it, bound his hands with wire, and had used the remains to troll for PBR sailors. Friendly Vietnamese fishermen had told Dai Qui Thom's men, and Dai Qui Thom organized a massive sweep of the area to secure the riverbanks as the search for remains continued until both sets were found.

Three days later the river rats on the YRBM-18 got to see Father McCoy once again at a memorial service, for the three 535th guys killed on June 22, and for another 535th sailor who had drowned after being knocked overboard at night when his PBR had collided with a Mobile Riverine vessel. As much as I liked the company of Chuck McCoy and the fine words of comfort for which he was noted, I really wanted that to be the last time I ever saw him. The most recent three occasions had each been for memorial masses and had come too frequently. While at the service, I already knew that the next day I would be going down the Mo Cay Canal.

Chapter 20

I was correct in my assessment of how easy it would be to finish up my Vietnam tour if I made it out of the Mo Cay Canal that June day. The Australian R & R never came. By July, Australia actually required *eleven* months in country. No sweat; the first week of July, I took off for Thailand for five days. Great food and warm tropical waters for four days and a day of fantastic shopping in Bangkok. I brought back a beautiful tiger skin, mounted head and all. When I got back, the tiger skin was the talk of the wardroom. I had to be very careful playing poker. Doc Dooher would have loved to bust me to the point where I would have to sell him my new *objet d'art*.

Patrols during July and August were long, boring, and of little interest. I did have an eventful night-patrol, drifting by sea anchor up Ambush Alley. The excitement came in the form of having the boats bounced around like shuttlecocks when the shock waves of several hundred five-hundred-pound bombs reached us through the water. A B-52 arc light strike had hit the nearby Ba Lai secret zone. Both "Boats" Shadoan, the boat captain on the PBR, and I felt that the big bombers probably were killing only fish and snakes. We thought the bombs would be more effective falling on Hanoi. I heard personal threats over the radio one more time. This time I was told, "Pineapple Bowl Charlie will never get back to Georgia." I guess this was a slight variant of my "not getting out of Vietnam alive."

I enjoyed really fabulous meals on two medcaps I went on with Dai Qui Thom's troops and Doc Dooher. I got to eat in both thatch huts and in an ornate wooden country home surrounded with tropical fruit trees and flowers. Inside the house was a picture of a smiling young Vietnamese man standing next to a T-33 jet aircraft. The lady of the house explained to us that the picture was that of her son, who was undergoing advanced flight training in Texas. I wished that every PBR sailor could have participated in those "get to know the people" missions. It sure would have made the Vietnamese seem less alien to the guys who cursed the "gooks," "dinks," and "slope heads" they encountered.

The most upsetting thing to happen to me during July was learning my new duty assignment after my tour in Vietnam was over; I was to go back to Vallejo as a river warfare instructor. The one command, the one job that I had specifically not requested. When I had filled out my "dream sheet" (more formally known as a duty assignment preference) in May, I had asked for East Coast shore duty. Since there was a strong rumor circulating that new Navy lieutenants with two or more years remaining of their service obligation (recently extended to five years from four by LBJ and company) were likely candidates for river warfare training duty, I attempted to nip that in the bud by a preemptive strike, basically telling the Bureau of Personnel that I would take anything except training duty back at Mare Island. Even Vietnam was better duty than Mare Island. If I had a choice between spending a year playing war on plastic boats in Vallejo or a year of actual war in the Mekong Delta, I would take Vietnam hands down. (Provided of course that I was guaranteed not to be killed.) Vietnam was interesting, even exciting at times. Mare Island, Vallejo, and the job of training river rats had no appeal whatsoever to me. It certainly had no career-enhancing potential if I wanted to stay in the Navy. I asked for a staff assignment, NROTC college instructor, or even recruitment work.

I was angry. I had about ten beers on the beer barge and wrote a very nasty letter to my junior officer detailer. So nasty in fact that Ron Wolin simply forwarded it with the words "contents noted," while Ron's boss, Lt. Comdr. Harlan Cust, wrote that my letter was, among other things, "unbecoming and unprofessional." Whatever the letter seemed like, it did the trick: my orders were changed. I would be staff officer for River Warfare at Commander Amphibious Forces, Pacific Fleet. A job based in Coronado, California, just across the bay from San Diego. A great staff job in a subtropical paradise.

The third week of July had a few combat incidents not involving me personally but interesting just the same. The first was when I came off a routine sampan-searching day-patrol on the Ham Luong to see a SEAL team disembarking from a couple of Rich Sloane's 535th PBRs. I recognized a SEAL as one of the two survivors of the ill-fated Mike Platoon. He was cradling an M-2 carbine with a broken stock and blown-away trigger guard. I asked him what was so important about that old busted-up rifle. The sailor proudly handed the weapon to me and said:

"It's significant to me because I put an M-72 round through the trigger housing while a Viet Cong tax collector was holding it at port arms."

The SEALs and Rich Sloane's 535th boats had just come back from a fabulous success. Ten or so SEALs had hidden in a commandeered junk taken from the Cho Lach marketplace and set out through a three-mile canal headed for the Co Chien River. The enemy controlled the canal. A particularly nasty VC tax collector with fifty armed men stayed in a small hamlet area near the middle. Every time Dai Qui Thom's Ruff Puffs swept the area they suffered heavy casualties from snipers and booby traps. Captain John Sabattinni called in John Doyle for Navy support. Jack called in the SEAL team from My Tho. The SEALs were each encouraged to come up with a plan. Some plans called for nighttime insertion by boat; some called for a daylight assault by helicopter. QM2 Gene Wardrobe, one of the survivors of the Mike Team disaster, conceived the most original plan. (Gene had been the SEAL left back in My Tho the night Patrick had been blown apart.) Gene's plan called for subterfuge, audacity, firepower, and airpower. It was the plan that was implemented. It worked beautifully. Right after the VC tax collector hailed a familiar thirty-six-foot junk, Gene jumped up, pushed back his conical straw hat, and blasted the chief tax collector in the belly button with an LAW. Seawolf gunships arrived overhead as the SEALs stormed ashore from the junk. Rich Sloane's PBRs rushed down the canal with flanking fire. Fifty Viet Cong were killed with no friendly casualties.

The second incident started while I was relaxing with Doc Dooher out on the beer barge around 1800. We were drinking beers and watching a small South Vietnamese Navy PGM (patrol gunboat, medium) make its way upriver. The eight-ton steel vessel was within a half mile when we observed explosions erupt on and around it; .51-caliber machine guns and recoilless rifles clobbered the little ship. Immediately, sailors scrambled into PBRs and within five minutes my buddy Doc was performing triage on the ten or so wounded Vietnamese sailors brought back to the YRBM-18. One had been killed and three had to be medevacked by helicopter.

August was a month of hail and farewells; Ron Wolin, Bill Earner, Jack Doyle, John Smock, Pete Richards, and several others completed their tours. Others came to take their places. The usual pomp and ceremony accompanied the change of commands for the river sections. Lieutenant Rich Monash replaced Ron. Another lieutenant, Tom Jones, replaced Bill Earner. A visiting lieutenant commander named Jack Elliot, river division leader out of Binh Thuy, attended the change of command ceremony. It was the only time I ever saw the man who became one of the greatest brown-water heroes of all time.

The names of the sailors changed also. Patrol officers and boat captains Evans, Raymond, Engle, Briggs, Burney, and Milkier were replaced by new guys named Youngblood, Wagner, and Whidden. Whatever their names, the new guys appeared competent and professional. Some of the old salts, including Tony Summerlin and his forward gunner, Wayne Forbes, extended for an additional six months or a year.

On September 2, 1968, I was reunited with Cliff Willis at the airport in Saigon almost precisely one year after we arrived. Cliff looked tanned and had more lines in his face. I'm sure I looked the same way to him. We enjoyed a couple of beers while waiting for our charter flight back to Travis Air Force Base.

I spent less than a week on leave in Atlanta. I was to relieve my predecessor by September 20, which was fine with me. I could locate only a couple of old friends. Time for me to go west and meet new ones. Because of the few nights of barhopping in Coronado while I was undergoing training over a year ago, I was looking forward to meeting a whole lot of new friends, especially of the female persuasion.

My job in Coronado was basically to be the Navy's PBR expert—in current operations in Vietnam, training requirements, logistical requirements, operating costs, performance parameters, and other areas. One day in late September, I had to brief Rear Adm. Elmo Zumwalt on PBR operations in Vietnam. I had never heard of Zumwalt but was told by my immediate boss—Capt. John Faulk, USN, the COMPHIBPAC special operation officer—that Zumwalt was a "hard charger" on his way to relieve Rear Admiral Veth as COMUSNAVFORV. With his insights and good questions, Zumwalt truly impressed me that day. I soon realized that the man was not going to be doing business as usual with the brown-water navy. Zumwalt asked about PBR sailor morale. I said it was headed south after a high during the Tet Offensive. He asked about the basic mission of patrolling the rivers. I replied that it was getting too boring. He asked what could be done. I said seal off the Cambodian border with both the Mobile Riverine forces and game warden PBRs. That aggressive concept was actually quite popular with a lot of the young sailors, who wanted to see some progress in the war. It was also extremely popular with Navy planners bucking for one more promotion before retirement. What I told the admiral was stuff that he had heard before and would hear again.

Zumwalt hit the ground running in Vietnam. He did anything and everything to shake up the status quo. He addressed the morale issue by promoting river section OinCs to commanding officers of river divisions. River division commanders became river flotilla commanders. Even lowly patrol officers and boat commanders got new respect. They were authorized to wear a newly designed badge, a speeding PBR, on their uniform as a kind of "command at river" honor. He hoped the measures would encourage additional volunteers for what he thought might be the brown-water navy's toughest year.

Zumwalt *knew* the next year was going to be tough because he was committed to doing the nearly impossible. He was on a mission to turn the brown-water navy over to the South Vietnamese within a year while buying time to train the South Viets by pressuring the NVA in their Cambodian sanctuaries from just north of Saigon all the way south to the Ca Mau Peninsula.

In November 1968, Zumwalt came up with his grand plan. He called it SEA LORDS, for South-East Asia Lake, Ocean, and Delta Strategy. Whatever it was named, the strategy called for mixed units of PBRs and RAGs (river assault groups) to seal the Cambodian border in and around the infamous Parrot's Beak and Swift boats from CTF-115 (Operation Market Time) to come in from off the coast and start operating in the rivers and canals of the Delta to replace the PBRs, which would be "forward deployed" along the border in narrow rivers.

River Divisions 534 and 535 comprised two of the three ten-boat PBR divisions initially allocated to Operation Giant Slingshot, so named because on the charts the river branches of the Vam Co Tay and the Vam Co Dong resembled a giant slingshot when they reached the Soi Rap River just southwest of Saigon.

When I saw the message traffic assigning the 534th to that operation, I said some silent prayers for my buddies still there. I read every combat action report from PBRs in Vietnam. Already, by late October, things had picked up for the 534th. A SEAL BMC named Frank Bomar had been assigned to run the PRUs and what remained of Jack Harrell's Kit Carson Scouts out of Ben Tre. River Division 534 PBRs picked up a squad or two on a nightly basis at the Ben Tre ferryboat landing. The PBRs then inserted them close to their known targets. The Kien Hoa VC infrastructure was taking a beating. Frank Alla took the time to put out a monthly newsletter to old hands back in the States, such as myself. His reports amplified what the combat action reports said. The Kien Hoa VC sappers came back to their old tricks. They blew up the Ben Tre ferry landing. They also almost destroyed the USS *Westchester County*, a modern LST assigned to the MRF just outside of Dong Tam harbor. Twenty-three sailors and soldiers were killed. The *Hunterton County* was hit in a rocket ambush just south of the Mo Cay Canal as it steamed upriver. Five sailors were killed. John Sabattinni took a rifle round in the ankle while riding a 534th boat. By November, River Division 534 was also beginning to experience a few old-fashioned firefights up the Ben Tre River. One day four 534th boats spent eight hours protecting Mobile Riverine supply boats at the junction of the Ben Tre and Ba Lai Rivers. A big fight took place in which the PBRs had the uncomfortable experience of 40mm cannon shells from MRF gunboats flying over their heads as enemy and friendly fire erupted in many directions at one time.

But that fight up the Ben Tre would seem like a walk in the woods compared to what the 534th river rats experienced the first six weeks of Giant Slingshot. On December 5, 1968, the YRBM-18 moved up to Tra Cu on the Vam Co Dong, and Giant Slingshot got under way. Half of the 534th and 535th boats were shifted to what were called ATSBs (advanced tactical support bases), i.e., several ammi pontoons towed upriver, lashed together, and moored at a Special Forces camp. The pontoons carried fuel, ammunition, food, and tents for those preferring to sleep inside the wire of an armed camp rather than on a little plastic boat exposed on a fifty-meter-wide river. The living conditions for the sailors at the ATSBs were downright primitive compared to the luxury of the "barge."

Just getting to the ASTB at Go Dau Ha near the Cambodian border soon became an adventure for the 534th sailors. The stretch from Tra Cu to Go Dau Ha on the Vam Co Dong River soon became known as "Blood Alley." Within two days of beginning the operation, the 534th sailors were getting into an average of two firefights per day. And the enemy was not just a few patient Viet Cong; it was hundreds of regular North Vietnamese who did not expect the little boats. By night the 534th sailors decided to turn the tables on the NVA. The boats would establish ambush or "bushwhack" positions by burying a PBR's bow completely in the nipa, cutting its engines, and waiting for the NVA to come on down. Down they did come since, unfortunately for the PBRs, the banks at the favorite crossing sites were steep.

On the afternoon of December 14, Tony Summerlin, by then 534th patrol officer, had a two-boat patrol slowly going up the upper Vam Co Dong. As the two boats reached a point where the east bank rose rapidly to a high green wall, the NVA initiated their most successful attack on Giant Slingshot units to date. The boat carrying Summerlin (the 7-20 boat, boat captain BM1 R. K. Sonnenberg) was hit by three RPG-7s. A hail of heavy automatic weapons fire that included at least one .51 machine gun followed. The cover boat, the 7-17 boat, took most of that fire. As the boats cleared the ambush site, BMGN Wayne Forbes left his forward machine gun mount to help the wounded on the stern, where the after gunner (BM2 David Lehman) was dying from multiple wounds, Tony Summerlin's head was soaked in blood, and another gunner was out of action. Forbes was the only sailor on the 7-20 boat not wounded. As soon as Forbes had finished bandaging up Summerlin's head wounds, he had to run back to the after .50 machine gun to take care of a dozen or so NVA who appeared on the bank with raised rifles and rocket launchers. Forbes's accurate fire knocked down seven NVA and messed up the aim of the others to the extent that the two PBRs could clear the ambush site. The results were one sailor KIA and six others medevacked. Wayne Forbes earned a Bronze Star that day. He finished his tour a couple of months later with yet another Bronze Star.

By the end of the first two weeks of Giant Slingshot, forty sailors of the three divisions involved had been wounded. Most of them were 534th and 535th sailors.

When Frank Alla finished his tour in January 1969, I requested that his orders be modified so that he could stop by Coronado and personally brief me and my command about the Giant Slingshot operation. That was the last time I saw Frank. He was not his old self. I guess Giant Slingshot had had an effect on him. Over the years we have remained in touch. He helped mightily in getting this story of the first year of combat by the first MK II PBRs published.

Epilogue

In October 1969, River Division 534 was one of the first PBR units to be turned over to the South Vietnamese Navy. The Vietnamese sailors had replaced the U.S. river rats sailor by sailor, job by job, over a period of weeks. The South Vietnamese were given the best boats in country and trained by the best sailors. Admiral Zumwalt really wanted his ACTOV program (accelerated turnover to the Vietnamese) to succeed. At the same time I was notified that my position, staff assistant for River Warfare, was to be eliminated as part of the general force reduction during that winding-down period of the war in Southeast Asia. I was offered a slot in the next available "destroyer school" class. The prospect of spending six months of extensive training in surface warfare operations during the nasty-weather months of November through March in Newport, Rhode Island, did not appeal to me. I requested a release from the extension of my minimum active duty obligation and was released from active duty in December 1969.

Soon every PBR sailor leaving Vietnam was going back to the blue-water navy or the civilian world. There was to be no active-duty PBR force or training force to keep their experience alive. The reserves did maintain several PBR divisions for contingencies (if insurgency war broke out in Panama, for instance) throughout the 1970s. By the early 1990s the only PBRs on the Navy's rosters were those of the Special Warfare (SEAL) Special Boat Units.

It took months to track down old shipmates for their assistance in writing this book. For the most part it was a joyous journey down memory lane; there were also some sad moments along the way. The following is a brief summary of what I learned from some of my old buddies:

Ron Wolin retired from the Navy with the rank of lieutenant commander. He operates a military memorabilia business—a hobby that he has enjoyed for decades. Some small shrapnel fragments still work themselves to the surface of his back from wounds suffered in Vietnam. He is in some discomfort and is thinking about yet another operation. (I can relate to this. I have had six eye operations for head-trauma-related problems, probably due to the concussion I had when I was wounded.)

Bill Earner retired with the three stars of a vice admiral. His last active-duty assignment was Deputy Chief of Naval Operations for Logistics. He is currently a senior executive with the Navy Federal Credit Union.

Frank Walker spent several months in naval hospitals before receiving a medical discharge in 1968. He is a businessman in Clinton, Louisiana, and is the proud father of two students at LSU.

Jack Harrell spent a couple of years more in Southeast Asia after leaving the Navy. He worked as a contract officer for the CIA. He currently is a gentleman farmer and businessman in south Georgia. He spends a lot of time conducting a Christian ministry for inmates of Georgia prisons and keeping in touch with Vietnamese families that he helped relocate to the Atlanta area after the war in Asia ended.

John Smith was promoted to lieutenant commander just before his 100 percent medical disability retirement in 1969. It was not the AK-47 round that disabled him, but the sloppy follow-up operation on his back in 1969 that led him to spend over thirty years in a wheelchair. He is not in the best of health and is probably more than a little bitter. I know I would be.

RD2 Robert Wenzel received a 100 percent disability retirement (and promotion to RD1). His last known address was in Las Vegas.

Ned Caldwell retired as a chief GM (G) and is a community college professor in his native North Carolina.

Tony Summerlin retired as a master chief boatswain's mate—the enlisted equivalent of Bill Earner's three-star rank. Tony is enjoying traveling.

James Shadoan retired as a senior chief boatswain's mate and is currently a law enforcement officer in his native Utah.

Earl Milliken retired as a chief quartermaster in the early 1990s. He passed away two years ago. According to his brother, Earl was the victim of an Agent Orange–related rapid-growth cancer. Milliken was one of three river rats I knew who died suddenly from cancer over the period of writing this book. Surviving relatives all claim Agent Orange was the suspected cause of the cancer. Vietnam is truly a viper that keeps biting.

SN Marty Vice left the Navy after Vietnam and is an executive for a pipeline company in Los Angeles.

Wayne Forbes left the Navy after Vietnam with a handful of medals and memories. He is a USPS letter carrier in his native Pennsylvania. He is active in veteran affairs dealing with Agent Orange issues and is a Gamewarden Association member.

Robert ("Handgrenade") Hunt retired as a chief quartermaster. He spent most of his service after Vietnam as a deepwater (hard-hat) Navy diver. He writes and travels with his wife, a retired Navy commander.

Frank Alla left active duty after Vietnam and returned to the Boston area. He had just recently left a management position in an eight-hundred-pound gorilla of a high-tech company for a more visible position in a small firm.

Pete Richards left the Navy after his three-year obligation and is a businessman in Atlanta, Georgia.

John Smock left the Navy and is an executive with a large international consulting firm in Chicago.

Rich Sloane and **Jack Doyle** are retired Navy captains with new careers. Jack is a high school teacher in Virginia. Rich runs the chamber of commerce of a mid-size town in central Florida.

Jerry Letcher retired from the Navy as a commander. One of his last billets was that of commanding officer, Special Boat Squadron 11, Vallejo, California. Jerry was the first and only non-SEAL designated officer to hold that command. Jerry is a marine-engine consultant and lives in Wisconsin.

Index

Read all about the elite LRRPs of the 1st Cavalry as they hunt—and are hunted—by some of the Viet Cong's crack divisions in the vast triple-canopy jungle near the Cambodian border.

LRRP COMPANY COMMAND:
The Cav's LRP/Rangers in Vietnam, 1968-1969

by Kregg P. J. Jorgenson

Published by Ballantine Books.
Available at a bookstore near you.

Not many soldiers fighting in the VC-infested rice paddies of the Mekong Delta can say they were in direct contact with the Oval Office. Read about one who can:

WHY A SOLDIER?
A Signal Corpsman's Tour from Vietnam to the Moscow Hot Line

by Colonel David G. Fitz-Enz, U.S. Army (Ret.)

Whether above or below the water, the men of UDT-13 took the fight to the Viet Cong in the deadly river and coastal regions of Vietnam. Here's the true story of one of these unique divers:

JUST A SAILOR

by Steven L. Waterman

Published by Ballantine Books.
Available at a bookstore near you.